BRAITHWELL
The Village Where I Belong

Joyce Milnes

BRAITHWELL

The Village Where I Belong

by

JOYCE MILNES

*A Century of the Social History
of a Farming Community
in South Yorkshire*

JOYCE MILNES
in association with
Twiddlesmith Publishing Ltd 1997

First published in Great Britain in 1997
by Joyce Milnes
Steetley House
Braithwell
Rotherham
S66 7AF
in association with Twiddlesmith Publishing Limited
Whitton House
11 York Road
Beverley
East Yorkshire
HU17 8DP

A CIP record for this book is available from the British Library

ISBN 1 901853 20 9

Typeset in Sabon by ABM Typographics Ltd, Hull
Printed in Great Britain by Redwood Books Limited,
Trowbridge, Wilts.

DEDICATION

❧

Written in memory of our parents
Ethel (Poppy) and Edwin (Ned) Dunstan
who gave us such a wonderful childhood

CONTENTS

Foreword

Introduction

ACKNOWLEDGEMENTS

Special thanks to Malcolm Arnold for deciphering my hand-writing, suggesting I have it published and typing this book for me – *and* urging me on to finish it. Without him, it would never have been finished let alone published. When Malcolm and his wife Glen were here for lunch one day, I mentioned that I was still writing down memories of my childhood and had been doing it for 25 years – all on odd little bits of paper. Glen said "Malcolm will type it for you." I laughed and said he'd never read my writing. She replied "We're teachers. We can read anybody's writing." And they did! And that's how it started. I shall always be indebted to them for the many hours of work they have put into this as well as their help in putting all the bits into some sort of order.

My cousin, Allen Smith – for his help with the Inclosure Act, his drawing of the farmstead, all his research on the Village history and editing of this book.

Lord Scarbrough – for allowing me to use his Archives and helping me in the search. I'm sure I sometimes must have been a damn nuisance to him.

Alice Rodgers – a very keen amateur historian, for helping in my searches at Sandbeck Hall and for deciphering documents I couldn't make head or tail of.

Gordon Pell and his son Howard – for memories of William & Aimée Marshall (Hare-hound House) and William's hand-written life story.

My brother, Derrick Dunstan – who put me right when he said I was "straying from the truth".

My brother, Dennis Dunstan – for his tales when my memory failed me.

Harold Clarkson – for information on the Clarkson family.

My cousin, Joseph Dunstan – for his tales and memories.

John Swift – for tales of the Village.

George Owen – for newspaper cuttings.

"Sheff" (Ted) Houghton – for tales of the Village and help with the Wells.

Pam Carling (nee Picton), Avril Ashley and Violet Holmes (nee Grindle) – for village photographs.

Robert Alvey Houghton – for his photographs.

Tom & Jessie Cutts – for helping with names and places.

Rev. Ernest Eccles – for being kind enough to search out the old church school documents for my godson (Nicholas Letts) to borrow for his dissertation at college and then letting me keep them to copy some interesting items.

Les Pugh – for his papers on Ruddle Mill.

DMBC Archive Staff – for their sympathetic assistance.

And, last but not least, my husband Malcolm, who must be sick to death of hearing about my wonderful childhood.

FOREWORD

SANDBECK PARK
MALTBY, ROTHERHAM
YORKSHIRE

Braithwell is a village which, at the end of the 20th century, still remains a community – to use that word in its proper sense. Mrs. Joyce Milnes has lived in Braithwell all her life and half this book is her record of the village's history for which future generations of Braithwell inhabitants will be grateful.

The other half is a glorious description of life in the village in the 1920s. We too easily forget how things have changed. This book should be read by all ages, both for enlightenment as well as huge pleasure and enjoyment.

THE EARL OF SCARBROUGH
October, 1997

INTRODUCTION

BRAITHWELL, BRETHWELL, BRAYWELL OR BREWELL
from p426 of White, "Directory of 20 miles round Sheffield" in 1852

"BRAITHWELL, 6½ miles E.N.E. of Rotherham and S.S.W. of Doncaster, is a village in an airy and pleasant situation and has in its township about 450 souls, and 1920 acres of land, including MICKLEBRING, a hamlet half a mile W. of Braithwell. The soil belongs to various freeholders. The Church (St. James) is an ancient structure and the living is a vicarage, valued at £330, with the curacy and Great Tithes of Bramley annexed to it. The Lord Chancellor is patron and the Rev. James Reece incumbent. The school and poor have several small benefactions; and here is a Wesleyan chapel. The Earl of Scarborough *(sic)* is lessee of the Great Tithes of Braithwell, under the Crown and they have been commuted for £370 per annum."

The Village of Braithwell existed before the Norman Conquest, its ancient origin is very obscure. In the Domesday Book, it is known as Bradeuuelle (pronounced Braywell), also Bradwelle, then Braywell, Brewell and, in 1309, Braythewell. Brewell is now the name used by some of the older local residents. "Braythewell" means "Broad Stream." (In 1673, at the West Riding Quarter Sessions held at Barnsley, Elizabeth Revell, a spinster, described as "of Braywell", was ordered to be whipped for petty theft.).

Set in an elevated position in the midst of fields and lanes, 3½ miles from Conisbrough station, 2½ miles from Maltby station and 168 miles from London, the Village has seen a fair amount of development over the years. Although people think of South Yorkshire as an industrial area we, despite the fact that we are only two miles from two collieries, Maltby and Edlington (now closed), still think of ourselves as a rural, open Village although many of the farms and smallholdings have now gone.

The Parish of Braithwell still covers 1,920 acres and is 350' to 400' above sea level. It was fully enclosed later than most parishes – people say because we were a difficult lot with no squire and so many small farmers and smallholders that the enclosure took a lot of working out. Alice Rodgers, interested in Local History, told me that Braithwell has always been known as a backward village. I replied that I knew people outside the Village said we were bloody-minded but not backward. Alice said: "Yes, you hate change. It's exactly the same thing. That's why you were so late being enclosed."

The present Lord Scarbrough lent me a book in the 1960s of old Braithwell, which gave me lots of information and fired my enthusiasm to find out more. The Scarbrough family gave the land on which the Cenotaph is built and for the new Churchyard, which was Low Farm stackyard. They once owned several properties here but in later years were left with only one cottage, sold in 1994 to my great nephew, Scott Dunstan. They encourage all who search for history of this Village and have been good friends to us over many years. The present Lord Scarbrough (the 12th Earl) gave the old trough for the "new" Village Pump and performed the opening ceremony in 1952.

Villages and their surroundings have changed dramatically over the centuries. The inhabitants and their customs have changed too. I am writing this to show how Braithwell Village has changed in my lifetime. I hope that my love of this Village and my affection for the people here will shine through as I write my story of life as it was in my childhood and my father's lifetime and some memories as passed down of his father's life in this village of BREWELL.

I also hope that my son David's family will know Brewell and that David, Allison and my five grandchildren Ruby, Pearl, Max, Bonny and Olmo will be proud of where they come from – true Yorkshire village stock – wherever they may end up. When Ruby was born and I was told her name, I said: "Oh! When I was little I had a lovely cat called Ruby." When Pearl was born my brother Dennis said to Allison: "Lovely name lass – best greyhound I ever had was called Pearl." Then followed Max and my friends had a dog calles Max. Bonny came and one of the last Shire horses we ever had was called Bonny! And then Olmo. Allison phoned me to tell me his name and said: "I guarantee that NOBODY in Braithwell has a cat, or dog, or a horse called Olmo."

Through my memories and the tales from other people in the Village, I have built up a picture of how this Village was in the late 1800s and early 1900s.

JOYCE MILNES
BRAITHWELL
OCTOBER 1997

PART 1
THE FAMILY LIFE

❖

CHAPTER 1

I remember, I remember
The house where I was born
The little wonder where the sun
Came peeping through at morn

When I was just 18, I volunteered for the Womens Land Army. I was sent to the Isle of Ely and thoroughly enjoyed my time there, living in a hostel with 25 other girls and working on the land – something I loved. I was there three months before I got my first leave. I came home on the train to Doncaster and told nobody at home as I wanted to give them a surprise – I was in my uniform, of course.

When the No. 18 bus turned into High Street, tears started in my eyes. Asked what was the matter by Ernest Dickinson sitting beside me, I could only shake my head. I jumped off the bus and ran up the farm drive, crying all the while. My mother was so upset – she thought something dreadful had happened to me but I'd never been away for so long from the Village before on my own. Coming back had just overwhelmed me. I realised then how much the Village and the farm really meant to me. I vowed when the war was over never to leave it again. I just can't imagine myself living anywhere else. To me, it's the only place to live.

In a village, the discussion of their own and their neighbours' affairs was very important but 100 years ago, due to lack of transport, lives were lived out under very hard circumstances. Even so, village people never pitied themselves. There's no denying that most villages are hot beds of gossip but, when the

1

need arises, the same people turn out to help. We all know the skeletons in each others cupboards. We don't air them because very few families are without some skeletons of their own and none of us want them exposed.

Cirumstances made village life a very close-knit affair. Particularly a village such as Braithwell, where there was no Lord of the Manor. It was a Village of farms and smallholdings. When I was a child, there were eight smallholdings and farms on the west side of the High Street. Why only on the **west** side and none on the **east** side? Perhaps it was because Great Field was on the west side just behind these houses and so access to it from the farms and smallholdings was easy before the Inclosure Act in 1857. There were nine farms in the area when I was small but many smallholdings. Five of the farms were dairy and our farm also had sheep. The other four were arable and a few also had sheep and some had beef cattle. Hall Farm, Ashton Farm, Elmfield Farm, Cedar Farm, Manor Farm, Orchard Farm and Well House Farm, Fox House Farm and Low Farm all had horses for work, transport and pleasure. Each of the farms had a small orchard with mixed fruit trees. We had pears, apples (eating and cooking), plums and damsons. These were only for home use and given away to farm workers and friends, as was most of the produce from Village orchards. Much chutney, apple jelly, blackberry and apple jelly and pies were made. Most of the "keepers" were put down in the cellar wrapped in paper and were good even until well after Christmas – Bramleys even into March!

There is no doubt that the agricultural labourer of today is much better off than he was in years gone by. But in my young days the farm was his all – as it was my father's, who ate slept and talked of nothing but farming. The farm supplied all his needs – the food, the shooting, riding, hunting, the gossip – everything . And so it did for the farm labourer. His farm was his life, his gaffer his friend and confidant. Oh what a happy secure and pleasant life we lived. How thankful I am to have lived through the times of never having to fasten your farm house doors night or day – of trusting everybody, wandering anywhere and always feeling safe, safe, safe. We have lost this wonderful feeling today. I write with great affection for the farm labourers I knew. I respected and loved them as I am sure they did my brothers and I.

I was born on 31st May, 1924 when the lilac was in full

bloom. My mother's bedroom window overlooked the drive where purple and white lilac, single and double, bloomed in the drive. My father's favourite shrub. Although a farmer, he was a wonderful gardener. I think my mother was happy when I was born – she already had two sons. My brother Dennis (Ambrose) was two years old and my eldest brother Derrick (Granville) was five. My half-sisters, Audrey Vera and Doris May were 14 and 15. They helped in the house – Doris often outside, always at harvest and hay time and helped with the poultry; Audrey only ever worked indoors. Why did I only have one name? I've always regretted it – I should like to have been called Joyce Charlotte.

How lucky I was to be born on a farm in Braithwell and to be a Yorkshire Lass. What happiness living on a working farm brings, with a loving, kind and generous mother and an optimistic, strict and happy father, who had a real "live and let live" view of life. What fun we had with the animals and our pets. With two older half-sisters and two older brothers, my young life had all the advantages and no disadvantages.

My mother's three younger brothers, Harry, Arthur and Harold (Lal) also lived with us. They were all unmarried and when their mother died, my Auntie Violet kept house for them at the Manor House in Micklebring which was their home. When she married, the brothers came to live with us at the farm and the Manor House was let – my grandma Ada left it in her will and that it couldn't be sold until Uncle Lal (the youngest) was 21. There were ten of us then living at Hall Farm.

There were eight children in mother's family – she had three sisters and four brothers. The eldest was Auntie Violet – she visited us often with her family. Uncle Joe Day and children Marie, Vernon and Phyllis. Dad, Mum my brothers and me sometimes walked to Maltby on a Sunday night for supper with them. Uncle Joe's family lived in and owned the Old Plough at Micklebring. He was the eldest son and married Auntie Violet, the eldest daughter from the Manor House almost opposite.

Auntie Renee – lived at Conisbrough and visited us often. Her husband was Uncle Herbert Foster. They had one daughter Kathy (we always called her) – she likes Kathlyn. She still lives in the house they built in Conisbrough – Kathlyn Villa. Kathy, as an only child, was always beautifully dressed. I was six years younger – usually very dishevelled when they called because I was always playing on the farm. I think Mum despaired of me and always fetched me in to tidy me up if she knew we were having visitors.

Uncle Willie had a stroke when he was in his forties and was paralysed and in a wheelchair. They had one son Alec who stayed most of the summer holidays with us and got his fingers in the turnip chopper and lost his middle finger. Mum said: "That's it. I'm having nobody else's kids staying here." But of course it didn't last long.

Auntie Molly, Willie's wife kept them going by running a small grocery business on Balby Bridge. She was small, plump and pretty and mother and her were great friends. She could tell fortunes from tea cups and cards and knew all sorts of folklore and funny things which we always found very amusing. As a girl, she'd worked in the mills in Manchester and was very superstitious. When uncle Willie died, she and Alec went back to Manchester and Mum and I visited her quite often and really missed her.

Uncle Arthur was a schoolteacher and became head of a school in Wilburton on the Isle of Ely. Auntie Ethel and he had two children Freda and Rex. They came every summer for their holiday with us. Where did they all sleep? I really can't remember. I know we had a beautiful mahogany four-poster bed and when there were a lot of girls staying, we slept sideways in it. I think six at one time – did we ever sleep? Dad eventually chopped it up because Mum had to make all the sheets etc. for it, as there was no such thing as king size and of course the rooms were quite low and it took up an awful lot of the bedroom. It was huge. Strange that during the war I was stationed in Ely and worked at a farm in Wilburton right opposite the schoolhouse where I visited them as a child.

Uncle Harry was the local hairdresser at Maltby. He and Aunt Evie lived in Braithwell so we saw them often. Aunt Evie was leader of the W.V.S. and a local Councillor in fact the first lady Councillor ever in the Village and a founder-member of the W.I. and the Darby & Joan. They had two sons Allen and Michael.

Uncle Lal was late marrying Ruth and lived with us for many years. He later lived in Maltby and has one daughter Elaine. I don't really remember the farm without him.

Sybil – my mother's youngest sister, married Stanley Hatfield and lived in Kilnhurst. They had six children – Doris, Derrick and Arthur (twins), Fred, Irene and Enid – and used to walk to

Braithwell with the littlest in the pram and the others walking and taking turns to ride. I can't remember how they got back – did Dad take them in the trap? What did they do with the pram? Doris, the eldest, was a bit older than me and often stopped for weeks on end with us. We were great friends.

Auntie Sybil courted a young man called Charlie Roberts. He was a butcher's son and lived at Maltby. They fell out – her family never knew why but heart-broken Charlie emigrated to America. He did extremely well there and prospered, buying and selling cattle and eventually had his own ranch. He married Ann and had one daughter, Betty. He returned every year to England, always visiting my mother. When she died, he still visited my brothers at the farm whenever he came over. His last trip was in the summer of 1988. In December 1988 the following letter arrived at the farm – I thought it touching and a poignant letter for a man who lived life to the full and counted our family among his friends.

4905 Pacific Ave
Pleasant Grove
CA 95668

John Charles Roberts
October 10, 1900 to December 6, 1988

Charlie Roberts died Tuesday morning December 6, 1988 from a heart attack at the Rideout Hospital in Marysville following minor complications from a car accident. Charlie died as he lived – fast and sure – and with a purpose.

Respecting his wishes the family chose not to have a funeral memorial service. Charlie has never been to a funeral in his life and it would be a shame to make the first one he had to attend his own.

We were all fortunate to have known Charlie. Ann, his wife, spent 63 years as his companion. And although this is a sad time, we have much to be grateful for. Charlie, who was never sick a day in his life, went quickly and peacefully. He had just returned from seven weeks in England where he saw most of his family and friends in a delightful visit. We had a wonderful Thanksgiving holiday together. Charlie is survived by his daughter Betty; two grandchildren, Susan and Ralph; and, two great grand-daughters who at one and a half and two years old already display his spunk and spirit toward life. And, maybe most importantly, even though Charlie was 88, he died before he got old. We should all be so fortunate.

We know that you will feel the loss of his passing. He won't be pulling up in that big brown Mercedes, and he won't be looking for a place to put his cigar. And you won't be hearing about the low price of cattle and the high price of the British pound. Except that Charlie will live on in our hearts and our minds and we can certainly be proud to say "I knew a fellow named Charlie Roberts and he was quite a man."

Many of you we haven't ever met and yet we have heard so much about Charlie's friends. You added a special richness to Charlie's life because Charlie truly valued a friend. So in his memory, raise your glass and toast to a life filled with good family and friends. Charlie would have liked it that way.

ANN

When my father's first wife died (she was Elizabeth Pawson and great aunt to Arnold, Derrick and Maureen) my father was left with two little girls, Doris 4 and Audrey 3, not yet at school. They lived in a cottage at Micklebring. Miss Storey and her brother Ernest, a bachelor, lived next door to them. She was a spinster and said she would look after the children for Dad in the daytime. This only lasted a short time as she was not used to children and found it hard going, so Audrey went to her grandmother who lived just up the road at Pawson's Farm. Doris had then started school (Church school at Braithwell) and so it was much easier for Nan so she stayed with Nan Storey (as we all called her) and came to the farm to her grandfather's for her dinner every day – her father too was there, of course. Both of them came for Saturday and Sunday dinner with their father, grandfather and grandmother Charlotte. Soon after Dad re-married – my mother came from the Manor House at Micklebring – Grandma Charlotte (my grandfather's second wife) died and Mum and Dad came to live at the farm with grandfather Robert. Audrey came to live with them but Nan Storey begged to keep Doris with her. Her brother had died and she was getting older and lonely. She was a very private person and didn't make friends easily. So that continued. When Doris left school, she came to help at the farm but often went back to sleep at Nan's. When Doris died, she asked for her ashes to be scattered on Micklebring Lane as she'd walked it so often. She loved walking and working – she always helped with the poultry and harvest time on the stacks, passing sheaves to the stacker. She had a lovely nature but had a real temper if crossed and if we saw it coming we removed ourselves very quickly.

Most girls married local men and Doris married the local milkman, Arthur Hawksworth and they had two children, Leslie (still in the Village) and Margaret (Chapeltown). People always thought Audrey was delicate. She was pale with blonde hair – she was a very good knitter and an expert needlewoman. She always tried to teach me but to no avail. I preferred being outdoors. She married our farm foreman Empson Houghton another local lad and they lived at No. 37 High Street. They had two children, Doreen (still in the Village) and Donald (Edlington). Ida Baker told me that her sister Connie worked for Grandmother Charlotte and one day when Ida visited the farm – I understand everybody was made welcome there – Connie was ironing Grandpa Robert's back with an iron and brown paper – he had backache – a novel idea. I suppose the same thing as a heat lamp now.

❧

CHAPTER 2

Early Childhood Memories and Lasting Impressions

It was the end of harvest in 1925. I was 16 months old and not yet walking. My mother was visiting a sick friend. I was playing quite happily on the rag rug in front of the fire. My sister Doris mashed the tea for the harvest field teas as usual in a gallon tea-can and slipped down to the cellar to fetch the milk. I crawled to the table, pulled myself up, grabbed the table cloth and pulled the boiling tea on top of me. I think my screams could be heard at the top of the street.

Imagine the panic, horror and fear on that day. My father rushed in from the stackyard, saddled his horse and dashed to Maltby for Doctor Duffty, a wise and clever old doctor. A few weeks before he had attended a young boy, Georgie Picton, who had fallen into a pansion of hot pig fat. Mrs. Picton, his mother, was putting away the pig they had killed – this was a long and tedious job, cutting up fat and putting it in big tins in the oven. Then when it was rendered down it was poured into the pansion on the hearth side. Poor little George fell into it. He was rushed to hospital but unfortunately he died – partly due to shock. His mother walked to Doncaster every day to see him.

So when the doctor told my mother I would have to go to hospital, she refused to let me go. He said afterwards normally he would have insisted but after George's death he thought being separated from his mother hadn't helped George to recover, so he agreed to my staying at home. My mother never left my room for more than a few minutes at a time for six weeks. The doctor told my father that I couldn't possibly live but after two weeks he said I may pull through but that my right arm, which was scalded to the bone, would be useless. Thank God they were all wrong but I still bear some scars. The local nurse, Nurse Mummery, lived at No. 2 Maltby Lane Cottage. She was my godmother and came in every day to dress my burns. I never took to her after that, as I was so terrified of the pain when the dressings were removed.

All the gates were padded with sacks to stop them banging and the drive was covered with straw so the carts and traps made no noise – common practice in those days, so I understand.

After I recovered, I was spoilt to death. I was a pale, thin, tall girl, with long, wavy, light-brown hair. My legs were really skinny and I was given Sanatogen wine every day to build me up. I always say that's why I'm so partial to sherry. I was made to wear combs (combinations) – like pants and vests all in one, in a creamy-coloured wool. They buttoned down the front, had a hole in the rear for your ablutions. I hated them and eventually, as I got older, refused to wear them. Then I was put into liberty bodices, which most of my friends wore. These were like the top half of a vest but with buttons down the front and very thick. You did, of course, wear a vest under this and elastic-legged knickers to go with it. Wow!!

My first memory is walking down the croft with my mother holding her hand – I was three years old. She had a bucket in her other hand and had been feeding the hens which, of course, were free range and housed in a big wooden hut in the middle of the croft. The yard man had let the tup into the field. When the tup saw my mother with the bucket he headed straight for us, head down. My mother was small and plump and no runner. I was very nimble, even at that young age. My mother dropped her bucket, lifted her skirts and we both headed for the gate. There, two of our farm men were standing grinning. "Look, missus", they said, pointing to the tup. There he was with his head in the bucket. These tups can be very aggressive, as my mother knew but this one was after the poultry feed. She told my father off in no uncertain terms. When he told the men, they replied: "Eeh! gaffer, it was only 'cos we saw t'Missis's pink drawers that she were upset!"

I was about six years old when a circus came to Braithwell and they asked my father if they could have the orchard for their next two shows. We children were so excited and my friends could sneak in with me and have a preview. It was 3d for adults and 1d for children. The thing I remember vividly is the horse that told the time. The Ringmaster led out a small pony. It had a long cream mane and tail and was a beautiful creature. He shouted: "It's 3 o' clock." and the pony pawed the ground three times and then threw back its head and whinnied. When it did 12 o' clock we were all clapping and cheering. I went both nights and thought it was heaven – that was Thursday and Friday. Saturday, they were moving off to Rotherham. When Dad went outside on Saturday morning, they had gone – lock, stock and barrel. He was furious – no payment and lots of rubbish left behind. He rushed to the stable and saddled up Darky, his mare. He took her at a gallop towards Rotherham and caught up with them at Silverwood. After lots of arguing and threatening, the owner gave him the foal belonging to the mare who told the time in lieu of money. She was a lovely little thing and we all grew to love her. We called her Stella. I was bitterly disappointed though because I thought she too would be able to tell the time and tried often to make her – to no avail, of course! They have to be trained to do that. Dad broke her in to ride and to the trap. I rode her often round the Village. We loved her.

My brother Derrick used her in the trap with his friend, Arthur (Artie) Smith from Ashton Farm. One day a buyer, Norman Smith, arrived and Derrick was told to saddle her up and show her paces. Norman was a local gypsy and, like all gypsies, knew a good horse when he saw one. Derrick and Artie sat in the trap very morose, seeing their favourite transport removed from them. The dealer made a bid of £10. My brother said: "You couldn't buy a bloody hair out of her tail for that, Mista" and gave a great crack of the whip. She was always flighty and very fast and not used to that treatment, for we weren't allowed to swear and certainly not to use a whip. She lifted up her back legs and kicked the bottom straight out of the front of the trap splintered wood hanging down and then set off like a bat out of hell up the croft, with the lads' legs dangling through the floor and leaving the buyer and father standing there in amazement. Needless to say, Dad didn't sell her then and never did but it took my brother quite a while to stop her in her gallop. She died with us at a grand old age.

⤙

CHAPTER 3

Four-legged Family Friends – Fly and Darky and Cats, Cats, Cats

A scene that stays vividly in my mind, I would be about seven years old, is getting out of bed one morning and, as always, going to the window to look out at the fold yard with the cattle mooching around. The stable door was open and strange men were there with my father. Suddenly in the doorway appeared the body of our beloved mare, Darky – she was a beautiful dapple grey. We had been waiting for her to foal – she had had her foal during the night and had died foaling. She had all her bed (uterus) hanging out – an awful sight. My heart ached for her and my father. I had never seen my father cry but as they pulled her body through the stable door, he wept. And I wept too, for many days. We called her foal Tommy Boy – had it been a filly, we could have kept her but not a colt. As soon as he was broken, Dad sold him. We all cried bitterly. He tried to explain to us that this is how he made his money and we lived because of it – of course when you're young, this is very difficult to understand.

The mother of Darky was called Fly. I never knew her. She died when I was just a baby but she was often the subject of conversation. My father bought her in a sale. She had a damaged left leg, otherwise he couldn't have afforded her. They used to talk about her having "legs like band". She was a thourough-

10

bred. Dad used her in the trap and my mother was very proud to drive round the Village with Fly. Once she went to Rotherham with her to pick up the groceries – sacks of flour and sugar etc.. Coming home up Winny Hill, the Salvation Army Band was playing. Fly started to dance and prance about and poor Mum was nearly thrown off the trap. They had to stop the band playing. One of the Salvation Army men then led her past, much to Mum's embarrassment. She never took Fly again but stuck to her old pony to go to Rotherham.

Later that year a man from near the Plumpers Hotel near Sheffield saw Fly out in the trap. He enquired about her and offered Dad £25 for her. Dad agreed and he was to fetch her next day. Mum was furious but Dad said he'd made the deal and needed the money. The man came with saddle, bridle etc. and rode her home – very happy with his purchase. At ten o'clock that night, Dad and Mum were in the kitchen and they heard a horse whinney. Mum said: "That's Fly." She was coming down Maltby Lane behind the house. Then she came galloping up the drive, whinnying all the way. Mum and Dad rushed out and there she was. She nuzzled up to them and Mum cried and said: "You can't send her back." But Dad had spent most of the money on wages. My grandfather (mother's father) gave her the money and Dad rode over and returned it to the buyer. From then on, she considered Fly was hers. The buyer told Dad she'd jumped the hedge to escape.

The Tithe Barn at the farm would be built along with the house. The big barn doors from the stackyard open opposite another pair of doors which lead into the fold yard. Here, in the 17th. century, the corn would be put on the barn floor and beaten with a flail. The corn would fall on the floor and the chaff would blow through into the fold yard. The hay and straw were also stored there and what a job it was passing the sheaves and loose hay through the barn windows. Farm men had to be very strong in those days.

The horses were stabled just opposite the house, across the yard. In winter, when all the cows were in the cow-house and yard and the horses stabled, there was a lot of mucking-out and feeding to be done. The pig sties were on the north side with the pond behind. The horses came in from work and always walked into the pond for a drink and the mud was washed off their legs too. Water was carried to the pigs but the cows drank at the big tank in the open yard. This was filled

11

from a pump in the back kitchen. A pipe ran under the drive and much pumping it needed to get the 200 gallons into it each day. On really hot days in summer we kids sat in this tank on the bar which ran across it – it was lovely. Sometimes we ducked under and when we bobbed up, we frightened the poor old cows to death who were just putting their heads over to drink.

Bob Houghton worked for my father from leaving school at 14. He is deaf and dumb and so certain jobs on the farm he didn't do but he worked with the pigs and did most of the dairy work. One day he was cleaning out a young sow, throwing the manure out behind him through a partly-open door, keeping the pig in front of him. I went bursting in to tell him Dad wanted him. I threw the door open and out shot the pig, straight through my legs and carried me straight onto the muck heap. I fell off with my legs in the air and did I stink! Bob came to look what was happening and laughed and laughed. I was furious.

On the floor in our kitchen were old Yorkstone slabs. Through constant scrubbing and wearing they were beautifully smooth. In one, by the side of the fireplace, was a perfect hole about 4" diameter and about ½" to ¾" deep. This we used to play marbles, Derrick, Dennis and me. We lined up the marbles with many pleadings to Dad sitting in his Windsor chair by the fire. Nobody else sat in this if Dad was in the kitchen and we scarpered if we were in it when he came in. Mum had a wooden rocking chair on the opposite side of the fire – this was hers although as kids we loved to get in it and have a good rock. Anyway, I always thought my brothers were taking advantage of me and had their marbles nearer than mine so Dad was the referee, although he'd rather have been left in peace to read his paper. Marbles were held between fore-finger and bent thumb, against the nail, with knuckles of the hand resting on the floor and then you shot your marble. If it landed in the hole and stayed it was your first turn and then you started the game "proper".

The ordinary marbles were lined up in a row and then an alley was used – this is a large marble. This was shot down the line to dislodge as many marbles as possible. There was also a special marble called a blood alley – it had pink stripes and was very superior. Hence the expression "You're a blood alley" (very special). Also there were "potties". These were made of pot instead of glass and everybody would play with that kind –

never glass and pot together. We played at school, on the street and in the farm-yard but my favourite place was always the farm kitchen on winter nights, when mother was getting tea ready and everybody was indoors. Oh! Happy times. A huge coal and log fire burning in the grate. What joy an open fire brings. Gas, electric, central heating – not the same! As one of my friends, Marion Byron, said when she was ill at Christmas: "There's no comfort there – especially if you're feeling poorly."

Our milkman was Mr. Wadsworth. He bought our milk from the farm and hawked it. He lived at Springdale House (Holywell Lane) with his mother and I visited them often with my father. He was a very nice man (he was Joan Addenbrooke's father) and, of course, came with his white pony Billy and float each morning. He loaded all the milk in big ten-gallon churns and travelled to Maltby with it. He then transferred this to a smaller two-gallon churn and went round from door to door, ladling out the milk in a one-pint measure. Some people left jugs on the step, some people basins, some came to the cart to collect theirs. Old white pony, Billy, stood quite still and moved on when "Gee up" was called and stopped at the command of "Whoa!" When Mr. Wadsworth retired, he gave "White Billy" to my brothers and I and he lived at Hall Farm until he died of old age – about 20. We all loved him and many a tear was shed when he died. He pulled a trap, we rode bare-back on him and he was always there to be patted or cuddled. Dear old Billy, such happy memories he brings back. Mother always knew where we'd been – we were covered in his white hairs.

As a child, for my seventh birthday, my mother bought me a doll – I called it Kalutas. I can only imagine that this was the name of the firm that made it and it was on the box – otherwise where would I get a name like that from? Mum bought it, I understand, because I was always playing with the cats. I had a beautiful long-haired ginger tom called "Fluff". He was born at the farm and became my special cat – most of them, there were about twelve, didn't come into the house but Fluff was mine and where I went, he went. I told you I was spoilt. I had an old pram and dressed him up in a dress and bonnet and pushed him around the farm with a blanket over him. He'd lay there for hours and I never ever got the same pleasure from a doll as I did from my cats. I think Mum used to think he'd pass on diseases. Cats had worms and kids had worms too. We used to take choc drops with coloured bits on top for them. This was supposed to purge you and clean out all the little blighters. We used to hear tell of people with tape worms. They said they were a foot long and sometimes broke off halfway out and if it was the bottom part, the head stayed in your stomach and ate it away. Ye Gods!! We must have frightened each other to death!

My cat before Fluff was a tortoiseshell female called "Tibby". She was big, fat and lazy and always having kittens. Couldn't get away from the tom I suppose, or maybe didn't want to. Anyway, she often had litters in the house – in a cupboard, under the settle, and once when I was away from school with a cold and sitting on the settle by the fire with a rug over me, she jumped on my knee and gave birth to five kittens. I was fascinated as she licked them all clean, these were blind little objects – well, they had their eyes closed. Audrey came in, she was looking after me and she was horrified but I insisted on her leaving them there and really learnt very early in life about birth and, of course, about death when three of them were drowned – common practice in those days – with many tears from me as to where they'd gone. Of course, to heaven was the answer.

All the cats congregated at milking time. First thing Bob did in the cowshed was squirt the milk into their dishes or he would have got no peace. Cats were never fed – their job was to catch mice but they got plenty of milk. Whenever I went through the door and he saw me, Bob always lifted the cow's teat up and squirted the milk in my face. I hated it – it was warm and sticky and he, of course, always thought it was a huge joke. He couldn't hear me coming but always seemed to have a sixth sense that somebody was there.

The milk was carried over to the dairy and syled (strained) through muslin to take out any bits. Some was put into churns for the milkman. The rest was put in big panshions in the cellar (on the stone slabs) and these were skimmed for making butter and for our porridge. We always had cream on everything – mother and Dad never had tea without a tablespoon of cream in their cups. The skimmed milk was given to any of the poor families in the Village who cared to call. The rest was given to the pigs and that's why I could never buy skimmed milk – pay out good money for "blue" milk, as we called it? My father would be horrified at the thought – he'd "turn" in his grave, as the saying goes. Dad also loved a pint of milk boiled and poured over a thick slice of bread cut into cubes. This was sprinkled with sugar and grated nutmeg and was his supper most nights.

I often had to take a turn at churning the butter when my sisters Audrey and Doris were busy with other things. It seemed to take ages and then it would turn (into butter) – you could see the small globules of fat appear on the glass top and you knew it was finished. It was taken out and washed and then salted and patted into ½ lb. pats. I didn't mind this job, as you could have great fun with the butter pats, making really small round balls and then eating them.

When the men couldn't get on the land, all the cow houses, pigsties and stables were mucked out and whitewashed. The men used to be covered in white spots. Lime was also used in the house. All the ceilings were done with it twice a year, Spring and Christmas. The cellars and dairy also. What a job! My sister Doris was really good at this and used to get her oldest apron and her mop cap on first thing in a morning and really get some work done. And surprise, surprise, she really enjoyed it! She said you could always see where you'd been. She then liked two boiled eggs – preferably duck eggs – for her tea with toast.

In 1946, Malcolm, Eileen (my sister-in-law) and I stripped our kitchen beams and ceiling of lime. It took us weeks and the dirt and dust was horrendous. We often wished, during that time, we'd never started but, once started, you can't stop. But think – there were 300 years of lime on there – and two coats every year. No wonder it was hard work. The dust even got into the attics.

❖

CHAPTER 4

Ah! Happy Days

The guns were always kept in the kitchen at the farm. There were five hanging from hooks on the beams. From being very young, my father impressed on us always to take care when handling guns. It was the only time I ever remember my father hitting me when I took a 16-bore gun down and pointed it at a friend. I just sobbed: "It wasn't loaded." He replied: "How do you know it wasn't loaded? It could have been." Mr.

15

Smith from Ashton Farm once went into their kitchen to hang up his gun. Putting it down, he caught the trigger and it went off and blew a hole right through the chimney breast. His wife was standing at the oven. It missed her by inches. He thought both barrels were empty. This sort of accident happened so often, as my father well knew. My father was a wonderful shot but never went in for clay pigeon shooting. He'd think it was a waste of cartridges – not as popular then as now. He shot rats, rooks, rabbits and pigeons, and hare, partridge and pheasant for the pot.

One day uncle Lal, Arthur Hawksworth (Birkwood Terrace, Seven Houses), Jack Saxton (Dam Cottage), Epe Houghton (35 High Street, now "Ridgeway") and Ralph Walker (Lambcote Grange, who was an excellent shot), were down in the "Hosswoods" (Austwoods) shooting clays for 1/- a time. Ralph also had several of his shooting friends with him. Derrick and Dennis and I were watching. Dad came down with Mr. Gurney and Jack his son from Well House. They stood watching a while and listening to these lads boasting. They were all in their teens and twenties. Mr. Gurney said to Derrick: "Run home lad and fetch your Dad's gun and a few cartridges." Derrick was off like a shot across the meadows into Holywell Lane, across the field called Vicarage Yard (where the Holywell Crescent houses are now built), over the wall into the farm. He was back flushed with excitement. I was just nervous. I kept saying to Dad: "Suppose you can't hit them." Dad laughed but Mr. Gurney, a great friend of Dad's, said:

"Don't you worry lass. Your Dad will knock spots off this clever little lot." And of course he did. We youngsters all got 3d each but I was starry-eyed.

Dad was a religious man but not "holier than thou". His father was a local preacher and he could quote huge chunks of the Bible at the appropriate time. At harvest time, when his farming friends were worried about their crops, he would say: "Don't worry. As the good book, Genesis Chap. 8, verse 22 says: "While the earth remaineth, seed time and harvest shall not fail." When anybody was acting childishly, he said: "Corinthians Chap. 13: When I was a child, I spoke as a child, I understood as a child, I thought as a child, but when I became a man, I put away childish things." And when he thought somebody was being mean, he said: "And now abideth Faith, Hope and Charity – these three but the greatest of these is Charity."

Mother too had a great faith and I suppose this is why we, as a family, are all believers. Is it heredity? Learnt at your mother's knee? We always had to say our prayers. Or is it something you grow up with and because of your happy memories you continue with it? I don't know. I only know that I have a simple belief in God and I always feel God is with me – it helps me. I often use Sir Jacob Astley's prayer: "Lord thou knowest how busy I must be today. If I forget thee, do not thou forget me.". People who are pious irritate me and people who go to church because "it's the done thing" infuriate me. Perhaps I go because it's a habit that's difficult to break but I do know that, usually, I feel better for it. If I don't, it's usually due to the fact that the hymns don't suit me – but then I always tell the Rector!

Uncle Albert too was a religious man and a regular chapel-goer but he wouldn't allow his family to do anything on a Sunday – no knitting, no sewing, nothing; this was the usual way with Methodists. Dad wasn't like that but he wouldn't allow the horses or men out to work. Just the milking and feeding the animals – these were a necessity.

When Mum and I wanted something new, a necklace or an ornament or a new dress, Dad used to say: "Think of what the Good Book says – Matthew Ch. 6 v. 19 "Lay not up for yourselves treasures upon earth where moth and dust doth corrupt." We used to reply:

"You don't want us to spend your money Dad." and he'd just grin. He hadn't a lot to spare. A man in the Village was boasting how he'd sold a tup – he'd got a good price but hadn't told the youngster who bought it that it wasn't much good. Dad said to him: "What doth it profit a man if he gain the whole world and lose his own soul?" He stamped off very upset. And to gardeners worried about their allotments, Ecclesiastes Ch. 3 v. 1 "To everything there is a season and a time to every purpose under the heaven." Or "A time to plant and a time to pluck up that which is planted." One of our men bemoaned the fact that his daughter had a young man he didn't approve of – "It's no good gaffer," he said to Dad, "I shall have to tell her." And Dad replied:

"Bill, there's a time to keep silence and a time to speak." Bill thanked him later when they married and he became very fond of his son-in-law.

"I might a' put me foot in it boss if you hadn't told me one o' your wise sayings." And when somebody died – we thought too early in their life – he'd say:

"There is a time to be born and a time to die."

He used to say that when he first started farming Hall Farm on his own, sometimes Mum and he only had 1/- left after paying the wages and buying the groceries. Of course there was always plenty of good food – we never went short of that but no money for spice (sweets) etc.. Dad said if you had a good fire, a good bed and good food, you didn't need anything else. And that was the way he lived his life.

One of Dad's sayings when he came to bring us a cup of tea in the morning at 6am was: "Come on, get up, it'll soon be dark." He was always an early-to-bed, early-to-rise man, often at 4.30am. In later years I often passed him on the stairs. I was just going to bed – he was getting up. I'd say: "Goodnight dad." He'd say: "Good morning Joyce."

Dad never slept away from home and never went on holiday. I once told him I should like to travel. "Why?" he asked. I said:

"They say it broadens the mind." He laughed and replied:

"Love, you won't find people any different anywhere in the world. They're happy or sad, generous or mean, kind or unkind, good or bad. Wherever you go, human nature doesn't change – Braithwell people are like people all over the world."

He always wore a black bow tie and a pork pie trilby and when he was going out he always had a buttonhole from his garden – winter and summer. This was in a silver holder which held water and so kept it fresh. I've never seen one since or known anybody else who owned one. In summer it was always a rose – he had about 300 roses in his front garden and people came from miles around to look over the wall or stand at the gate to admire them. Sometimes he asked them in but only if they were also interested in farming.

✢

CHAPTER 5

To Plough and Sow, to Reap and Mow

As a child, one of our great days was when the stallion came. He was a huge Shire usually 17 or more hands high. With his beautiful coat and movement, we loved to see him prancing up the drive. The stallion man, who was in charge, was always a small, wiry fellow – I never saw a big one. He had a wide circle of farms to visit and, in those days, he walked. He called at each farm to serve the mares which were in season and returned to check if the mares were in foal. The stallion was always very fit and took some handling. My father, once in his career, went with his father's stallion. He said some of the digs were dreadful. He stayed one night at a farm that was very scruffy. He spent the night on top of the bed because of fleas but when he went to use the chamber pot, it had been used much earlier and not emptied and the top was covered with green, fluffy mould. He said he peed through the window. He never went again – he liked his home comforts.

When the stallion called round on its yearly visit we were always despatched to the house so never knew what went on. But of course were delighted with the result – a foal. Always wanting a filly so that we could breed from her and keep the same strain of these lovely Shires at the farm. Dad always did the haltering, breaking and working them himself. He was wonderful with horses. When they were broken to the reins, he would put them with an old horse and fasten them both to a railway sleeper. Then he would drive them round and round in the croft – backing, turning and stopping. I used to sit on the gate and listen to the sounds of "Auve" (to the left), "Gee", "Gee back" (to the right), "Back, back", "Come back" (back up), " Woa". His voice would echo through the evening air. And that after a hard day's work in the fields. Later the pair would then be put in the harrows – the first job for a young horse. Eventually on to ploughing but always with an old horse to keep them steady. The old horse walked on the unploughed land and the young horse in the furrow to keep it in a straight line.

Farming runs in the blood – once a way of life but today, with all the form-filling, irritating regulations and interfering of officials, sons following fathers need a lot more education and are no longer in charge of their own acres. To plough and sow and reap and mow are long gone from farming. It's really become a business and sadly lots of farms no longer have even a few chickens in the stackyard, pigs in the sties nor cows in the cow shed. So making a living from the land is how much money one can get out of so many acres. It's a business.

Although as a farmer's lass I saw cows calving, ewes lamb-

19

ing, etc., I don't think I ever associated it with the mating of the bull and cow or the tup and ewe. The stallion I never saw "operating". Perhaps the only thing which eventually made me "cotton on" was the cats. The mating and then the kittens came quite close and at last I associated them together. But by then I was much older and wiser.

The farm labourers of my childhood always had a natural dignity. Because of his association with the land he never seemed frustrated, irritable, never craving for material things. In most villages, families are inter-connected by marriage. Offend one and you offend them all. One of my brothers told one farmer not to take implements from our farmyard without telling him first. After that, this farmer completely ignored both my brothers and never spoke to me again – he cut us all off. He, of course, was the loser as he couldn't borrow any more implements.

In those days, thrift, hard work, pride in the job and craftsmanship were rewarded. They were healthy because they ate good food they grew on the land and reared stock themselves. They were happy and lived life in a close-knit agricultural community. They also helped each other especially in hard times, births or deaths etc..

Farmers always worked together, borrowing horses and equipment. My father worked with Mr. Smith of Ashton Farm. He was a big, fat, jolly man with a big moustache and his daughter Jessie and I were great friends. Artie (Arthur), his son, and my brother Derrick were pals too. Men were loaned between farms for potatoeing, pea picking, thrashing etc.. Money was very scarce but food was always plentiful. We had a rabbit warren in the middle of the croft and it was great fun to sit and watch the rabbits playing round the warren. When I clapped my hands they all ran for their hole, soon to re-appear and slowly move farther afield to eat. Dad would take down his gun once a week and hey presto! – we'd have rabbit pie for dinner.

The first job any small boy did on the land was bird-scaring. Often he took time off from school to earn a few pence for his family. He stood all day with a clap board, rattling it when birds – pigeons, rooks etc. appeared. Dad often went up to the corn field with his gun after drilling and then there was pigeon pie. When children were used on farms for bird-scaring, this rhyme was sung:

We've ploughed our land
We've sown our seed
We've made all neat and gay
So take a bit and leave a bit
Away you birds away.

He always took me rook-shooting to the Manor. I collected the rooks and bagged them up as he dropped them with his gun. Friends shudder when I tell them these tales but, as a country girl, I knew that this was essential to keep down the rook population, otherwise they would ruin the crops. I used to have a 16-bore gun to shoot pigeons from the corn field but I was never a very good shot – the noise scared them off though. I inherited a lot of things from my father – love of the country and home, love of old furniture and bygones. Flowers and gardening were a joy to him. The rookery, I'm sorry to say, has long since gone. It was in the big elms at the Manor Farm, Micklebring Lane. Rook pies were very good – you used just the breast cooked with shin beef and a good crust. You slit down the middle of the bird, pulled off the skin with the feathers and, putting your fingers under the breast meat, pulled it out – simple.

Farms in those days carried all stock and so were very self-sufficient. We always had our own bull – no artificial insemination in those days. He was a beautiful creature. Lots of farmers with only a small herd would use him. He was penned in one corner of the fold yard. They were contrary things and we were always warned not to mess with him but we could never resist teasing him when we passed. He was a pedigree Friesian called Westphalia Mustafa – what a name for such a noble animal. We also had a cow named "Dunshade", a prize animal who gave eight gallons a day.

We had an old man staying with us, Mr. Page. He was in his nineties and deaf. The father of a friend of my mother's, he came for a holiday and stayed on. He loved the farm and feared nothing. The Bull hated him. He had a stick and used to go up and bang the railings, rattling along them. The bull would paw the ground and bellow and, try as my father might, he couldn't stop Mr. Page. One day, the bull went beserk. Luckily, Dad was there. He broke down the fence and charged round the fold yard. The noise was horrendous. Dad tried to lassoo him to get a rope round his neck but to no avail. Eventually the knacker man came and shot him. He was a beautiful Friesian bull and a big financial loss to my father but this did happen quite often. They pulled him out with a horse and a chain round his neck. Sometimes the farmers were lamed when a bull went mad and one cowman in the area got killed by one. The men were never allowed to take him out without a pole. This was attached to a ring on his nose and if he got difficult, it was pulled to keep him in check. It hurts when the tender skin on your nose is pulled – you give in. Once a bull went beserk in Doncaster Market and caused havoc. It was cornered well away from the market after scaring the people of Doncaster half to death. Another bull kept a local farmer up a tree for several hours until somebody had the nerve to rescue him by ticing (enticing) the bull away with cow cake.

❧

CHAPTER 6

Every little helps

Each day seemed to go on for ever. Each day that dawned in the summer holidays was a new adventure day. Things to do, things to see, horses to ride, cats to cuddle, hens to feed. I've never understood why people call them chickens. People nowadays always talk about keeping chickens. Chickens are babies, small fluffy things; hens lay eggs. They're pullets first, then hens, then boiling fowls and in the pot.

In our Village, lots of people kept hens. In those days, a few hens scratching about the yard kept you in eggs – and a boiling fowl to boot when they finished laying. You replenished by letting a hen go broody (she stopped laying and started cluck-clucking, puffing out (fluffing up) her feathers) and she was left to sit on the eggs and bring off her own chicks. If, by any chance, you preferred her to lay, you shut her up in a small coop with slatted front and bottom. A hen that wants to sit has a very hot breast and, of course, keeps it this way in a nice, warm, nest but putting it into this coop with a mesh floor soon cools that. We always said: "This'll cool her ardour." And it usually did – within two or three days she'd be back to laying. The local pheasant rearers used to come round asking for broodies to sit on their pheasant and partridge eggs. Many a good shilling was made this way by my mother but usually she preferred to hatch out her own chickens, ducks and geese with her broodies.

Something I've never heard or seen anybody but mother do. When she had young pullets, they sometimes got snuffles. I didn't know if it was cold or just the dry meal – we mixed our own always from Dad's own ground oats, fish meal, maize etc.. Anyway, when mother saw this happening, she'd take me up to the hen-house, put a partition across and then I'd catch the pullets and Mum would wipe their noses with a piece of rag dipped in permanganate of potash. She said it stopped it spreading. They always seemed to improve. Remember, these were her pin money and in hard times even the grocery money. Once, when Mum left me to mix the meal, I decided to improve it with a little more fish meal, as she had said it was good for them. All the customers complained that their eggs tasted of fish – they couldn't understand it. So did ours – I got a good ticking-off.

Collecting eggs was quite an art. The hens wandered the farm scratching and clucking and we were always told if we heard one making its egg-laying noise to get in there and find the eggs. The most unlikely places – the dog kennels when the dog had gone out for the day – the cart shed under the most awkward piece of machinery and the meal house amongst the sacks but most of all the stacks – they could be left for days there if nobody saw them leave the nest or cluck-clucking away. Then of course they all had to be cracked – who knows which had been laid first? Egg custard, lemon curd – all were made when a nest was found. Some were bad – what a stink!

One day, mother was chatting to a lady of the Village who'd called for eggs. Up the drive came a young woman who, six months before, had lost her small two-year-old son with diphtheria – a dreaded disease this. She chatted and laughed with Mum. When she'd gone, the old lady said: "How can she laugh and joke? She only lost her little boy a few months ago." My mother rounded on her and replied: "Remember Mary, there's many a broken heart behind a smiling face." How true this is – I often think of my wise mother's sayings.

Mum plucked and dressed her own poultry for extra money. Whilst she was doing one for our dinner, she'd do an extra one for sale. She also made marvellous potted chicken – a real delicacy. I loved the days we had boiling fowl when I came from school. It was thick broth with lots of veg. in and a whole loaf of bread cut into squares in a big basin on the table. A good handful was put into a soup dish and several ladles of hot chicken broth poured over. Then the hot meat in a lovely white sauce (made with the stock and cream), served with leeks, carrots, parsnips, sprouts and lashings of mashed potatoes – lovely! Happy memory!

My mother was an excellent cook. How lucky my friends were. She took them all to her heart, fed them, slept them, loved them. It gave me great joy on meeting again two friends I hadn't seen for forty years. During our happy recollections at the home of my schoolfriend Anne Staniland (Kelly), they both remarked at separate times how they had such a great respect and love for my mother. "Such fond memories of her.", Gladys Jevons, visiting from Wales, said. "She was so kind to us. We did enjoy her cooking.", said Stan Shephard, now living in Australia. "Her suppers in that farm kitchen were wonderful.". He also said: "How lucky you are to have found contentment in the place where you were born. I had to travel thousands of miles to find it."

My mother pickled eggs in big stone jars in the cellar. All spare eggs were put down in isinglass – these were used in winter for baking when eggs were short and the eggs from the hens had to be sold to pay for the feed. In later years, she reared Broad-breasted Bronze turkeys. Cussed birds these were. It was in the days that they died at the drop of a hat – blackhead was a nightmare with turkeys and there were no proprietary feeds then as now. We fed them chopped lettuce and dandelion leaves and chopped hard-boiled eggs when they were small – quite a tedious job. There was no cure for blackhead but the greenery was supposed to be a deterrent. Going into the pen in the morning and finding turkeys dead on the floor was a devastating thing for my mother who depended on these birds, plucked and dressed for Christmas, for all those little extras – new clothes, a few bottles of port, bottles of rum for the rum sauce. We all in the family still have rum sauce and not brandy.

Killing of the turkeys was my father's job. Geese and ducks were bled by a knife in the neck, then scalded to make them easier to pluck. Mother got so fed up with asking the farm men and my Dad to kill the poultry that she eventually decided on a do-it-yourself job – she put their head in the fold yard door shut it and pulled and it broke their necks – very effective, except one day, my mother killed and plucked a boiling fowl for dinner, put it on the stone in the cellar before drawing its innards (insides) out. When she went down the cellar, the poor old thing was running around! It had only been stunned. It took some catching and made such a mess, as you can imagine! She was terrified and never killed another.

We always made crab-apple jelly at home to eat with the hare and pheasant. The apples came from a tree in the hedge at Birchwood Close Field and I liked the job of removing the stalk. This was the only thing necessary, apart from washing them. They were then covered in water and put into the oven until they broke down into a mush. I used to love seeing the pink liquid running through the bag (a flour bag – flour came in cotton bags then!) which was tied to stool legs to drip into a bowl. It was such a beautiful colour but these were wild crab apples from the field trees. I still make this jelly but the cultivated ones never seem to have the same flavour.

We never bought a cake or bread. All jam, marmalade, pickles were home-made, lemon curd, mincemeat etc.. Chickens, ducks, geese were fattened, eaten and the surplus sold. Sheep, pigs, bullocks and goats were kept. Some went to the local slaughterhouse (Mr. Jim Parkes, John Parkes' grandfather) and were brought back for us to eat – in the case of the bullocks, we had a huge roast of lift (topside of beef) from it, usually weighing about a stone (14lbs) and the rest Mr. Parkes sold. No money changed hands – we had meat each week instead until the beast was paid for. Fruit was bottled and stored for winter. Pears, plums and damsons were picked and bottled or made into jam or pickles.

We all used to love it when a cow calved. Then we'd have "beastling" custard for dinner. This was the first milking from the cow after she'd calved. The beastlings mixed with sugar and put into a deep pastry case and grated nutmeg on top. This was then cooked in the oven exactly like an egg custard. It was beautiful. It is really delicious and it sets without effort.

When Dad had finished his dinner he'd often sit back and say: "King George hasn't enjoyed his dinner better than me." I used to say:

"But Dad, he can have anything." Of course now I know exactly what he meant but he'd just smile and say:

"You'll understand one day."

Mothers of course wore corsets and long brassieres. These hooked together. A lady used to come round and measure mother for these – we always called her Mrs. Spirella as they were called "Spirella" corsets. She was a handsome woman – tall and well-built but of course beautifully upholstered. Her bosom was huge and her tummy well held in – I'll bet she breathed a sigh of relief every night when Mr. Spirella undid the laces at the back of her corsets. They had bones (whalebones, I think they called them). Did they come from a whale? They had huge laces which were pulled hard to flatten all you'd got. My mother was small and plump, so had quite a lot to fit into both corsets and brassieres. These, too, were made to measure.

I used to feel sorry for my friends who had thin mothers and thought: "Fancy having to cuddle up to that."

❧

CHAPTER 7

Live as though you'll die tomorrow
Farm as though you'll live for ever

We went for picnics in the pony and trap. It seemed miles away. Now I realise, of course, that it was only about 1½ miles from home – Dale Hill Field or Foxholes, full of buttercups, daisies and moonpennies. There were always gypsies in the fields – nobody ever moved them on. I had roast hedgehog with them once when my brother Derrick went visiting them and took me – I daren't refuse. It tasted good – like chicken. They were camped in Fidler's Field up Maltby Lane, a long narrow field at the end of Birchwood Lane on the east side of Maltby Lane going down the hill. Further along, there were woods running right down into Maltby. They were kind and friendly people – true Romanies with beautiful caravans and piebald horses.

In Dad's youth, the farm men who lived in never sat in the kitchen in the evenings. They sat in the stables. The farmer and his wife sat in the kitchen – the front room was only used on Sundays. Bed at 9pm. Up at 5am. Out to milk before breakfast, which consisted of a bowl of hot milk with fat bacon in it. Monday dinner was cold meat and potatoes with pickles. Suet or rice pudding seemed to be the pudding. Sunday dinner was a stone of beef, practically all fat, potatoes and veg.. Tea was bread and jam – Sundays there was a sponge cake. For supper bread and cheese. None of the old farm workers ever recall anything in tins, not even tinned fruit. On most farms the brasses the horseman cleaned belonged to them personally – not to the farmer. The Head Horseman had the best horse and cart The Second Horseman the next and so on. Each man owned his own brasses and decorated his own horse. If he left the farm, he took his brasses with him.

Going out at night, when it was dark, to "supper up" with the horseman and foreman Empson Houghton (Epe – he became my brother-in-law), settling them all down for the night, staying up with them a while, listening to the farm men chatter, play cards, tell tales, sing songs in the clean "standing" where the straw was kept, playing the mouth-organ and smoking – very careful with this too. This was where they spent their evenings. Some cleaned harness, some cleaned brass. I never realised that these farm lads had nowhere else to go. No money for the pub. They spent lots of evenings in the stable. Saturday night was the one night they went out – usually to the pub or a local hop (dance). It was always warm with the horses in the stable and clean in the straw.

Always there seemed happy, easy laughter. When the talk turned to girls, they sent me back to the house. Across the yard, all dark after the stable lamps' yellow glow. Indoors, the paraffin lamps were burning. Mother sewing, Dad reading the newspaper. I don't remember the wireless at all. Then up to bed with a candle after visiting the outside toilet – a two-seater. Mum or my sisters sat to wait for me on the seat of one whilst I used the other – such hygiene. A museum piece today.

Upstairs, I could hear them talking downstairs because the floors had holes right through. If I pulled back the rug, I could look right down into the kitchen. Those floors dated back to the house being built in the 1600s and I heard many a secret that way.

The only time I remember the Shire horses being difficult was when they had a foal. After a while, the mare had to return to work and leave the foal at home on the farm. They hated this and whinnied all the way to the field – the foal whinneying back until they were out of hearing. One day, I was in school when we heard this terrible noise – no rubber tyres on carts then, they were iron wheels. This horse and cart, which was tipped up, came thundering past the school on Micklebring Lane without

27

a driver. We all stood up shouting and frightened, I more than anybody because I saw it was our horse, Daisy – she went galloping down the High Street. She wanted to get back to her foal Blossom. She had set off when the back of the cart was tipped up in the field for muck-spreading, thrown Epe off the load and lost half of the manure in the gateway. My father was in the farm yard. He heard her coming and knew what had happened, jumped the farm wall and stopped her by grabbing the reins. I cried and insisted that I went home. I kept sobbing: "Daisy may be hurt." Miss Athron let me go but she couldn't stop me crying. Of course, I didn't go back to school that afternoon. Poor old Epe broke his arm but I was only worried about Daisy.

In the open yard by our pigsties stood a big barrel of phenol (we pronounced it phenile) with a big wooden lid which was always kept on top. This was a very strong disinfectant used for many jobs around the farm. Disinfecting hen perches, pig sties etc.. My mother bred her own goslings, ducklings and chickens. They all ran loose around the farm with their mothers. Sometimes, when she had enough eggs, she used an incubator which was heated by paraffin to produce the warmth of the mother's body and the eggs had to be turned and damped each day as the hen would do to stop the chickens sticking to the shell. Going out one night to lock up her stock she put the hens and chickens in the coop, the duck and ducklings in the duck-house but could only find the goose and one gosling. She put them in the shed and went inside to find Dad, telling him the tale. Before he could speak my brother Derrick, who was about five, said: "I saw 'em Mummy. I put em in't pond and de drowned." She took him outside and said:

"Show me where you put them." He pointed to the phenol barrel – now with the lid securely on. On removing the lid and putting a dipper into the barrel, there were nine dead goslings killed by the fumes. Obviously he couldn't catch the last one and somebody had been negligent leaving the lid off the barrel. Nobody ever admitted to it of course. They would have had the sharp end of mother's tongue. Another time, mother only managed to rear one gosling from a clutch of eggs. This small gosling became a family pet and we kept him on the lawn in the back garden and we called him Jaffet – I don't know why. He was a particular favourite of mine and I took him all the scraps and fed him up until he was quite fat. Dad started talking about Christmas and we were very indignant. I was in tears and Mum promised he would be spared so we went to bed happy. But five days before Christmas, Jaffet disappeared. Obviously somebody else had their eye on a Christmas dinner. We mourned him like a long-lost friend and I cried myself to sleep.

Other animals we became fond of were the lambs. When an ewe died, or one had more lambs than she could feed, Dad always tried to get other ewes with only one lamb or who had lost lambs to take to them. This usually entailed skinning the dead lamb and putting the skin on the motherless lamb to keep the scent that the mother knew and recognised. Or fastening up the ewe by the neck and getting the lamb (always interested in any mother's milk) to suckle her. In this way she couldn't tup them off. I was always very upset to see these poor little things, only a few hours old, knocked down time and again by the ewe, who knew they didn't belong to her. Sometimes of course she just wouldn't take to them and they had to be hand-reared on a bottle. This I loved. Neither Mum nor Dad did, as it was time-consuming for both of them. In those days there was no pre-pared feed on the market as there is today and they went on to cow's milk mixed with water. This often gave them skits (diarrhoea). The feed had to be the right mix, heated to just the right temperature (blood temperature) as for human babies). When I was getting a little older this job fell to me. One day twins were born and the mother died. Being unable to pass them onto another ewe, Dad passed them on to Dennis (my brother) and me. We called them Billy and Betty. Dennis soon grew sick of this job. He had his goat Topsy, who kept producing kids and his alsatian Crafty, so I took on the job alone. Quite a job for a seven-year-old, particularly as they got bigger and used to push forward and nearly knock you down for their food. The day came when I went in to the back garden to feed them and they rushed up to me and Billy knocked me flying. It was a wet, miserable day and I landed flat on my back. Of course I rushed into the kitchen "rooring (crying) my eyes out" as the expression goes. Mother said: "That does it. They'll have to go." I shouted:

"No! I'll be alright." But their fate was sealed and come Saturday off they went to market. I was sent off whilst the deed was done. Of course I was told they'd gone to a good home with bigger girls and boys who they couldn't knock over and, stupid little fool that I was, I believed them.

CHAPTER 8

The Farmer's Year
(with apologies to Sarah Coleridge)

January	Furrow filled with snow
	Horses ploughing cannot go
February	Wet and rainy too
	Fields are dormant just like you
March	The winds they heave and shriek
	Trees blown down and branches creak
April	Is the month of lambs
	Mother ewes and father rams
May	The month of sun and showers
	Work the land for all the hours
June	Is haytime, hay to store
	Winter feed, need more and more
July	Cutting is beginning
	Winter corn is worth a shilling
August	Harvest sheaves are led
	There's no time to stay in bed
September	Harvest suppers bring
	Then do all the workers sing
October	Sun is such a gift
	For potato crops to lift
November	Can be wet and warm
	Cattle gather near the farm
December	Turkeys, cockerels, geese
	Plucked and ready for the feast

Farm boys were roused by Ploughboys' song:

It's past 4 o' clock boys
So rise with good will
Your horses want hay
Their bellies to fill

It is said that a ploughman walked eleven miles to the acre after a 9" furrow plough – no wonder my Dad was whacked when he came home from a day's ploughing with horses! In one decade farming and attitudes to farming changed dramatically. Tractors replaced horses, manpower was no longer needed for many jobs, combine harvesters now take all the backache out of harvesting, potato planters and potato harvesters out of potatoeing and do away with potato pickers and potato spinners and hoovers (the machines for lifting potatoes) – so many machines, so much change. No longer are men needed on the land. Machines have taken over. Farms are not labour intensive. Farm labourers would have been much happier to have stayed on the land instead of going off each day to factories or pits.There's no chance now of a man becoming his own master on a small farm. If farming wasn't a way of life, it was a drudgery and that's very hard to all concerned. A man must always care for the land – not exploit it.

In the late 1800s, early 1900s, all schoolchildren could find a job on the farms and were allowed to leave school at twelve if they had passed the exam. and had a job to go to. Hoeing, striking turnips, stubbing thistles – all jobs to be done by hand – they were very labour-intensive. Things had changed very little for many years – opening up the fields with scythes so that the binder could get in, hedges to be cut with a brushing bill or "slasher" for cutting thick growth and a Yorkshire bill-hook for laying, cows milked by hand twice a day, land ploughed, sown and harvested by horse power.....

Getting to the market, at either Rotherham or Doncaster, was a good day out for all farmers. On the way, they viewed other people's fields from their pony and traps and commented on the crops. Ploughing and sowing was always on view to others, any poor crops the farmers gossiped about. When ploughing, they were always keen to keep a straight furrow for neighbours to view. Winter ploughing seemed to go on for ever. Day after day my father followed the plough whenever it was fit to get on the land – he used to come home exhausted. This was with a single-furrow plough with two horses to control and be sure you kept the furrows straight because the neighbours were always ready to comment. "Nice bit o' ploughing in t'Foxholes Ned" or: "Aat' tha loisin' thi touch then lad?" (Are you losing your touch then lad) if they didn't think it was so good.

Then of course, the drilling.

One for the Rook, one for the Crow
One to rot, and one to grow

Drilling was done by the seed drill drawn by one or two horses. Oats were grown then for cattle and horse feed; these aren't grown very much now but were then a big part of any farming crop. Wheat and barley, turnips, swedes and potatoes (planted by hand, of course, by women brought in from neighbouring villages). Peas also, pulled by hand. Paid 6d a 40lb. sack. Hard work. Dad asked the ganger (she got the women together) who her milkman in Maltby was to send word with him when he needed them again for pulling peas. She said she didn't have one. Twenty women – and not one bought fresh milk! They all used condensed milk. Wow!!! – milk and sugar all in one!

I can also remember my father sowing seed with a hopper. It was October when this started, often straight after the ploughing and if it was wet land it went on into January. What a beautiful sight this is. To see a man with perfect rhythm broadcasting seed. He carried the steel hopper round his neck on a leather strap and broadcast seed from left and right. A fiddle drill (like a fiddle – the wooden "bow" had holes in, which dropped the seed) was used by some farmers but this didn't need the skill of a hopper and my father was a joy to behold. He was so proficient with the hopper. My brothers sometimes still do this job even now for small areas but I always tell them they are not a patch on dad and they agree.

As children, we made many scarecrows. My brothers more than me. A 5' stake was stuck in the ground – usually in the middle of the field – especially where peas were sown. Another smaller piece was put crossways about 1' from the top. A jacket was put on the "arms" this formed. A piece of string was put round the middle of the jacket and the arms and top were filled with straw. The head was formed on the top piece with straw and stuffed into the top of the jacket, which had the collar turned up. This again was tied with string. A cap or hat was then jammed on the head. The biggest trouble was if the jacket or hat was better than the local tramp's – it would be gone next day. He or she never left their old one either! We didn't have too many old jackets as they were really worn out before discarding and then cut up for rugs.

> A swarm of bees in May is worth a load of hay
> A swarm of bees in June is worth a silver spoon
> A swarm in July is not worth a fly

The smell of horses and new-mown hay! Lovely! Horses with broad backs, glistening with sweat, pulling the carts to load the hay – their winter feed. All praying the sun would keep shining to dry the crop. It was cut by a reaper pulled by two horses, sometimes more. The reaper knife laid the grass in long rows and when dry this was raked up by a horse-rake pulled by one horse. If it rained, it had to be turned with a fork by hand, then left to dry again. It was then stacked into hay cocks in the field and left again. When the farmer thought it ready, it was led loose from the field on drays – with hecks attached (wooden structures at each end to hold the hay in). It was unloaded in the farm yard and stacked, usually in the barn or Dutch Barn. Otherwise it was 'strawed' (covered in straw as thatch) in the stackyard to keep out the rain.

Woe-betide anybody who led it too early. It heated up and could fire. A long tool was kept to check for this. It was pushed down into the heart of the stack and checked for heat. Sometimes the stack had to be moved if it was a real fire risk, much to the horror of the farmer and then re-built – a rotten job! When it was needed in the winter for feed, it was cut by a hay knife into squares (quite a hard and heavy job, as was most farm work) and then shaken out and fed to the animals in their hecks in the cowhouse and stables and sheep-pens.

Then followed harvest. When the corn was ripe, Dad or Epe, our foreman, rode the binder and watched if the knotter failed to tie the sheaves. Three horses pulled it if it was a heavy land like our farm – Metal, Daisy and Captain. The stookers followed as the sheaves were ejected. A sheaf was picked up under each arm and the butt end of the sheaves was shoved into the ground, the corn heads uppermost, balancing the first pair and then the other six were added to make a stook. Wheat and oats were preferable to barley, which had ains (sharp whiskers) which stuck into clothing and skin and really irritated. Of course there were often thistles too. No sprays in those far-off days. All crops hand-weeded. Often the knotter didn't tie and there was great consternation – a great worry and sometimes broken down for hours with everybody getting irritable, particularly when the weather was good – very frustrating. I have heard it said that the man who invented the knotter on the binder became so frustrated at the problems with it that he committed suicide. I know how furious the men used to get when again and again it failed to tie. The loose straw came tumbling out. They swore at the machine. Think of trying to perfect this!

When the stooks had dried out, which could take a long time (if it rained, then the stooks had to be moved as they grew into the ground) they were led from the field by horse and dray with hecks. One man was on the dray loading and each sheaf had to be placed correctly on the load, butts out and centre filled, otherwise the load would fall off on the way home. There was pride in this work and the sheaves were pitched head first to facilitate the loading. The horse moved forward at the words "Gee up" and it stopped at "Whoa". You can't do that with a tractor!

Horse and load safely home, the sheaves were unloaded in the stackyard. Stack-building was an art – Dad was the stack man. Sheaves were carefully laid layer after layer, butts outward, middle filled – every sheaf had to be forked correctly. Long hours were worked at harvest time by horses and men – only darkness or wet weather called a halt. But what an experience to have been part of that. How satisfying. A job well done. As the last round of corn was cut, the hares bolted from their cover. Many a youngster was soundly sworn at by the men with guns as in their excitement they chased the hare across the field – they had no chance of catching him, often tripped and fell and they used to come back shame-faced, having made the guns miss their target or not even get a shot in.

Harvest Teas were always taken to the field at 4pm. Home-made bread and home-cooked hams. Teacake or scones and then cake to follow – "cut-and-come-again" cake, Parkin, Bakewell. All demolished with gusto by hungry farm men. The tea always had lots of milk and sugar in so everybody must have taken both in those days. Usually several miners from the local pit at Maltby would come to help in the fields. They didn't get paid but they got a good tea and enjoyed the fresh air. And of course they were used to hard work. They said the fresh air did their lungs a power of good. As children we used to climb on the dray, sit down, hold onto the hecks and hold the basket with the food in. The men would be in charge of the big gallon can of tea – we all had tea together in the field.

It was always a great delight to me to be allowed to lead the horses anywhere, anytime, but a special privilege at harvest-time, when everybody was so busy and you really felt you were helping Harvest Home. At harvest time, we rode home on the loads from the fields. Once the load slipped. We were on Boggy Lane, Bub and Kath and me. We landed on the floor, very shaken but luckily unhurt amongst the sheaves. The poor old horse, Bonny, fell down and couldn't get up. The dray had to be unhitched and she had to be unharnessed and helped up. I can remember still the pitiful look in her eyes and the way she shook herself when she was free. Sometimes horses ran away and headed for home with men in hot pursuit. We had many horses, how I loved them all – Captain (with the broken wind), Daisy, Flower, Blossom – the greys, the bays, the chestnuts. Riding on them bare-backs from the stable to the trough for drinking.

I get to thinking sometimes that I'm glad I was a lass
When horses ploughed the furrows, and pigs ran out on grass
When eggs were laid on grassy banks
And often on the stack
And sometimes 'fore you found them
The shells had all gone crack
And out had popped a chicken
All ready for the fray,
To scratch around the stackyard
Cockerels hailing a new day
Oh! Life was good and sunny
The smell of new-mown hay
The horses homeward wending
At the end of a hard day,
Oh! God who sends the sunshine
And the rain to make things grow
May I thank you now, and always,
For the Village life I Know.

CHAPTER 9

One potato, two potato, three potato, four

Harvest over, usually in September or October and then straight into potato picking. What hard and busy lives they all lived. Misty October mornings is my remembrance of potato-picking days. A week before it started Dad would send word by Mr. Wadsworth (our milkman) to tell the ganger who lived in Maltby we wanted twelve pickers for the following Monday. Stints were marked out early in the morning with wooden markers – you picked your potatoes between these two markers. Of course only eleven pickers arrived, or thirteen, not twelve as asked and then the markers all had to be moved again. There were always arguments that some had more length than others to pick – especially if one or two finished early and had a sit down on their buckets. Some were so slow the horse and spinner had to wait for them to catch up. The others breathed a sigh of relief and enjoyed their rest. They brought their own buckets to pick in and then tipped them into big baskets. The men then came round with a horse and cart and emptied them into the cart. Things settled down when the sun came out and a gallon of sweet tea was brought from the farm. Then everybody became more affable and the women teased the farm lads, often making the young ones blush. Many a potato-picker ended up as a young farm lad's wife egged on by the older women, who liked to see some romance blossoming. As I said, the women brought their own buckets and as one of the perks always took a bucket of potatoes home. Many farmers tried to stop this but were never successful. One thing they did stop was several buckets being put into sacks under the hedge and fetched out later – our pickers were always fetched and taken home by cart so hiding them was rather more difficult.

The potatoes were then pied in the field – not as now, taken back to the farm. They were put in a pile and straw from the harvest, always wheat straw, packed round them and then covered in soil to keep out the frost. Many a farm man earned his reputation because he was a good "pie-er". People used to say if Harry or Tom did the job: "There'll be no frost gits in theer." Later in the winter the pie was opened up and a riddling machine taken to the field and the potatoes thrown on with a sippet (a special fork with blunt tines). The small ones then fell through the ridddle. These were later boiled in the copper and fed to the pigs – the bad and damaged ones were picked off by hand and the rest slid into 8-stone hessian sacks at the end and were weighed and tied up with binder twine ready for market. Usually a cold job but a great time for tale-telling and gossip as at most jobs farm men worked on their own, so to get together was a time for laughter and teasing. In later years Derrick hated being with the pickers so Dennis always got that job and Derrick helped with the potato pie.

One evening in October 1932, it was raining hard. Two travellers came knocking at our door looking for work – a ginger-haired, cheerful, pale-looking man in a trilby and a dark attractive woman. Shabbily dressed, they told a pitiful story of having nowhere to go or sleep. My mother, always soft-hearted, persuaded my father to set them on for potato harvesting. They were taken up to the corn chamber and a tray of hot soup and ham rolls disappeared in no time. Their names were Jack Kirshaw and Dolly. We thought husband and wife. Of course they were, as I heard the Villagers whisper, "livin' o'er t' brush". This expression puzzled me for years. They lived up in that corn chamber all winter – Dolly helped with housework and poultry, Jack on the farm. Mother gave them table and chairs, rugs, curtains, a bed and blankets etc. and an oil stove for heating. She cooked their main meals, which we carried out to them, or Dolly fetched. I visited them in the evening and played cards, usually Newmarket, a favourite game, with buttons for money. They moved on in the following winter. We heard that Jack's wife was looking for him! I wonder if they remember us as vividly as I remember them. I had long, curly hair – I could sit on it. My mother thought it was sapping my strength as I was very thin (such old wives' tales) but nobody in the Village would cut it off, not even my uncle Harry, who was a hairdresser. She took me up to Jack in the chamber and he cut off all my hair and I wept. Next morning he was gone. No wonder I remember him so clearly.

I remember going with my father to "supper up" as a kid with the paraffin storm lantern. This meant seeing all the animals were alright for the night. Once, we found a cow choking and I had to hold the lamp whilst Dad pushed a rubber tube down the cow's throat. It had a potato stuck. The noise was awful and she began to swell up. Luckily, as it filled with gas, the tube did the trick. Another night, we found a cow calving, my brothers were both out, so I was again holding the lamp. I eventually hung this on the beam and ended up on the end of a rope, which was tied round the calf's legs, pulling for dear life to get the calf out. Great joy when it was an heifer.

> The thrasher comes in through the gate
> The farmer wonders why he's late
> The driver says: "Now steady, mate."
> We're here, and ready now.
>
> He sets the chocks, he feeds the coal
> He shovels it into the hole.
> The great big, gaping mouth he feeds
> With harvest corn, the golden sheaves

It separates the chaff and straw
With chaff sheets open on the floor
The ripened corn upon his back
"There's 16 stone to carry, Jack."

Up the chamber steps he goes
Empties the sack and the corn flows
A dirty job and really hard
A job well done is his reward.

Great excitement as thrashing day approached. A horse and cart was sent to Maltby pit to fetch a load of steam coal – *then* the thrasher arrived. It travelled very, very slowly – a huge, huge, steam-driven engine with two great iron wheels at the back and two smaller at the front. This pulled the drum which did the actual thrashing of the corn; then followed the chopper, followed by a tyer to re-tie the batts of straw. There was great difficulty in getting this equipment into the farm yard – even more difficult to set it up by the stack. It took a lot of hard work to level it with chogs of wood.

At 6am the next morning they'd be back, stoking coal into the fire-box to get the boiler raised to steam level. This all over-seen by the man in charge – The First Man. The drum which did the actual thrashing was a revolving drum with beaters inside – all inside a big wooden casing – with lots of flywheels down the outside. The driver always brought his own second man. There was a man on the stack who moved the sheaves from their original place as built by the stacker. There was a picker, who took it from him and passed it (the correct way round) to a third man on the drum. The sheaves were fed into the top of the drum by the cutter, Bill – he came with the thrash-er. It was always the second man's job to feed the drum, stand-ing on a platform with a knife with which he cut the binder band (twine) binding the sheaf. Holding the string in his hand, he slowly fed the sheaf into the drum.

This then beat out the corn from the straw. The straw went into the back of the machine and was re-tied into sheaves and stacked for use as bedding. Oat straw would be fed into the chopper and made into chopped straw for feed for cattle or horses which was mixed with meal or turnips and molasses (black treacle). Chaff was the cover from the ear of corn and was carted into the foldyard on a huge sheet of sacking. It was an awful job for the chaff carrier – dusty, dirty, prickly. This was usually Herbert Walker from Stone, who walked to wherever the thrasher was working and then walked home – it could be Bawtry, Wadworrth, Tickhill, Ravenfield, Braithwell etc.. Bob did this job on our farm. His eyes and face and clothes were filthy at the end of the day and remember – no hot bath to go home to.

There were always nests of mice and rats in the stack. They were pink-skinned – no hair and squirmy squiggly little things. I hated them. The men would toss them off the stack and the cats would devour them. It always made me cringe. I could never pick them up as they did. The hens would gobble them up too. I used to get out of the way quite terrified they'd drop onto my hair.

Sometimes, the belt which drove the drum would slip and I was despatched to the kitchen to fetch the treacle tin and a stick and they spread this onto the belt to hold it and make it grip again. The drum could be heard right through the Village. It was a constant, pleasant noise (hmm, hmm) unless Bill, the cutting man, missed feeding the sheaf in slowly and dropped it in whole instead – the noise of the machine changed and this would make it go "bump, bump, bump", and the lovely, even, rhythm was broken.

Barley was the worst thing to thrash as the ains stuck to everything and were most unpleasant. Clothes, caps and whiskers were covered in them.

The corn ran into the sacks hooked on the back of the drum and, when taken off the hook and weighed (16 stone!), they were then put on a lifting barrow which was wound up to the height of the man's shoulders for carrying and were carried up to the corn chamber – two men did this job, always up steep wooden steps, a hard job and particularly so when it went on all day. They must have been very strong – I never heard them complain of backache. The sacks for the corn were hired from the railway company – this was the usual practice and when empty, they had to be returned in a given time.

The first and second men came into the house for dinner. The rest of the team had snap (sandwiches) and tea taken outside to the barn. Later a ruling came out during the war that wire netting must be put all round the thrashing area so that no rats escaped. This used to cause great excitement, as lads (and lasses) with sticks and terrier dogs and other "Heinz" varieties would come in to kill these. A man from Maltby, Joe Bell, collected a bag of live rats and took them on the bus from

Braithwell to release in the pit wood and train his greyhounds and make them keen. Asked on the 'bus what was in the bag, as it was seen moving, Joe said: "Rats." and everybody got up and quickly moved away – leaving Joe in isolation on the front seat greatly amused!

It took twelve men to do the thrashing – other farmers loaned men for the day and then, when they needed help, our men went to them. We always helped and worked with Mr. Ron Robinson of Elmfield farm, also Mr. Smith from Ashton Farm. Dad and he also grew peas together.

Three men who followed the thrasher were: Arthur Storey and Ollie (never knew his surname) – these men lived in the Village and Cyril who lived in Fox House Cottage

The thrashing man I remember was Mr. George Davison. He was very well respected by farmers and farm labourers alike and he loved and knew his machines. He had come from East Yorkshire (Muston, near Filey) to work for Mr. Ted Knowles, who lived and worked from Austwood House Farm. I presume he was "poached" from his job in the East Riding by the better wages and a new bungalow for his wife and three daughters, built specially for them on Doncaster Road, Braithwell and called "Muston Lea" after the East Yorkshire village they left. He certainly knew his engines and could repair anything. In this Village, they still talk of him, he was a wonderful worker. (His grandson is Phil Wadsley, another man who's a wizard with engines. Genes will out, as they say). He had few breakdowns, even with the wartime spare part situation – he could make parts when needed. He was always known as George by everybody, although he was christened William. His daughter (Kathleen Leigh) tells me that he had the same name, William, as another worker on the farm in East Yorkshire, so the boss there said: "We'll call you George." and it stuck and George he was in Yorkshire until the day he died aged 78. He ended his days at Micklebring, where he lived with his daughter Eva Wadsley.

At busy times of the farm – thrashing, harvest etc. when every able-bodied boy or man was called upon to do his bit, many a youngster found himself absolutely whacked before knocking-off time. If he complained of being shattered one of the old hands would say: "Nivver let thee muther know she bred a jibber." A jibber of course was a horse that didn't pull its weight with the cart, the plough etc. – jibbed at work. A lovely expression I always thought.

CHAPTER 10

Christmas is coming, the goose is getting fat

Most people baked their own bread, teacakes and cakes etc.. There was very little tinned or bought food used by Village people. One Village girl told me when her father's mother came to chapel, she called on them and always looked in the dustbin to see if there were any tins in. Almost every cottage kept a pig – all the scraps were fed to it and potatoes boiled and meal mixed in to make a good feed. These were always killed for Christmas, the slaughterman coming to the house.

The copper was lit first thing in the morning. The pig was brought squealing from the sty. It was stunned by a pole-axe and then pulled up on a rope over a beam and its throat slit, scalded with water from the copper and scraped to remove the hairs, then left to cool and set (new meat is soft – it sets when cool). Next day it was cut up into joints etc.. There was then food in that household for many weeks – brawn and pork pies, "frys" were sent to neighbours. These were a slice of liver, heart, a piece of pork and kidney put onto a plate with a fat veiling over – this veiling was just like a veil with lumps of fat in it. You used the veiling to extract the fat to fry the meat. You don't ever see this today, of course, because pigs are slaughtered when they're very young. Remember, these pigs (ours was always the best of the bunch) would weigh 20 or 30 stone or more and be full of fat. This fat was cut up and rendered down and used for baking and cooking. The crisp fat bits that were left were called scraps and were eaten with bread and butter for tea; now put into packets and called pork scratchings. The bladder was blown up and used as a football. My grandfather Robert won five first prizes at five shows with a 15-month-old pig weighing 50 stone. Think of the fat from that. It was always said with a pig you used everything but its squeal!

When you got a fry from your neighbour you never washed the plate. Usually the children went round with the fry. They got a sweet and a dirty plate back – if you washed it, it was bad luck. When you killed a pig, you did the same for your neighbour. In the days without 'fridges, this was free fresh meat on a regular basis. The hams and sides of bacon were salted for winter in the cellar – on the stone slab with saltpetre and salt.

Salt was bought in blocks measuring 18" x 8". These had to be cut up and then crushed with a rolling pin. This was then used along with saltpetre to preserve the meat. Later the bacon sides and hams were dried and hung on the hooks on the beams in the kitchen, wrapped in mutton cloth. The bacon sides were taken down each morning and many slices cut off, then hung back – plenty of fat for frying eggs and bread!

I went to take a fry to a Village family. I knocked and shouted: "It's Joyce, Mrs ——". The lady of the house shouted: "Come in lass." I went in and she was kneading bread. She took her hands out of the dough to get a plate and her nails were filthy dirty. When I went home and told my Dad he laughed and said that was how some of the women got their nails clean. I never had any bread at that house again.

Whole hams were boiled in the copper for Christmas. They always had plenty of fat. A pig was always killed around Christmas at our house so that home-made pork pies could be served for breakfast – we still all have pork pie for Christmas breakfast. Dad said that on some farms hams were kept from one Christmas to the next. As sometimes the new hams wouldn't be ready in time for Christmas, so last year's ham was used. This was kept in the corn chamber under the corn 'till needed and the boy was sent to find it. My uncle Harold (Lal Smith) told me that as a boy this was always his job to find the ham at Manor Farm in Micklebring. He said you could smell it cooking right across the yard. Pork was never eaten in summer because, with no freezers, it wasn't a good keeping meat – it was said because the skin was scalded to remove the hairs. Pork and goose were served for Christmas dinner, always with sprouts and carrots and salted beans. A huge Christmas Pudding, with masses of rum sauce. Tea was drunk – coffee was only Camp coffee – awful stuff! and home-made wines (dandelion, cowslip, nettle). Usually the only bought wine was port and neighbours would call in for a glass and a mince pie. We always had a holly tree from the fields hung upside-down in the kitchen from the beams but presents were always put in a pillow-case at the foot of the bed – this was the first thing you saw when you woke up, if it was light. Otherwise, with no electric light and candles removed, there was no way of seeing what you had until day broke. I remember my uncle Lal one year buying me a blow-up goose. He had blown it up and put it with its neck and beak over the end of my bed. In the half-light, it terrified me. They were all waiting for my screams and laughed heartily, as did I when I saw what it was. I had great fun floating it on the pond. When it broke away and got out of reach, my brother Derrick used to wade out for it. Then he was in trouble covered in mud. But it gave me lots of pleasure until it punctured.

All farms and cottages had big hooks on the ceiling for hanging hams and bacons. When a pig was killed it was not for pork but for eating of bacon and ham. Then the pork pies were made, usually about six. The biggest was huge and was always kept for Christmas morning. The meat was chopped, not minced – a little sage and parsley, salt and pepper added and a raw egg beaten and added to every pie filling. Hot water crust made, meat put in, lid on and then slowly cooked in the side oven by the fire for several hours.

The jelly from the brawn was boiled up every other day, so it would keep fresh, until some was needed to jelly a pie. This was only done very carefully through the hole in the top when you were going to eat the pie next day. It has puzzled me for many years how, without refrigerators, did these pies keep? They were put on the cellar stone slab until used. We never got poisoned and there was no preservative added. Of course, they were only made in winter: pigs were only killed in winter. Brawn was made with the hocks, face, chaps, pigs' feet and shin beef. Cooked slowly in the oven, then the meat stripped from the bones and chopped. Salted and peppered and put into dishes with the liquid poured over. This then set into a jelly. We always ate it with salt, pepper and vinegar, mustard or pickled beetroot.

Besides this pig-killing, my mother would have cockerels, geese and ducks to dress for Christmas. The men would pluck or scald them but what a busy time it must have been. She then had to take their "innards" out, pen them (remove the quill stumps) and truss them with string ready for the oven. Whilst plucking the ducks and geese, the breast feathers were put together in an old pillow case. Later these were washed in the bag and hung on the line to dry, then finished drying in the oven when it had cooled down. When completely dry they were made into pillows and cushions. Ticking (feather-proof material) was bought by the yard in Doncaster at "Pinny's" and made up into cushion covers or pillowcases. Soap was damped in water and then rubbed onto the inside of the ticking case so the feathers didn't come through – called proofing. Sometimes when an eiderdown had seen its last days, my mother opened it up and took out the feathers for pillows. All time-consuming jobs and very messy. Feathers stuck to everything and we always had to do this work up in the stackyard where a few feathers more or less didn't matter. Of course we always slept on feather beds. If you slept alone it was lovely snuggled down and it rolled round you but if friends came to stay, you were in a heap together in the middle. Always stone hot water bottles or a baking sheet from the oven for your feet.

❧

CHAPTER 11

Open House – Open all Hours
and a Woman's work is never done

Dad was always generous to other farmers with his equipment and advice. Farmers only had to ask and he would go out of his way to get the job he was doing finished and let the smaller farmer have the cart, the harrows or the loan of a horse. At my father's funeral, Mr Willie Cooke, who had farmed Ashton Farm, came to me with tears in his eyes. Holding my hand he said: "Lass, your father was a friend to me. Without his help with machinery and advice, I shouldn't be where I am today. I owe him a lot." He had then moved to Rainborough Grange, Hemingfield, a much bigger and better farm. Before he took Ashton Farm, he had been in charge of the horses at the pit and had his own smallholding. He saved and saved and did without to rent his own farm. He worked himself into the ground. Mrs. Cooke was a lovely lady and we saw her often – bread baked, dinner over, house cleaned, with a hoe over her shoulder striding up Maltby Lane to hoe turnips or stub thistles or pull wild oats out of the corn. She was a great help to him. They had two sons Dennis and George. During the war, Dennis, who was at Leeds University, volunteered and became a captain in the Indian Army and was saving money from his pay, hoping to buy his own farm when he came home. I wrote to him all through the war. Sadly he was killed in India. George (Bunty we always called him) attended Braithwell School with us. Late in life, the Cooke's had a daughter Kathleen. George and her now live in Barnsley.

44

Mr. Cooke's funeral was one of the last I went to where they kept the body at home in the front parlour until the burial. We did this with Dad – it was common practice then.

Nobody went to a funeral parlour or Chapel of Rest. When you arrived at the house for the funeral, you were asked if you'd like to see the body before they fastened the coffin lid down. You filed past to pay your respects. People thought it very strange if you said "No." When the time came to go to the churchyard, *all* curtains in the Village were closed until the funeral had passed and all men stood with hats off until the cortege had gone by. At my father-in-law's (Charles Milnes) funeral in Maltby, many miners stood in the street with caps off, as he was so well known with his ironmonger's shop. It brought tears to all our eyes. Now quite often traffic doesn't even slow down. How things have changed.

A regular visitor mother had was a schoolteacher friend from Rotherham. She and her husband, also a teacher, came often. They were quite wealthy but childless and both rather pale and delicate. When she came alone to visit mother, we always had afternoon tea in the small sitting room and nearly always had fresh prawns, peeled by my mother, with home-made bread of course, which Mrs. Jackson loved. I was always fetched in, washed, dressed in my best and told to mind my manners but my brothers escaped that. Mrs. Jackson was a lovely lady. I loved her and I love prawns too. Sometimes they brought her nephew Ernest. He was like them – thin and pale and delicate. My brothers thought he was a real weed but I thought he was lovely – gentle, kind and a real little gentleman. I suppose I was a bit smitten. I wasn't used to real polite little boys who helped you up steps and over stiles. Mrs. Jackson's mother was dead and when her father, Mr. Dixon Page, got into his eighties, he had quite a serious operation. She asked my mother if he could stay with us to recuperate as she was still teaching. A room downstairs was made into a bed-sitting room. It had an outside door and he lived and slept there and had his meals there too. He then said he'd like to come and have his meals with us in the kitchen. When he recovered enough to go home, he begged my mother to let him stay. He said he'd never been so happy since his childhood and he loved the farm. My sisters really looked after him and I'm sure the money he paid came in very handy. He lived with us until he died at ninety-five and seemed one of the family. He was buried in Braithwell churchyard. Then my grandfather (mother's father) came to live with us and stayed until he died at eighty-four.

As children with many friends, we must have driven Dad wild. Everybody was welcome at our house and children flocked. We had ponies, cats and dogs, rabbits and guinea-pigs. Dad had a wonderful smooth-haired old sheep dog called Ramp who always followed him all round the farm. He was a natural with dogs as is my brother Dennis but Dad always had sheep dogs. When Ramp went blind, he laid hours by the back door; as soon as Dad came out Ramp was off behind him. As long as Dad was there he instinctively followed him. He died at 14 – much missed. Then followed Scamp, Wul and Rex. Dennis had his own dog Crafty (an alsatian). She could jump anything and used to round up his goats with him. Then Mick, also an alsatian, who terrified the neighbourhood and kept away all strangers from the house if he was loose. Dennis is still an alsatian man and I suppose he always will be.

We learnt to dance up in the Chop Chamber. You climbed up stone steps from the Fold Yard and then nobody knew where you were and we danced and danced. All the young teenagers gathered here – my brother Dennis and me, Kay Davison (Leigh – Doncaster Road), Marion Wells (Byron – Maltby Lane), Brenda Ward (Harden), Susan Bailey (Cardwell Cottage), Alice Green (High Street), Lal Weyman (Cardwell House), Dennis Cooke (Ashton Farm), Charlie Cutts (Cremona Villa), John Swift (High Street), Harry Parkes (Fox House Farm).

One day Dad, coming to feed the horses below, heard us throwing the chop about. John Swift saw him coming, shouted a warning and threw himself down the chop hole – head first – he knew Dad's temper. This was the hole in the corner where the chop was shovelled down into a huge bag which was hung from this hole with bottom slit open. This was then tied with binder-band and each day filled from above with chop. When the horses' feed was to be mixed, this bag was undone and out shot the chop into the big wooden bin below. The meal etc. was then added and put into the skep to carry to the horses' mangers. We loved to slide down the chop hole through this big bag when opened and land in the bin – it was a great game head first – but poor old Johnny hadn't realised that the neck was tied – Dad had been doing that when he heard us. Johnny lay there quietly. We others made our escape after Dad had told us all off good and proper. Dad proceeded to fill the chop bag –

nearly smothering Johnny who never made a muff. Then Dad went down and untied the string and he shot out with the chop like a cork from a bottle.

We were always told not to climb up on the beams in the cart shed. Dangerous and absolutely forbidden. These beams had wood stacked across them and hide and seek was a favourite game. We hid there of course. Dennis hid there one day and I went to find him. I poked him with a hay-fork handle and moving quickly he fell down. Right on top of the binder – he cut his arm quite badly on the cutters and blood flowed profusely. I wanted to fetch Dad but we were all very scared and gathered round him. Eventually, I fetched my sister Doris under some pretence. She fetched bandages etc. and bound him up – she was very efficient but her telling-off was nearly as bad as Dad's. Of course he eventually found out. Dennis was terrified of getting a thrashing. Whenever he got a cut and saw blood he always shouted: "Shall I die, Mother?" We always shouted back: "Yes. You will."

One day we were all playing on the stack after harvest-time. During harvest-time, Dad used several of us kids to tread the stack down. This consolidated it and was common practice. After that, when the stack was finished, we were supposed to keep off but there we all were, burrowing down into it – removing sheaves, throwing them at each other, hiding and jumping small distances onto lower stacks. My brother 'Der' decided he'd jump to the bottom and dared us all – to no avail but, to our horror, he jumped. There was thick straw below but he fell heavily – it was about 16' high, quite a jump!. Terrified, we hurriedly climbed down and he lay still with his eyes closed. I thought he was dead. I just rushed down to the house shouting: "Come quick Mum, Der's dead." Poor Mum. She shot after me – sisters, Dad, uncles, everybody following. He was sitting up nursing a sprained ankle.

"I'm not dead, Mum." he said in a small, miserable voice.

Every day had a set job in the house. This was the only way that everything got done. Monday washday and ironing; Tuesday baking day; Wednesday bedrooms; Thursday downstairs rooms; Friday kitchen and baking again. Often when it was harvest or haytime Mum baked bread and teacakes and cakes every day. No labour-saving equipment – "cut and come again cake" was very common. Made in a big tin 12" square it was a sponge with cherries or sultanas and cut into squares or sometimes it was plain and iced. Always made for thrashing days and Harvest Teas. What a busy life. Yet she always had time for us and our friends.

Most houses had a wash-house or shared one. We washed in the dairy. Dad lit the copper at 4.30am and mother was up at about 5am sorting washing into piles. The whites went into a big zinc tub with warm soapy water to soak. The soap was just a block – yellow and hard – and was grated off into the water on the coarse side of the kitchen grater. The boiling copper water melted this and then cold water was added. These clothes were possed up and down in a metal dolly tub of hot water. The posser was like an inverted copper collander with a long handle at the base. Whites were possed first, then these were boiled in the copper. Then followed the coloureds – all going through the same procedure.

Some people preferred a dolly – this was twirled round and back, round and back and was like a small four-legged stool with a handle through the middle and a cross-piece at the top. You held it by this and twisted it round and back until your arms and back ached. These clothes were then put into the copper to boil. It was all hard and wet work – the floor running in water and steam filling the room. They then all had to be rinsed in clean water (in our case, hand-pumped up from the well below the dairy) and then blued and starched. The Dolly blue came in little round bags and cost a penny and made the water a lovely colour. This improved the whiteness of clothes and the colour of your washing in a village was very important.

In any Yorkshire village, spotless washing was always a matter of pride. After you'd used the dolly, you scrubbed the clothes on a rubbing board, a wooden ladder frame with a metal corrugated centre stood in the dolly tub. These jobs were hard and time-consuming. By the time you'd rinsed and mangled everything, through a huge mangle with big wooden rollers, you'd really earned your dinner – usually cold meat (from Sunday) and mashed potatoes and piccalilli at our house, followed by a huge rice pudding.

These clothes then all had to be hung out to dry. Always we prayed for a good Monday. Otherwise the clothes would hang about for days, drying on the rack hanging from the ceiling in the kitchen or on wooden clothes horses, getting in everybody's way and irritating the menfolk of the house. Also, everthing but woollens was starched. This was packet starch. Boiling water was added to the powder which had already been mixed with cold water and it turned the thin white paste to a lovely pale blue thick starch. The colour of your washing denoted the type of housewife you were. Many's the time I've heard, when a newcomer came to the Village, the regrettable comment: "Have you seen her whites?" Or "She's got beautiful whites." – therefore you were a good housewife.

All door steps were done on Friday with donkey stone either deep cream or white and woe betide anybody who stepped on it when it was freshly done. The donkey stone was dipped in the water bucket and then rubbed onto the edge of the clean-scrubbed step. How lovely this looked. How fresh and bright.

Friday morning was also kitchen-cleaning day with only a black-leaded fireplace with an oven on one side and a tank on the other side from which you ladled hot water for washing or washing up. Men got out of the way quick. All the flues to be cleaned and the stove black-leaded – quite a job. Soot which collected thick on the chimney back to be swept down – with coal fires this was always a dirty job. Then the black leading. One brush to put it on, one to polish it up and what a mess it made of your hands. My sister Doris, who often did the black leading, used to spit on the cloth – she used to say it moved the most stubborn marks and it always seemed to. The kitchen floor which was smooth Yorkshire Flagstones, was then scrubbed and everything within sight polished.

Sticks were pushed under the oven to heat it up quickly for dinner as everything was cooked on the stove – the only other means of cooking was a primus stove which was always in use for veg. etc.. But of course the oven was on the go every day for puddings or pies and dinner kept warm there until everything was ready and the men came in.

One day when Dad was about twenty he went past the kitchen door at 7am and Martha, their old maid, was scouring the step with donkey stone. He was astounded and said: "By Martha! You've got done early today." She replied:

"Nay lad, I'm that throng (busy) today and behind wi't work I've decided there's moor (more) pass by than come in and they'll think we've finished if I've dun 't step." Wise old girl!

"Waste not want not." A real Yorkshire saying. This was particularly true with clothes. Sunday best was eventually, after many years' wear, then taken by the farm men for work. Old shirts were worn without collars on weekdays – collars were detatchable. When eventually his wife decided that trousers and jackets could be mended no more they were cut up to make rag rugs for the floors. I spent many happy hours in front of the kitchen fire, sitting on the rug with my sisters, cutting up old coats and trousers etc. into 4" x 1" strips to hook through the canvas. We particularly liked it when we had ladies' red skirts or bright blue jackets to cut up. My sisters made patterns which I thought was very clever. Sacks of course were very easily obtainable from the corn chamber – these were washed and pegged out to dry. The only other necessity was a rug hook to pull the cloth pieces through the sacking.

Thrift was always encouraged and string and brown paper were always kept to be re-used. Newspapers lined shelves and were cut up for toilet use as well as lighting fires. Also made into spills for the smokers and hung by the fire or put on the mantlepiece in a spill-holder, or carried to light the primus stove – thus saving on matches. I can't imagine anybody today going to all the trouble to save money but it really was a necessity in the 1930s when many families were very poor.

Soap was always stored a long time until it went hard. Thrifty housewives had bars of soap stored to dry. Soft soap was made with left-over bits softened with boiling water. This was used for washing up or the copper. Mostly, washing up was done with soda – there was no Fairy Liquid. Think of the havoc soda does to the hands.

"Cleanliness is next to godliness." And lots of housewives practised this. Auntie Clara (Fenn) came often to the farm and said during the conversation about some Village girl newly married: "You could eat your dinner off her floor." I replied: "Who'd want to do a thing like that anyway?" Mother replied: "Little girls should be seen and not heard." and put me in my place.

If anybody told my mother that something did you good, mother would buy it and you were "on it.". Taking it three and four times a day. This is how I came to be on Sanatogen wine. Another thing was Fennings Fever Cure. If we showd any sign of a temperature, out came the bottle. It was foul-tasting so we kept quiet unless we felt really ill. I felt really bad one day but said nothing. Next morning I was covered in spots. The doctor was sent for and I was kept off school and in bed – feeling rotten. The doctor thought I had scarlet fever (very common in those days) but as we had a milk herd, it would have meant me going away to the fever hospital at Conisbrough (near Stringer's

Nursery). Every two hours through that day and night, I had a dose of this vile medicine. I kept saying: "Not again, Mum" and she replied:

"You don't want to go away do you?" Down it went with a sweet to follow. Poor old Mum can't have had any sleep. Next day, when the doctor came, he said:

"I can't believe it. She hasn't got a temperature at all." Nobody told him I'd drunk a big bottle of Fennings Fever Cure!

Mum was of the opinion that if it said 'one spoonful', then two was much better and every morning we had Scott's emulsion before we went to school (another well-wisher – it does you good). Derrick hated it. It made him gip. So we were then all put on to Cod Liver Oil and Malt. Really, we should have been the fittest family in the area! If Mum thought your bowels needed attention you had a good dose of Syrup of Figs on Friday night to clear you out for Sunday. Sometimes if it was cold Mum would put a paraffin stove in the bedroom before we went to bed. This was one of those round black valour stoves. I would lift my nighty and stand with my bottom to it. One night, my brother Dennis got sick of me hogging the stove and gave me a push. I sat on it. Wow! Did it hurt. I had the pattern on my bottom for days and had to sleep on my front. He got a good whacking. I was very pleased. Horrible child.

Many visitors gave advice on ailments and when one of the farm lads had chilblains he was told to bathe them with his urine. Bogey Watson said to him: "First thing in the morning before you put your socks on put your feet in the piss-pot lad." I never knew if he did. Warts were cured by rubbing with a piece of raw meat and then burying it; or a snail rubbed on was a good cure – then stick the snail on a thorn of a hawthorn hedge and as the snail withered, so did the wart. Boils were common. Mostly youths seemed to get them on the neck or bottom. These were poulticed with a bread poultice. Bread scalded and put between two muslin cloths and laid on the boil then tied with another cloth right round the neck. Of course boils on the bottom were more difficult. I heard of fathers warming bottles in the oven and then putting the neck onto the boil to draw it. One lad said: "He might a' drawn t' boil aht but my – he burnt my backside wi' t' bottle end." We always knew who had boils just there – they couldn't ride a bike! You were given brimstone and treacle as it was said you were run down.

When a woman had a hysterectomy, she'd say: "Eeh, I 'ad

51

everything takken away Missis." The mind boggles. We kids used to imagine a great empty space and everything slopping about. People always used to love talking about their operations. It was a great subject of conversation.

If you had a cold, woe betide you. Each night the goose grease came out of the cupboard, was warmed by the fire and then rubbed on your chest. A cloth was put over so that your nighty wasn't all greased up. Hot home-made elderberry syrup was downed and you were tucked into bed with a stone hot water bottle to sweat it out of you.

Of course no house had central heating but all rooms and most bedrooms had fireplaces. I loved being ill and having a fire lit in the bedroom. Mother fussing and bringing up special treats and the fire making patterns and funny shapes on the ceiling, when it became dark, due to years of whitewashing. When I was ill in bed with a fire burning and mother and sisters busy downstairs, Mum would give me grandmother Dunstan's box (a Victorian wooden box inlaid with mother of pearl) to look through. There were all sorts of pieces of old jewellery – rings, necklaces, brooches and I loved it. When mother died this came to me and I treasured it for many years. When my nephew Granville emigrated to New Zealand to farm there I gave it to him as a little bit of Hall Farm to remember us by.

Coal and logs were, of course, the fuels of yesteryears but the coal came in great lumps – huge black blocks that were broken by a coal hammer. There were no bathrooms and we had a big tin bath filled from the copper. This was put in front of the fire on a Friday night – with a screen round. I was lucky, being the youngest and a girl, I got first go. Huge towels, warmed on the fireguard were wrapped round you as you stepped out in front of a roaring fire. What bliss! Hot drink and bed!

People rarely sent for the Doctor but tried all the old wives' remedies first. Doctors cost money – no NHS. Farm workers had little money to spare and you had to be proper poorly for the doctor to be sent for.

The same with dentists. People had very little dental treatment if any and I remember many old Villagers with mouths full of bad teeth. Some didn't even go when they had really bad toothache but put up with it – filling it with whisky was a well-known remedy, or at least a better alternative. Most people were terrified of the dentist. Of course there weren't the modern aids there are today and many gruesome tales were told.

When children had teeth loose a piece of sewing thread (cotton) was tied to the door handle and the door shut quickly. This removed the offending tooth. People used to tell me that if they had an aching tooth they went to the blacksmith. He sterilised his pincers in the fire, cooled them and then grabbed the offending tooth and yanked it out. Wow!

As for false teeth – well many a man or woman spent their life without teeth. Once they were all taken out, you had to wait several weeks for your gums to settle and heal – not like today – teeth fitted instantly. By that time, most of the old ones found they could eat just as well, cutting the meat up fine, without them. Some got them and the teeth spent their life in a cup in the cupboard. Some I'm sure bought them second-hand by the way the teeth fitted and they kept dropping down – click. "Drat these things." old George used to say and immediately removed them into his handkerchief – or a bit of rag it usually was. Later he was in the hayfield, took his rag out to wipe his sweaty face forgetting the teeth and dropped them. He got home, found his teeth gone and went back with his friends and searched diligently but never found those teeth. He was very philosophical and said: "Dratted things nee'er were any good anyroad." He spent the rest of his life toothless and happy. He always said you got much more taste to your food "wi'out those bloody china things filling yer mouth." One old girl told me when she took her teeth out after she'd been out it was like taking her shoes off to ease her corns.

"You can laugh lass." she said, "Wait 'till it happens to you." Luckily up to now it hasn't.

Glasses – well, most people's eyesight just failed and that was that. Many went to Woolworths and bought some from there. You tried them on – if they improved your sight you bought them, paid 6d. and left rejoicing. They never had the addiction to the newspapers that we have today. Most of them were quite happy with the Village gossip and tales of their neighbours.

I don't think lots of things have improved from my childhood but certainly doctors, dentists and opticians have. Those old folk wouldn't believe that injections, pain-killers etc. could make life so much better for the sick, the aged and the infirm. Most of the other pains were put down to "rheumatics" (or "screws").

Our nearest Workhouse was at Balby – now knocked down and houses built. The sick, the aged, orphans and physically or mentally handicapped were all given shelter here. The unmarried mother and the homeless – it was the last hope of most people. All had to work when they got there. Cleaning, cooking etc. If people in the Village didn't work hard, they were threatened with: "You'll end up in the workhouse." and it was dreaded by everyone.

❧

CHAPTER 12

Long Before Television – Those were the Days

We had a "house" in the stackyard – it was a workmen's caravan and it was there quite a while. We had great fun in it. Then it went – I presume back to the workmen and we were very upset but Dad said we could have a pig-sty. When we went to see it it was full of pig muck. He said: "Well, clean it out and it's yours." We did. We forked out the muck into barrows – one pushed the barrow to the muck heap whilst another was filled. Four of us usually could keep it going but due to dropping it, stepping in it and general messing about, we all ended up smelling piggy. Dad did let one of the men whitewash it after we'd chucked pail after pail of water over the floor and scrubbed it with a stiff brush. After the whitewashing, we scrubbed it again and hey presto! – a lovely house to play in for weeks. Then Dad would say he needed it for a pig to farrow. Several weeks later we'd be offered another – my clever old father knew how to keep us occupied and also do a bit of useful work at the same time!

When we played on the stack we used to get terribly-scratched legs – never felt it while we were playing but wow! when we got washed at night my legs were so sore I used to cry. I vowed never again to play on the stack or run in the corn field when it had been cut because then you had red prickles all round your ankles. Boys too – they had long socks but all boys wore shorts. They didn't go into long trousers until they left school at fourteen and sometimes if they were from a poor family they wore shorts even then – or otherwise dad's cut-down trousers. Many a child got tormented for this – it was very embarrassing for them. And of course we girls wore knickers with elastic in the legs. If pulled down they came nearly to your knees – usually brown or navy blue. Real passion-killers! I don't suppose we knew what passion was in those days – certainly never heard it mentioned.

One of my favourite sights as a child was seeing the horses return from a day's work in the fields. The men would return with their own team almost at the same time. They would be riding sideways on the horse's backs – Bob on Blossom, Epe with Daisy and Captain, Bogey with Violet and Metal. They would slide off their backs and slip off the horse's harness at the stable door. The horses would toss their heads – pleased to be free and make straight for the pond. There they wallowed in the cool water – drank their fill – whinnied often and stayed for ages. Then the men would shout: "Supper up." and they'd turn and make their way into their own standing. There were many horses over the years – Metal, Captain, Daisy, Blossom, Bonny, Stella, Billy, Tommy, Violet, Fly, Darky, Flower, Prince, Royal and Duke. We generally kept ten horses, most heavy-legged but some half-legged and ponies for traps and light work – and riding of course.

> *The cuckoo comes in April*
> *He sings his song in May*
> *In the middle of June he changes tune*
> *And in July he flies away*

My brother Dennis and I have always bet each other as to who would hear the cuckoo first. We still do this. I always hear it now from across the meadows in the wood that leads to Ruddle Mill. But when we were children, there was a woman called Trilby who lived at the Hawthorns. She used to go out into the field near to her house and run round the field, always at the end of April and shout: "Cuckoo, cuckoo, cuckoo." People would say:

"Oh! I heard the cuckoo this morning." and we'd reply: "It would be old Trilby." We could never decide whether she wanted to fool us or if, when the spring weather came, she just felt elated. Poor old Trilby, dead these many years.

In lots of old houses there were Blackclocks (beetles), which came out at night when it was dark and were gone next morning as soon as daylight came. Horrible things. They looked like large rain beetles. We had them at the farm as we had underground cellars (not in use) and I presume they came up from there. We used to dose them with Carter's "Strike 'em Stiff" – what a name! We sprinkled this round the hearth each night and always had many dead ones to sweep up in the morning. They made a cracking noise if you stood on them.

As children, we used to go into the hen house at night when it was dark. Der and Den with a torch and me. I had the torch, they each had a big stick. I'd shine the torch into the nests and often out would jump a rat – been eating the eggs. I'd jump back and they'd hit it with their stick. What a game! 1d each for them from Dad. I'd never do that now. Dogs and sticks kept the rat population down. When you think that a rat can breed every six weeks and can be pregnant again even whilst suckling its young the mind boggles. It is said now that there is a bigger rat population than people.

We kids loved winter with the ice and snow. We always made slides on the ponds. Pickin's Cedar Farm was the favourite one as being exposed to the elements it froze first and we would slide all day long. I never remember anybody having skates. Sledging also was wonderful. We went across the public footpath in Birchwood Close and sledged down Lambcote Grange Field. If you weren't careful, you ended up in the stream at the bottom. Many's the time we've had to go home and change – wet through and very cold from landing in there. We also sledged down Ruddle Mill Lane in the first field on the corner at the side of Granny Grindle's Lane. What joy – we took Dennis' dog Crafty to pull the sledge back up the hill. She loved it – dashing down beside us scattering the snow then hauling the sledge back for another go.

Summertime meant home-made pop. Big bread panshions put in the cellar with lemons squeezed and the whole lot then put in with sugar, boiled water and ginger. Yeast on a slice of toast floated on top and left to work. Cor! What joy waiting for it to be ready. It was strained and put in huge stone jars and glass bottles and left to finish on the stone slab in the cellar. Often the corks would go bang and out would pour this lovely liquid onto the slabs. Sometimes horror of horrors a glass bottle would burst – glass all over and all contents wasted. But the taste of this was absolutely scrumptious. We drank gallon after gallon. It was always taken on picnics and to the hay and harvest fields. The farm men would remark: "Eee by gum lass, that does me a power o' good!"

56

The stream from Holywell Spring runs through the Horsewoods (Austwood Field). As children, my brother and his friends dammed this and swam there. It made quite a big pool when the sides were dug out. Many hours of fun were spent there and Dad and Mum and me would go down in the trap and take our tea and watch them on hot Saturday afternoons in Summer. The greatest problem was getting out. It was so muddy – by the time they'd scrambled out, their legs and hands and arms were covered in mud. Then they got a bucket of water and washed themselves down and all had tea with home-made pop, sitting round whilst they dried off in the hot sun. Remember that stream was ice cold. I never ventured in.

We always had a local policeman living in the Village. He was tall and slim and good-humoured – Bobby Yeomans. He had two sons Leslie and Kenneth. I always felt sorry for them. They always had to behave and could never join in our mischief-making for fear of being caught. If we were caught doing anything amiss, the lads got a clip round the ear and the girls a good ticking off. Next time your dad was told, to the lads this meant a thrashing – to the girls kept in at night. I had a lovely dog called Tess, a golden retriever. I was responsible for getting the dog license and Dad had given me the money but I hadn't bothered to go to the Post Office. Sitting in the kitchen one day I saw the policeman's helmet through the window. Mother said: "I wonder what Bobby Yeomans wants?" I knew. I shot upstairs, grabbed my money and my bike from the shed and rode up the street like a bat out of hell. Dashed into the Post Office and got my license – back home through the front door while my mother was searching for me upstairs. She said: "The Bobby wants your dog license." I said:

"I thought so. Here it is." and into the kitchen we went. He took it from me and said:

"That's lucky lass, you only got it today." My mother looked amazed.

"You cheeky young bugger! You've only *just* got it." he said. I had no idea they put the time on too. He laughed and said to my mother: "I shall have to report this as I've been sent out to look at it." We were fined 10/-. I was in big trouble.

PART 2
MY VILLAGE

CHAPTER 13

Braithwell, Village of my birth
Streets and lanes I know
Fields I wanderd in my youth
Dykes and streams o'erflow

Many houses have been knocked down in the Village over the years. In years gone by, there was no electric, no gas, no hot water. The houses were all very plain – none were "done up", tarted up, no sun lounges, patios, hanging baskets, glass porches. Most of them needed a coat of paint and the cottage gardens grew mostly vegetables. Every cottage and farm kitchen had a blackleaded fireplace with an oven on one side and a boiler on the other. A ladling can stood on this and hot water was ladled out from the side boiler for body washing, pot washing, floor scrubbing and hair washing and any other job that needed hot water. Usually people washed in cold water, not from a tap but water from a bucket carried from the pump in the village street or in the yard – often several houses shared a pump or well. We always washed our hair in rainwater. It was supposed to be good and give it a shine and make it strong and glossy.

Our Village was built of stone because that's the material that was available – limestone land, stone from the quarries – many houses would be built of stone taken from Roche Abbey. People didn't respect ancient buildings as we do today. Each village is very individual. We are all insular, always thinking our Village is the best for miles around. Unfortunately now our Village could never support its working population but 100 years ago, most Village people would find work in this Village.

There were farmers and farm labourers, quarry men, tailors, blacksmiths, hosiery-makers, cordwainers (shoe-makers), shop-keepers, water-carters etc.. Self-employed men clearing dykes and hedge-laying.

All hedges had to be cut by hand with a hedging bill ("slash-er") or Yorkshire Billhook for laying and it was a full-time win-ter occupation. And of course there were a lot more of them. The field next to me, which is about 20 acres and butts up to the Holywell Spring, had six small fields – all grass with tall hedges and huge trees under which the cows, horses and sheep sheltered from rain and sun. These have all gone – how sad.

People lived very simple lives and our expectations were very modest. A week's holiday a year was a real treat. Most people never got one at all and a day at the seaside with the Sunday School trip or at Roche Abbey satisfied people. What a change when now most people think if they haven't been abroad or "down south" they haven't had a change. We would have thought people were barmy when we were young if they'd said they needed a change or a rest. And if they'd mentioned want-ing their own space, we should have died laughing. We should-n't have known what they meant.

In those days, thrift, hard work and craftsmanship were rewarded and people showed pride in their job. They were healthy because they ate good food which they grew on the land and reared the stock themselves. They were happy and lived life in a close-knit agricultural community. They also helped each other, especially in hard times, births or deaths etc..

Country people used to rise at daybreak and go to bed at dark. Lighting was expensive – the work was hard and they needed their rest. We only had candles upstairs but paraffin lamps downstairs, which were trimmed (wicks cleaned and straightened) on the kitchen table and then filled with paraffin ready for night.

One thing that has changed dramatically in villages in the last 100 years is the status of people and their expectations. It used to be said in churches and schools: "The status that it has pleased God to call you." And you weren't expected to step out of that. It has changed now. I remember a "Lady" in the Village passing a young farm worker in the street and as he slouched past, she said: "Young man, don't you doff your cap to a Lady?" He replied: "Ai. When I see a Lady I do."

The greatest change I think in the Village has been new

people who live here but commute and so don't really integrate. They think it's a nice place to live but don't get involved. What a lot they miss.

The people who lived down at The Hawthorns, Holywell Cottage and Birkwood House got their water from the Holy Well, which bubbled up from the ground on the west side of the road – this spring water is still there with seven springs still rising, still running clear. The original well, unfortunately, has been taken into the main waterway. This is the rise of the River Torne and runs from here to Stainton, then Tickhill and Rossington, and Branton. The people of Birkwood Terrace (the Seven Houses) had a pump in the back yard. In 1983, when I was on the Parish Council, I asked Mrs. Appleyard, who owned the houses, if the Village could have this pump and erect it where the original Village Pump used to be in front of Well House. She was delighted to give it to the Village and attended the ceremony when this was completed.

The older you get the more you realise the significance of things. Funerals in a village are always well-attended. My uncle Albert used to attend all the Village funerals. I am the same. People say it's morbid but of course it isn't. It's a sign of respect and when you've lived in a Village all your life you know everybody. My family call me the Village Mourner. If anybody is ill people gather round to help with baking or some small gift. It's not often they go empty-handed to visit the sick.

To think people of my age have lived through the time of only horses and carts on the farm to combines, potato-planters and beet-lifters all in one operation. From earth closets, poes, lino on the floor (or bare boards and rag rugs) to fitted carpets everywhere. Then from water fetched from the well by bucket to hot water at the turn of a tap – I still think a bathful of really hot water with bubbles is a luxury. Of course I enjoy it more now with a book in one hand and a gin and tonic in the other! From battery-operated wirelesses to modern radios and televsion.

My husband's family were ironmongers in Maltby for eighty years until they retired in 1986. Charles Milnes, my father-in-law, came to Maltby as a building foreman to construct the pit in 1904. All the men he employed had to have their own tools. He used to have to send a horse and cart to Sheffield for these and then take the money from the men's wages, as they had no money to pay for them. He decided to set his wife, Alice, up with the necessary tools in a small hut he built on land he bought in High Street. The men from the pit then went and chose their tools. He still drew the money from their wages but no longer had to keep sending to Sheffield as he stocked the tools in the shop. He then progressed to other tools – plumbers', farm tools, other tradesmen's tools and so decided to stay in Maltby. That's how C. Milnes & Sons started. They supplied all the accumulators and dry batteries for wirelesses to the surrounding villages and re-charged batteries each week for 6d and took the old ones back to the shop for re-charging. This is how I met Malcolm – after the war when paraffin was rationed, my mother and I raised a lot of day-old chickens in incubators (needed paraffin for the heating). He tells everybody my Dad swapped me for five gallons of paraffin – what a dowry!!

Before the Milnes business owned a van, Malcolm's older brothers Eric and Hubert, who were in their early teens, would take a hand cart to Ranskill for tools. They would load this up at Skinner & Johnson's and with the help of their airdale dog Darky pulling with them at the front, they would return home to the shop at Maltby. About a 20-mile round trip. What youngster would do that now-a-days?

See a pin, pick it up
All the day you'll have good luck
See a pin, let it stay
Bad luck is yours all that day

Village people were very superstitious – they believed implicitly in the moon's influence. They talked about locals who were affected by the moon – even in my childhood. They turned their money over in their pocket or went outside to view the new moon so as not to see it through glass – that was really bad luck. Remember that the full moon played a great part in Village activities as there were no street lights.

Children would play in the streets – whip and top, hop-scotch, cricket, skipping or hoops, shuttle cocks – no fear of being run down by motor cars. The odd farm cart or pony and trap came through. Cricket was an important game and all the Village would turn out to watch the Village team – teas, sandwiches and cakes were served from a hut. This used to be in our field up Maltby Lane on the east side past Hoyle Croft Lane, then it moved to where Willow Place is built, in Allison's Field. But most of all, I liked hop-scotch. We made our pattern with chalk and played happily for hours in the street. One day whilst playing, one of my friends' elder brother came up to watch. After making lots of daft remarks when his sister had her turn, he put his foot out and tripped her up. He walked off laughing but she was furious. She shouted: "I'll get my own back." We all said: "How can you do that? He's far bigger than you." She looked triumphant and said: "I'll pee in his bath watter." Remember, in those days the family got bathed in the same water – and girls went first. I hope she did!

When I was about seven years old a boy from London came to visit relatives in the Village. He spoke with a cockney accent and we Village kids all stood around in amazement as he held forth. His small cousin was very embarrassed by his "cocki-ness" as we called it and when he had finished his tales about London, we locals (or yokels as you may think of us) all burst out laughing at his accent. He was furious, went very red and shouted: "You don't think I've come all the way from London to be 'larfed at'." We all found it very amusing. How silly he must have thought us. We really were very insular.

We do really hate being patronised and many people used to get cross with the vicar, who always wanted to know why you hadn't been to church. In fact, I know of one farmer, who was a keen churchgoer, who said to his man on Monday morning: "I didn't see you at church yesterday Tom." The farm labourer mumbled some excuse and the farmer said: "Well go home. If you can't go to church on Sunday, you can't work on Monday." – without pay of course. This never happened in hay-making or harvest but only when work was slack.

Mrs. Dick Robinson of Croft End, missing me at church and seeing me in the Village, asked why I hadn't been there. "Oh!" I said, "I have such good intentions Mrs. Dick but I never seem to follow it up and get there." She replied:

"Joyce, the road to hell is paved with good intentions." I always think of her when I miss church.

Teddy Dobbs of Low Farm told me of a new town bride coming to the Village. The young man must have travelled on his bicycle to meet her!! Her husband was a smallholder and a neighbour gave them a hen and a clutch of twelve chickens for a wedding present. The young bride was very thrilled and told her husband she would like to look after them. She kept the chicken coop clean and supplied water and wandered out often during the day to view them. A visitor called and she took him

62

to look at her present. Several lay dead, several looked sickly. "What are you feeding them?" he asked.

"Feeding them?" she said, "Doesn't the mother hen do that?" Another young town visitor to the Village was sent out by his aunt to look round the smallholding whilst she cooked the dinner. He rushed in, grabbed his aunt by the hand and said:

"Come quickly, those little pigs are chewing their mother's tummy buttons off." Could these tales really be true – were they kidding me or am I kidding you?

CHAPTER 14

Great Excitement – Electricity!
"We're Going to get Lit Up!"

As there was no electricity in the Village, there were no electric poles to spoil the surrounding countryside. The street light consisted of two – one on the Cross and one at the top of the street. These were fuelled by paraffin but only lit in winter. Albert Fidler was in charge of them. They were difficult to light and often they weren't working.

When electricity came to the village in 1933/4, there was great excitement. No more lamps to trim – no more candles to take upstairs to bed. The farmers dreamed of electric milking machines – and the wives of electric washing machines, fridges and cookers. Of course most of them didn't get these for years but they always lived in hope. Many didn't get electricity until well after the war due to the expense of installing it into homes – particularly if they were rented. Landlords didn't want that expense.

One young man coming home to visit his father, who was a widower, was delighted to pay for his father's electric to be fitted as he worried about the old man trimming wicks and going upstairs with lighted candles. "How are you getting on with the electric dad?" he asked.

"Alreet lad" was the reply "but I do wish I could tun it dahn a bit when Ah've finished ree-adin' mi paper."

An old lady was found by her son standing on a chair removing the electric light bulb from the bedroom ceiling. "Ah'm just takking this aht lad so I dun't ger electrified while Ah'm asleep in't' neet." she said. Now he knew why she still went upstairs every night with an unlighted candle and matches!

But the delight on the women's faces who acquired a hoover was a joy to behold – everybody invited in to see this miracle. No more beating of carpets and rugs. Needless to say some still hoovered and beat them as well. Old habits die hard!

And two electric lights were fixed in the Village – one at the top and one by the Cross. We youngsters didn't really take to them. I always thought it was more fun wandering about in the dark with only the two oil lamps – often not even lit. You didn't get caught that way did you?

One favourite place to congregate was the fish shop (now the hairdresser's). We sat on the wall in front. We saw everybody coming and going. It was a real hive of activity. There was a nice glow from the fish shop lights and everybody's chips were shared. If you hadn't any money, you still always managed a chip or two. As my Auntie Ada and Uncle Frank kept the shop, they always sent me in for fish bits – which came free with chips. We teased each other, flirted and watched whose mother went to the pub with a jug for ale.

Each pub had a "beer off" – a small area about 1½ yards square, entered through an outside door – you could buy your beer etc. without having to go into the pub itself. Women very rarely went into the pub to drink but many a tale could be told of the old ladies who came to the jug and bottle as this area was known. Some took empty bottles to fill in a basket – discreetly covered with a tea towel. Often after dark. Some just had a bottle or two in their pockets. Some took big harvest jugs or cans and had them filled. Then they had to drink the top off "to save it spilling" – or so they said. Many's the time I've called for my mother at the Mother's Union after school and heard one of them saying: "Not a drop ever touches mi lips." I'd open my eyes in amazement but at a look from my mother, I kept quiet. I'd seen them the night before leaving the jug and bottle with a jug full of ale and they'd supped the top off before carrying it home.

Most people had earth closets. Ours had a stone wall round it, with a small gate for cleaning out. Fire ashes were thrown in, often right under the seats. These outdoor, dry toilets (closet or privy) with two or three holes (two large, one small for children) in a white wooden seat over a large hole. Newspaper was cut into squares about 8" across and stuck onto a nail behind the closet door. A nice little job for the children in the evenings. One girl in our Village was sitting happily dreaming on the seat in the yard one morning when the farm man let the boar pig out so that he could clean out the pig sty. For some unearthly reason, it charged the closet door – why, nobody ever knew – poor old Mary leapt onto the seat yelling blue murder. What was so embarrassing was that she still had her pink knickers round her ankles when she was rescued. Rows of cottages often shared toilets. I know of one Village boy who went to use the shared closet. He opened the door and the neighbour was already sitting on one seat. He tried to shut the door but she grabbed him by his jacket collar and said: "Tha can coom in – I've seen all tha's got." He was made to sit next to her but he said it never happened again. He always kicked the door first.

We used to go into our outside toilet, friends together. One sat on one hole and one on the other and chatted. All our secrets were told here. Did we ever notice the smell? I don't remember. One thing I do remember is that a small banty cock used to sit on the wall that surrounded this ash pit and closet. I was always terrified that he'd nip underneath and bite my bottom. He always chased us as we came out and nipped our ankles. He was really beautiful but a little monster. One day, when I was sitting contemplating on the "loo", my sister Doris came from the house with the hot cinders and threw them under the seat – not knowing, of course, that I was sitting there. I shot up and yelled at the top of my voice – I frightened poor old Doris. I have one of these seats now in my garden for "decoration" and underneath the seat is all burnt black. This came from my husband Malcolm's home in Maltby and when we open our garden for charity, I always write out a sign "Malcolm Milnes Sat Here".

There was a night soil service where the outside closets were emptied at night by two men who worked all through the night with a horse and cart and led it away into fields, charging for the service. But lots of people emptied their own. I myself have found several treasures from a field of mine that was used for this purpose. Objects discarded from the house were dropped into the pit along with the ashes. I have a china doll, a horse brass, a brass dish, a "marble" pop bottle (a bottle with a glass alley in the neck), a baby's bottle and several stone jars and lids – all found when digging out a hedge in Holywell Field (Birchwood Close).

There were one or two bread ovens still left in the Village when I was a child, one at Rook House Farm, one at Orchard Farm and one at Ashton House where there was also a salt hole. These ovens were long, box-shaped, brick or stone, cupboard-like holes by the side of the chimney and with iron doors. Wood was put in, lit and left to burn out. When the back bricks of the oven within glowed white-hot, the embers were scraped out and the dough loaves put in to bake. I never remember these in use but was told how they worked – the one at Ashton House is still there.

Knife grinders and Rag-and-bone Men always visited the Village. All my friends had old wool for the rag and bone man but we hadn't any. I was devastated as they all came away with their balloons etc.. Dad gave me a sheep fleece to take. The rag and bone man was absolutely astounded – he said he'd never had one given before and I got 10 balloons and a stick to put them on.

Most Village people lived out their lives without ever going far from the Village. Doncaster and Rotherham were the farthest a lot of people ever ventured – it was either walking, pony and trap, or the waggonette.

❧

CHAPTER 15

MEMORIES

Do you remember when you were young
When you could buy a tuppenny bun
When gorgeous milk came in a can
When cream was served thick on a flan
Do you remember? Do you?

Do you remember when you were small
When there was time to spare for all
When horses stood in every stall
When hot baths were a weekly treat
When every day was meat to eat
Do you remember? Do you?

Sometimes Mum would let me drive Stella up the Village when we were going out. You can imagine me – cocky little thing, showing off. One day, a crowd of Village lads were standing by the Butcher's Arms corner. I was riding Stella and on my own this time and she broke wind – not just once but all the way from the Fish & Chip Shop. I was so embarrassed and even more so when one of the big lads shouted: "Nah Joyce. Tha's doin' some fartin' in't ya? Has t' had peas for thi dinner?" I tried to look dignified and said:

"It's the horse."

"Ah," he said, "tha'll tell us owt."

The boys always played 'knocking' on winter nights and sometimes they let us join in. No street lights. You went up to somebody's door, knocked and ran away. Then the next boy or girl did the same. By the time three had done it, the householder was furious and waited for you and came out running. This was the best part. They must have been sick and tired of our little game. If houses were close togther, we tied the door knobs with string. Albert Fidler and Ted Littlewood were our best targets – they'd always chase you.

On Sunday nights after we'd been to chapel or church, we went for a walk down the Village lanes. We all congregated to chat and laugh and there'd probably be five girls in a row, arm-in-arm. Then we'd meet up with the lads standing at the street corners. Then home to supper – we always had cold beef (from dinner) with horseradish and all the left-over veg. put into the oven and warmed up. Very rarely did we manage to eat this on our own as a family. We'd just be sitting down at our big kitchen table and up would come an Auntie and Uncle and family, or Village friends, or relatives and we'd all have to shuffle round to get them at the table and share the food. Luckily there was always plenty. At our house, Mum sat on the right side at the head of the table and Dad on the left, always in his Windsor chair. The youngest child stood in between them. As you got older, you moved round onto a stool next to Mum. I took over Dennis' place and he then moved to Dad's side so we were all under scrutiny. If you licked your knife or used your fingers, you got a tap with his knife. Audrey, Doris and Uncles sat at the far end. The family never depleted because, as my uncles married, Mr. Page arrived and he was followed by my grandfather, who lived with us until he died.

My uncle Harold (Lal), my mother's brother, started work on the land at 12 years old in 1916 and got £7 a year . He was released from school as he had a job to go to. My uncle worked with sheep. This meant rising at 5am and "living in" on the farm. My father too left school at 12yrs.. He had a job on his father's farm to go to with the cows. Uncle Lal started work at Manor Farm, Micklebring. He was the boy. During lambing the farmer, Mr. Bentley and uncle used to stay up all night in the farm kitchen. Mr. Bentley slept on the settle and my uncle slept on the pegged rug in front of the fire with the sheep dog Gyp. They went out every half hour to see if any of the ewes were in trouble with lambing. On the hour, Mr. Bentley went out and on the half hour uncle Lal. Mr. Bentley used to wake him – "Cum on lad. Ger up." He took the stable lamp and Gyp and crossed the fold yard to the barn. He wore breeches and leggings and he said the space between (they never seemed to meet) was very cold. How quickly these boys had to grow up and learn about birth and life and death. He said he was always very frightened crossing the fold yard.

He also tells of his "gaffer" going to Rotherham (Statice Fair in November) and signing on a cowman. He was bound for one year – £30 to £40 wages if he was very experienced. They shook hands and the farmer "fastened" him with half-a-crown (2/6d., 12½p). Also Lincoln Fair in May was for farm hands. All met and talked and decided on new farms to work – often the waggoner came from Lincoln. First waggoner would be on £40 a year.

Many wooden huts caravans and buildings were put up in the Village in the early 1900s when the ownership of a piece of land entitled you to put up a "building" and live there. There was a wooden building up Maltby Lane on the corner called Tofields. This building was built between two small fields. Knowing this Village and Yorkshire peoples' way of saying "two" this would inevitably become "Tofields" (pronounced "Toefields"). One at Ash Close on Cockhill Field Lane, one at 10 Doncaster Road ("Pip Ridge"), Granny Grindle's bungalow on Chapel Holes Lane, one caravan in the gardens down Holywell Lane – by the spring, where Liza and Fred Ward lived, with Cambridge the tramp living in a hut on the same land. Norman Smith, a gypsy, lived in a caravan in the small triangular field down Cockhill Field Lane. There was a farm track through the small field leading to Skellingdales – my father farmed this so we saw Norman often. He was a real horse-dealer. There was a caravan on land where the children's play-park is now – Big Fred the roadman lived there. But the latter few were all too poor to build houses for themselves.

There was a row of three terraced houses attached to the south side of the Village Store – the wall still remains. It was called "The Alley". There was also a house on the north side on the wall of Rose Cottage. It seems unbelievable that four houses could be built in this small area. Many of the families who lived there had six to eight children. They had one thing in common – they were all poor. I don't think they'd think of them as the good old days. What tales this Alley could tell of neighbours' quarrels and many problems, sickness and death. Some of the women stood to chat at the end of the Alley with arms folded and sacking aprons. To me they always seemed to be there when you went past but they were kind and jolly women and, of course, knew me well. They chatted to whoever was passing to the Village Shop. Lots of Village people had "tick" at the shop. They had a book and everything was written down. They paid up on Friday or when the husband got paid. This shop stayed open very late because often bosses (particularly farmers) didn't pay wages until late on Friday night. Sometimes even Saturday if the farmer had no money or had to take a beast or sheep to market to take him through the following week. Times were very hard for the gaffers also.

Bogey Watson lived in the middle one of these houses. He was tall and thin with a beard and moustache and worked as long as I can ever remember for my father. I don't know why they called him "Bogey", his real name was George. He loved his beer and spent most of his wages in the Butcher's Arms on a Friday and Saturday night. He always wore a soft trilby and smoked clay pipes. When he left farming because of ill health, my mother used to sometimes send his dinner up. Often I took it as I knew him so well. He was a pitiful sight – he'd changed from the man I knew. He was very morose and his trousers used to be turned up to the knees and his legs were swollen and sore. He wore just boots, no socks. Sadly he ended up in the workhouse. Poor old Bogey.

There was a lot of T.B. about then – a dreadful disease. People seemed to waste away. A friend of mine died of it and so did her mother. We were all very upset and frightened by this as so little was known about it. They slept outside in huts in the garden in the fresh air.

Farm men always wore leggings and boots. There were no wellingtons at that time. Well-to-do men wore spats with trousers. When a farm man got some overtime money at harvest and hay time, he invested in a new pair of strong boots made by the local shoemaker, Henry Hall, and new trousers made by the village tailor, Mr. Louis Colbeck and took the old ones to work in.

❧

CHAPTER 16

Hear All, See All, Say Nowt

Sunday was for church or chapel – twice a day. Your were considered not much good if you didn't attend either but, of course, some men preferred the pub. Lots of women who were widows, or whose husband spent his wage at the pub, took in washing or went to work on the land or for the farmer's wife. What a hard life it must have been – washing, drying thick sheets and shirts and then ironing with a flat iron heated in front of the dirty coal fire to be changed often to keep it hot – sometimes two or three days doing other people's washing.

They say the church's business is "hatching, matching and dispatching" and that people go at least three times in their lives for these. But like the church the pub also has a useful part in Village life – gossip is swapped there. Back-scratching is a way of life in the village and much of it goes on here. Bartering – never pay for anything if you can exchange it for some other commodity, even today. We're a thrifty lot. It runs in the blood.

One day on my way to church I stopped to talk to Fred, an old Villager and a frequent customer at the pubs. A regular church-goer passed us. "Aren't you coming to church Joyce?" she asked.

"Yes," I replied, "I'm just having a word with Fred." She completely ignored Fred and went on her way. He gave me a quizzical look and said:

"Lass, if she's a Christian, I don't want to be."

I know of one Villager, a widow, who worked at the local pub and on two farms. She went to the pub at 8am and cleaned through. Then did bedrooms. Her daughter went from school for her dinner but had to wash up afterwards – she was eight years old. Her mother cleaned in the afternoon and then the girl went back for tea after school, washed the tea pots and all the pub pots. For this, the mother got 2/6d a day. The girl nothing, not even a penny, only her meals. The same at the farms – sometimes walking 1½ miles in all weathers to do the washing at the farm. Finishing at 5pm after washing, scouring and walking home. Even in bad weather. Her husband died when he was thirty-two. Whilst her husband was in bed with the pneumonia from which he died, her small eleven-month-old son died in a fit in her arms as she carried him upstairs to see her husband. Her other son, eight years old, died of measles the following year. She just had her daughter left and struggled to bring them both up. No help from anybody and too proud to go on the Parish. She worked from morn 'till night.

Women doing housework always wore dustcaps – cotton material made into a small cap, often patterned, with an elasticated back which fitted over the head – almost like a shower cap but it had a wide band at the front about 3" high. This covered all the hair – housework was always very dirty – open fires, black-leaded cooking ranges – think of the black soot-bottomed pans to wash without hot water on tap; scrubbed stone floors, rag rugs to be shaken, old sacks for door mats to shake; white-washed ceilings (white dust always falling from them) and white-washed cellars – these down stone steps and with flagged floors to scrub.

When I was about seven and walking up the street to school, I always chatted to the people in the cottages (I've always been a big talker!). Mrs. Markham, who lived in Orchard Cottage south of Orchard Farm, was shaking her rag rug. I called: "Hello, Mrs. Markham." She was just turning to go into the cottage and, turning to wave to me, she caught her cap on the hook by the door. This not only removed her cap but also her wig. I was dumbfounded at this poor completely bald woman. Embarrassed, she rushed inside and I just stood there. When I dashed home to tell my mother, she was so upset and said I mustn't say anything to anybody about this. I can't remember ever doing so until now. Mrs. Markham had a son Charlie who loved cricket. I found out years later that he was adopted. When she died, Charlie left the cottage. I don't know where he went or what happened to him. Poor old Charlie, he was nice but rather a simple soul. Mrs. Markham did the laying-out when anybody died in the Village. Also she helped deliver the babies. She had three lodgers too – Irish Paddy, Josh and Sagey who all worked on the farms and the thrasher. I can't imagine where they all slept as it was only 2-up and 2-down. She was a real good hard-working soul. A typical kind and genuine Village woman.

A farmer's wife was in tears when a lady of the Village called on her for some eggs. They'd had a demand note for £5 for the rates and they had no money. She was worried sick and had visions of her husband ending up in prison. The lady neighbour, who had always admired the blue-and-white pottery that was on display in the parlour, said: "Would you like to sell the pottery? I'll give you the £5 for the rates for it." The farmer's wife was delighted and heaved a sigh of relief. The neighbour was happy and the deal was concluded. I see these plates and dishes adorning the walls of this house now and think about the poor woman, now long since dead, who exchanged her beloved possessions for the rate money and to save her husband, who was an idle devil.

One old lady in the Village we visited regularly – she had no hot water, of course, and made good use of the kettle when it boiled on the hob. She was always generous with her cups of tea and biscuits, which we enjoyed and she always made us welcome. We were very amused one day and rather shocked to see her take the kettle from the fire and put it into the bowl and add cold water, rinse her teeth in the bowl and then get a good wash. She then washed the pots in the same water – mashed the tea in the pot and asked us if we'd like a cup of tea. Needless to say, we were in a hurry and ever after had always "just had one thank you.".

I visited a local farmer's house in the Village and he had a tree trunk burning on the fire. His wife had died and he was a lazy man. He just sat there and as a piece burnt he pushed the trunk with his foot and went on drinking his beer. How he put it out at night I don't know. I presume he poured water over it but how dangerous and how idle can you be.

A very deaf old retired farmer visited a young man who used to work for his family. He sat down on a stool in the kitchen and when the wife turned round from the sink, she saw his trousers were undone. She turned back and muttered to her husband: "Do tell him to fasten up his fly." The husband shouted to make him hear this request and the old boy replied:

"Eeh. Tell her not to worry lad, dee-ed buds don't fly art a t' nest." (Dead birds don't fly out of the nest).

72

One old lady of the Village very upset when her neighbour had died in bed said: "I've telled George (her husband) if I dee in bed to mak sure afore he gets t' laying out woman in tha mun put mi teeth in an pull mi nightie down. I don't want catching unawares." I do hope he did this – she's long dead and I never dared to ask him.

Dad told me a lady who kept a smallholding on High Street got up in the night when she heard noises outside. She slipped and fell, breaking her leg. Her son, a nice but gormless (a bit simple) lad, was shouted out of bed and sent for the doctor. He took the pony and trap and headed for Bramley. He knocked hard on the door of the house and eventually got the owner up, who shouted: "What is it lad?" from the bedroom window.

"It's mi Mar sir." he shouted "It's Jimmy Turner." Down came the householder, opened the door and asked:

"Now, lad, what seems to be the matter?"

"Mi Mar's broken her leg. Can you come?" The man shouted:

"A broken leg? Well shoot the buggar."

"What? Shoot mi mother?" said the lad, dumbfounded.

"Your mother." said the astounded man, "I thought you said your mare. You're at the wrong house lad, I'm not the doctor, I'm the vet.. You want next door.".

In the middle of High Street, at the cottage now called Stoneleigh (none of the cottages had names before the war) lived Harry Allison and his wife. His farming skills have always been admired. He was an expert in ditching, hedging, stacking and any farm job that needed specialist knowledge. He was self-employed and my father employed him often and always spoke very highly of him. He was tall and thin ("spare" these people used to be known as). His wife was small and thin and had been a skilled cook in London. She came to the Village to look after Harry when her sister, Harry's wife, died. She stayed on and married him and was a wonderful wife and mother. Her daughter is Mrs. Muriel (Edith) Pearson. She worked hard and was often to be seen with her baskets of vegetables coming from the allotments at the bottom of the Village, where her husband tended a vegetable plot. One day she called at Leigh's furniture store in Maltby and said she wanted to choose a new bed. Her husband didn't know she'd gone as he was very happy with the old one and she said they had to deliver it when her husband was out. They took down the old iron bedstead for her and put up the modern one. She laughed and said: "Wait 'till he comes to hang his trousers over the knob at the end of the bed tonight when he comes home from the pub. He will be done." And he was!

Ossie Picton lived in the Village in Nailor's Cottage. His wife and Nance Holmes from Rook House Farm were sisters. They had five girls and one boy, George. He unfortunately was scalded when small and died in hospital. Ossie was a really good runner and one day in the pub, when everybody boasts what they can do after a few beers, either John Swift challenged Ossie or Ossie challenged John. There is some dispute about which. Anyway, it was yards for years. Ossie was years older than John. They raced on Boxing Day – always very competitive in this Village. I don't even remember who won their race. Ever since then, some race or challenge has happened on Boxing Day.

When Ernest Wadsworth started his milk round at Maltby, he bought the float from my father. When he gave the milk round up, he went to drive for Butler's (Quarries) and we got the float back. We always used this to go for family picnics to the Fox Holes or Dale Hill Field – it always seemed miles away when I was young. Mr. Jack Stones left the Manor in the early 1930s and came to live next door to The Poplars. He bought Ernest Wadsworth's milk round but delivered in a car. He was the first milkman we ever knew who used a car – an Armstrong Siddeley. Willie Palmer, of Elmfield Farm then started delivering milk on a motorbike – a Raleigh.

One of the old Village women fascinated me. She always had stockings round the table legs. It was a big Victorian table with polished mahogany legs. Her old lisle stockings had the feet cut out and then were pushed over the table legs. When I was very little I asked why the table wore stockings. She replied: "Ee luv, if I left them bare t' menfook would muck up t' legs in no time at all, rubbing their mucky trousers on 'em. This table were me mother's. She kept stockings on it and so shall I." I understand she removed them on Sundays. Most women kept chenille tablecloths on top of polished tables. I knew one woman who always used a clean sheet to cover her bed counter-pane so that it didn't get dirty. I never understood why she bothered with such a lovely counterpane as she never saw it and nobody else did either. She just said she wanted to keep it nice. It certainly would never wear out. I think her daughter still has it.

An old Village farmer asked: "Weers tha goin' lad?" when he

saw his son leaving the house with a torch.

"I'm goin' courtin'." the lad replied.

"I nivver needed a leet wen ar wint courtin'."

"Ai" said the lad "but look what tha browt hoo-am."."

❧

CHAPTER 17

Waggonette to Town

Oh, a happy man is the carrier man
Who plies between village and town
As he jogs along with his old brown mare
Whistling and singing with never a care,
Never concerned if he's late getting there
For a village will wait on the town.

R. A. H. Goodyear

People didn't travel very far in my father's day. Most Village people lived out their lives without ever going far from the Village. Doncaster and Rotherham were the farthest a lot of people ever ventured – it was either walking, riding a horse, or the pony and trap. Again, most of the people, even of my sister's generation, married men from the Village. On Saturdays Mr. Grindle (Granny Grindle's husband) took a wagonette. In later years, Albert Fidler took one. They went to the market in the morning and returned later that day. All for 6d. Lots of people never left the Village.

Mr. & Mrs. Herbert Allison ran the Butcher's Arms public house then – it was the old "whiteweshed" pub. Mrs. Allison did the cricket club dinner. It was hot beef and veg. etc.. Next day, all the gravy and meat which was left were put into the copper with fresh vegetables. This was given out to any poor Villager who cared to go along with a can or a jug to fill and take home. They then moved over to Maltkiln Farm and that is where I remember them in my childhood. He was always known as "Spoff" Allison – a real character. Tall and with a white moustache turned ginger by taking snuff. The nickname was given because of his love of cricket – Spofforth was a member of the touring Australian team of that time. He was always the

75

gentleman. His wife small and slight and always working. They had a smallholding opposite which went with the pub. When they left the pub, they took over the Farm from Nicholsons and like all farmers they struggled to make a living. Mrs. Allison still worked all day and was a lovely lady – never complaining

Tithe Dinners were held alternately in each pub – the Red Lion and the Butcher's Arms. They were held every six months in March and September. A dinner was served to the tenants of the land and the Tithes collected by the Earl of Scarbrough's agent of Sandbeck Hall. In 1898 Mr. Colbeck had the Butcher's Arms and the dinner cost Lord Scarbrough £3 for all the dinners of his tenants. In 1901 The Red Lion had the dinner and requested rabbits from the Sandbeck estate – this was a usual thing. In 1904 Herbert Allison had the dinner at the Butchers Arms and asked Lord Scarbrough, the 10th Earl, if he could provide the rabbits as usual – he also said a few hares wouldn't come amiss as the farmers preferred these and could they be delivered as he hadn't any transport (cheeky devil). One tenant was taken on one side by the agent who suggested that as his yearly Tithe was only 2/6d (12½p), he could perhaps pay it yearly instead of half-yearly. "Indeed not," said the tenant "I should miss me dinner then."

After the Allison's left the Butcher's Arms Mr. & Mrs. George Morrell took over. They had one daughter Marion. She was two years younger than me but we were good friends. Mr. Morrell had a marvellous sense of humour. Mrs. Morrell was very smart and attractive and in those days publicans and their wives always had different nights off as one of them always stayed to look after the pub.. Mrs. Morrell used to go with two friends, Mrs. Braithwaite (Manor Farm) and Mrs. Lawrence (Ashton House), to Doncaster for a drink in one of the hotels. Mr. Morrell used to infuriate his wife by remarking: "By lass! You've had plenty of gin tonight." She used to get very annoyed and reply:

"So what? I work hard enough don't I?" and flounce off upstairs. She thought she'd get her own back, so when he came in after a night out and in front of all his customers she said:

"George! You've had too much to drink." and he replied, putting his arm round her:

"I have lass. And by gum I have enjoyed it." She couldn't win.

Mr. Joe Copley built and lived in a small wooden hut on No. 10 Doncaster Road. He was a builder by trade and later built all the houses on Doncaster Road. The first one he built he lived in with his wife – No. 20, now known as "Bruncliffe". Very few houses had names in earlier years. He was a very good man for the Village. He was a councillor and a churchwarden and his wife ran the local drama group, which I belonged to for many years. The last play we did was "The Stray Lady". We had some good concerts in the school at the top of the Village where the new housing estate is now built – Birchwood Gardens.

At Harehound House (now partly demolished) at the bottom of Maltby Lane, lived Mrs. Martha (Mitty) Marshall. This was an ale house in my father's youth although, being a Methodist, he never used it but told tales often of people who did. He used to use this expression: "He only has to smell the barmaid's pinny (pinafore) and he is away.", meaning that it didn't take many to make him drunk and daft (silly). When I was in the W.L.A. I visited a riding stables in Cambridge as I missed riding my horse Tommy at home. The owner said he'd have to ride with me as he wasn't allowed to send people out until he knew they were safe. He chatted away as we rode and asked where I came from – surprise, surprise, he could tell by my accent that I was Yorkshire. I said: "A small village called Braithwell, you wouldn't know it". He said:

"Goodness me! I was born at Stainton." He was a Nicholson of the Nicholson jockey family. He told me tales of when he was a young man fastening Mitty Marhsall in the cellar. He thought she was going to kill them when she got out. And of jumping his horse for a bet over the iron rails that surrounded the garden. He said they were always betting each other to do daredevil things. On the hunting field too this went on. They hunted often from the Village before the motorways and many a man came home with broken limbs due to taking up the challenge to jump a difficult hedge or dyke. Luckily in those days farmers never used barbed wire.

I always found it strange when people returned to the Village who had "done well". They'd perhaps call at the Red Lion pub and buy a few drinks for people. The old Villagers, whilst drinking beer he'd bought them, would say: "Who does ee think ee is? Chuckin' 'is money abaht. His dad were a reight good 'ossman (horseman) an' all. Him showing off. He were at skuil (school) wi' (with) me – he were nivver (never) that bright neether (neither)." It is strange that some Village people never seem to appreciate anybody prospering. When somebody new came to the Village and was throwing his weight about, the old Villagers would say: "He ain't bin 'ere long enough to ger 'is backside warm."

I was told by Ernest Dickinson of Fox House Cottage, who was a keen cricketer, of a Village cricket match for charity – two Village sides, mostly farmers against farm labourers but with a few players from Stainton and the surrounding villages to make up the teams. A new Vicar had just come to the Village and was asked to play for the farmers. He walked out on the field to bat – beautiful white flannels, immaculate in all ways, he smiled round at his new flock and took his stand at the wicket. Tom, who was bowling, sent down a corker first ball and flattened the stumps. The vicar, looking crestfallen, returned to the pavilion. The captain, a local foreman, rushed over and said to Tom: "What do you think you're doing? You should have given him a chance. Don't you realise that's our new vicar?"

"Coorse (of course) I knoo it's new parson. I were at t' church on Sunday warn't I? I knoo he can't pree-ach but I didn't knoo he couldn't bloody bat an' all."

❧

CHAPTER 18

People and Characters

Yorkshire born and Yorkshire bred
In woods and streams to play
Oh! The joy of Village life
Were it still here today

At Elmhurst House lived the Houghton family. Mrs. Houghton was an invalid but Mr. Houghton was well known in the Village. The thing I remember about him – he loved to dance. He was at all the Village whist drives and dances. They were an old Braithwell family and Bob Houghton, who worked for my father all his life, is now ninety-three years old and still living with his daughter Rita Davis up Ashton Lane. Epe was my brother-in-law, Joe and Edward (Ted) – we always called him Sheff – were all his sons. They had eight children – the four girls were Edith, Julia, Kathleen and Maud. The building at the back of the house, which had been a stable, was known as the Ebeneezer Chapel and was used up to the chapel on Austwood Lane being built for services.

Flo Tomney lived in the house attached to Cremona called Pear Tree Cottage. She was a real character. Osbert, her husband, was a real Labour man and Flo was staunch Conservative. We never understood how they lived together so amiably as politics came often into the conversation. Everybody in the Village called her Auntie Flo. Flo always had a lodger and Miss Robinson, one of our teachers at school, lived with her in the 1930s. She was very pretty with red hair, freckles and very slim. We all loved her. She "courted" Jack Parkes for a long time and we used to tease her about when she was getting married. She used to blush terribly. Obviously something went wrong – they split up. Flo was jolly and people flocked to her house, young and old. She always had time for you and was much loved. The kettle was always on the hob. She loved going out, belonged to everything and every organisation and went on every trip that ever left the Village – and many others from other villages. Flo was very fat and often "not too well" but always managed to come round after a drop of brandy – wonderful cure. Every coffee morning, Mother's Union, etc. she was there. She was greatly missed when she passed away, leaving just one son Richard, the apple of her eye.

The school head was John Joseph Fox (known as "JJ"). He lived with his wife and two sons Kenneth and Gerald (always known as Bill) in a cottage No. 16 Maltby Lane. He and his wife were very keen gardeners. He was an excellent cricketer and the cricket and football teams at the school were top class. He brought them on a treat and gave lots of time after school coaching them. In those days we started at five and stayed at this school until we were fourteen unless you passed the 11+. He had three classrooms and an infant room and 140 pupils There was no hall or kitchen then. When a hall was needed, the big doors dividing the classrooms were pushed back. This is where we held school and Village concerts, dances, public meetings etc.. This is why we never bothered about a village hall. We had the school – our school, which sadly we have now lost, after having a school in the Village from the late 1600s. This, we all felt and still feel, was a real tragedy and nobody will convince us it was necessary. A village this size could support a school and particularly now when they've built thirty-seven houses on the same land and sixteen more off High Street – does it make sense?

There were three teachers and J.J.. One teacher taught infants – Miss Athron (5–6), Mrs. Cartwright taught juniors (7–9), Miss Robinson middles (9–11), Mr. Fox seniors. He did all the book-work, all the letter-writing, all the organising – everything that needed doing, he did. He could never get over the fact that so many people in later years were needed to run a school that only took pupils from five to eleven. When we had the school's Fiftieth Anniversary he came to the school celebrations and made a speech. Braithwell was very lucky to have him from the school opening in 1928 to 1958. When he retired, he built a bungalow in Cockhill Field Lane – Lea Haven. When he came down Maltby Lane in the morning, any pupils going to school took his hand and walked up with him. Sometimes he had six or seven infants on each side. What a pity we never took a picture. But he used the cane when necessary and kept everybody well in order. Swearing would have got six of the best. He would have been busy now-a-days. Good manners were essential and please and thank-you the order of the day. Sandwiches could be eaten at school. Pupils came from Foredoles, Birkwood Farm, Ravenfield, Ravenfield Common, Clifton and Micklebring and walked both ways whatever the weather – but local children went home to dinner.

My brother Derrick started school at the Old School House. The headmaster was Mr. Styrrup. He was a spare the rod and spoil the child man and Derrick often ran off home at playtime. If he got in before Dad saw him, Mum said he was ill but if Dad saw him coming up the drive, he literally chased him back – and Dad could run! After a week or two, Derrick got the message and stayed at school despite hating it. He left at fourteen with great relief but, of course, by then he had J.J. as head and enjoyed the sport. Dennis, my other brother, wasn't keen on school. I suppose it's living on a farm – there's so many other, more interesting things to do. He was a very good runner and enjoyed all the sport at school but was delighted when he could leave. He was one of the first pupils at the "new school" in 1928.

Mr Hill lived at No 8 Maltby Lane. He was a small, shrewd, hard-working man and eventually bought and owned quite a few houses and plots of land round about – quite an achievement in those days. He owned No. 8 (his own), 10 (next door attatched), 12, 14, 16 and 18 up Maltby Lane. Also the land where Dorian is built and from Martha Marshall he bought the field where Nettlefield House is built. When he died, Leonard Lawrence who lived at No.10 with his sister Clara Fenn bought the land and had pigs in the buildings by Harehound House and a pony and trap. Mum used to use it sometimes and take his sisters Clara and Ida Wells to Stainton in it to visit the Burdons who farmed Hall Farm there. They were always terribly nervous and when I went with them it always amused me. They'd be real back-seat drivers: "Be careful Poppy. Have you seen that dog, will it frighten the pony? "Mind that hole in the road." Oh dear, oh dear!

There were, as now, two pubs Red Lion and Butcher's Arms but then also an Ale House, Harehound House, which brewed and sold its own ale but didn't sell spirits. Also the Working Men's Club, which was then in the garden of Club Cottage, Holywell Lane. This was a wooden structure with corrugated roof, pulled down in 1947 when the new club was built.

Aimee Marshall lived at Harehound House. She had been the pianist in her husband William's travelling theatre and was a wonderful pianist and entertainer. She was very gifted and if we hummed a tune, she could play it. When we were young, we used to spend lots of time at her house and she used to train us to sing – drama, comedy – you name it, she could do it. Then we gave concerts in the church schoolroom, raising money for Charity. Eva Davison, Edith Allison, Joyce Harrison, Kathleen Davison, Carole Byron, Marion Wells, Margaret Stewart, Iris Davison and me were her Troupe and she did us proud and nothing was too much trouble for "her girls".

The sink was always full of pots and she always had to dust the piano keys with her apron before she sat down but she had a heart of gold and welcomed us all into her home. What's a bit of dust when you make so many young people happy and give your time and energy to that end? We sang all the old songs – "The Biggest Aspidistra in the World" and "Dandelion Daisy and Daffodil" were our songs – comic songs which she knew and loved. I was "Dandelion", Kay Davison "Daisy" and Joyce Harrison "Daffodil". We danced at the Garden Parties to make money for many charities. When war broke out we toured various halls in the district raising money for the war effort. She could produce the most fantastic costumes obviously from her travelling theatre days. She also played at cinemas for the silent films and very good she was too.

She kept us off the streets and gave her time – a valuable commodity. We loved her. She had four children: Flo – she was a beauty queen several times and we were fascinated when she appeared with different-coloured hair each week, John, the only son, was very quiet and a great friend of mine. I think I talked so much he couldn't get a word in anyway. A daughter Margaret (Peggy) and a daughter Ella – also a friend of mine. What fun we had. In later years she played for us at Christmas at the Red Lion when she could rattle off any carol you cared to hum and joined in with a very good voice. New Year's Eve she was always there for her girls to sing along with the locals at the Church School New Year's Party.

How I wish I had known about her days with the theatre when I was a child. What questions I would have asked. How sad I am that I never told her son, who I wrote to regularly in the army and his sister, how much I loved and admired their mother. She hated housework and cooking but gave her all to music and the young people of this Village. Oh that there were more of her calibre today. I wish she could know how much we appreciated her. The time and trouble she took with us. Sadly, that is life. If only and with hindsight we could tell people how we feel. They enriched our lives but at the time we didn't really appreciate it. What a pity we have nobody in the Village today with half her talents. I'm sorry she's not buried in the Village. I would like to have sometimes put flowers on her grave. Happily now I am in touch with her son-in-law Gordon Pell and two of her grandchildren, Howard and Christopher Pell.

❧

CHAPTER 19

Travelling Theatre Days

William Marshall, husband of Aimee, owned Harehound House, bottom of High Street. He inherited it from his aunt Martha, who ran an Ale House there in the early 1900s. He was born July 6th. 1885. His aunt Martha adopted Willie (as we called him) when he was six months old. His mother had five other children and her husband was a farm labourer and when Willie was born, his aunt said she'd take him to live with her at the "Plough Inn" at Micklebring where she was landlady, as his family were quite poor. He was well looked after – well fed with home-made butter and bacon and ham from their own pigs. He attended Braithwell School, where he was a friend of my uncle Frank's and my Dad. He came often to the farm to play with them – Hall Farm where my grandfather Robert Dunstan lived.

I always knew my father's mother was killed by a cricket ball at Braithwell when she was pregnant but I never knew when. Willie's grandson, Howard Pell, sent me the hand-written story of his grandfather's life, which he started on January 3rd. 1960 when he was seventy-five. He told of coming to a "do" in Braithwell Village. It was his birthday – he was eight. It was 6th. July 1893, the Duke of York's (later George V) wedding. A cricket match, tea and games were on in the Village, as a celebration, behind Orchard House Farm. My grandmother was sitting in a chair – it was half-time, tea time. Some drunks came from the Butcher's Arms and were knocking the ball about during the interval. One knocked the ball hard and hit my grandmother in the stomach. She died later that day – now I know the date. What a coincidence.

Willie tells of coming to Hall Farm to play and getting into trouble at home for not doing his daily jobs – carting water from the Village Pump at Micklebring to the poultry and pigs, fetching in the cow. He only found out he was adopted when his mother, father and family visited Aunt Martha when he was eight years old. They had five boys and a girl then besides Willie and he found out from the children. He never settled after that. He says he had the best of everything – wonderful food, good clothes but he wanted to return to his mother and family and several times tried to run away. Eventually when he was ten Aunt Martha realised he wasn't going to settle and, although she loved him dearly, she took him home to his family who now lived outside Worksop. How sad she must have been. He says his mother was pleased to have him home. They lived at Springfield Cottage near the canal. Fishermen came from Sheffield to fish there and his mother mashed tea for them and sold them home-made ginger beer to make a few shillings – they were still very poor.

He became interested in the travelling theatres which came often to Worksop but it was 3d to go in and he hadn't got 3d but he started to caddy at Lindrick Golf Club. He got 9d, gave

6d to his mother and kept the silver 3d bit to go to the theatre – he put it in his shoe. When he got to the theatre, he took off his shoe but he had a hole in it and had lost the threepenny bit. He sat dolefully outside. When the owner came out smoking his cigar, he saw the miserable little boy and asked what was the matter. On hearing the story, he said: "Come on in lad." and that was the beginning of a dream. To one day own a theatre.

From then on when he left school at thirteen he worked with this end in mind. He went down the pit. He soon realised he was never going to get his theatre that way – 1/6d a night for nine-and-a-half hours work. He continued at the pit but also helped out at any theatre that came to the district, sometimes getting paid. He did several months with a travelling theatre but fell out with the boss. He then moved to Silverwood pit but got sick of pit work and saw an advert in Taylor's (printers) shop in Rotherham which read: "Wanted. Harvesters for Canada. Fare from Liverpool to Winnipeg £6". He had a second-hand bike and a silver watch and chain. He was twenty-one. He sold the bike and the watch and chain and got £6. He was a keen gambler and went to a gambling school he knew in a field in Worksop and won a bit more to help him on his way. When the gang started to use a two-headed coin, he got out quick. As he left, he saw the police arriving to break up the school. Gambling of course was illegal.

He returned to Rotherham, bought his ticket, got a train ticket and took the train to Liverpool. He sailed on 10th. August, 1906. He did many jobs in Canada – working on the railways, snow-shifting, farming etc.. All hard work – sometimes very poor pay and poor conditions. He once even touted for customers for a Chinese gambling den in Vancouver. He also worked in the diamond mines and whilst there built himself a timber house and let off some of the rooms to other workers to make more money to make his dream come true.

Then he left there and went back to coal mining. He didn't say why – probably better money. He became the union man. He almost decided to stay in Canada but then home called and the theatre so he sold his house and returned. He sailed on the Lusitania and had £200 saved. He arrived home on May 24th.. It must have been 1910 as he says it was on the day of the funeral of King Edward VII. He was nearly 25. He went to see his mother at Worksop and then to his aunt's. She had sold the Plough at Micklebring and come to live at Harehound House,

Braithwell and ran an Ale House. She had a room ready for him. She must have loved him dearly.

He bought the magazine "The Stage" and saw a theatre for sale at Wells-on-Sea, Norfolk. He bought a second-hand bike and biked to Newark, where he stopped the night. He went on the next day to Wells and bought the theatre. He took on the actors and pianist as the company had gone broke. It was a wooden sectional building with a tent-like roof. The cast not only performed, they also had to erect and dismantle the theatre. They usually stayed a week at each town or village but always had to get a licence from the local magistrate before they could perform there. He lost his pianist and engaged a new one. The new pianist, Aimee, later became his wife.

He greatly treasured a letter from Ellen Terry when she was staying at Mawbyns, Little Easton, Dunmow, with Mr. and Mrs. H. G. Wells. She booked two seats in the front row for herself and Mrs. Wells and four seats in the eighth row for the servants for 17th. October, 1913 and wished him luck.

They always had to do East Lynne – it was the great favourite. When they hanged Crippen on the Monday, on the following Monday they were playing it at his theatre. Each of the actors wrote their own part from the report of the trial published in the "News of the World". How's that for improvisation?

He tells of people who were very much against the theatre and decried it. One mission society set up a tent in the same field as the theatre and tried to persuade the boys to go there instead. One father threatened his son if he went to the theatre. When he was disobeyed and he caught his son coming from the theatre and not the mission tent he chastised him and said: "Why did you disobey me?" The boy replied:

"But there's no difference, dad. In the mission tent they shout: "Stand up stand up for Jesus" and in here they shout: "For Christ's sake sit down.".".

John his only son and Flo' his eldest daughter were born whilst they were on the road with the theatre. William bought a pullman car and they all lived in that and moved it on the railway with the theatre when they moved to each new town. In 1914, William volunteered for the army and left his wife Aimee in charge of the theatre. The war hit the theatre hard and when he came home he tried to keep it going but things were difficult. He then had to let it go. Aimee had come to Braithwell in 1917

85

T.

The Manager
at The Barn Theatre =

MAWBYNS,
LITTLE EASTON,
DUNMOW.

Will you kindly reserve for
this address 2 front
seats for this evening, &
4 other seats in about the
8th row near
the middle = I enclose
payment & hope. you
will have a good house
With all good wishes
Ellen Terry

Friday
17. Oct -

with the three children and was living with Aunt Martha at Harehound House. However, he was philosophical and came back with to his wife and family at Braithwell. But he could look back on a life and achievement that, to most people, would have remained only a dream.

He worked at the Maltby colliery for a while and then bought another theatre but by 1929, after nineteen years on and off with the theatre, he gave it up. He became a bookie's runner with a bookmaker, a salesman selling hoovers, cutlery, etc. but never got the theatre out of his blood.

They used to talk about Willie in the Village – they always thought he was a romancer as he often talked about his travels. How little they knew! I remember he was in the Red Lion with the locals one Sunday lunchtime when Aimee came to the door. "William," she said, "we're ready for you to carve." He picked up his glass, emptied it, put it firmly down on the bar, turned to them all and said:

"How do you carve a bloody lettuce?" Then walked out. Never much of a cook was our Aimee but we all loved her.

❧

CHAPTER 20

All Things Bright and Beautiful
All Creatures Great and Small

One of the things that older people miss today are the wild flowers of yesteryear. The field where I now live was full of moonpennies. Holly Croft Lane (Hoyle Croft Lane) was blue with violets under the hedge – I never understood why they grew better on the right side than on the left of this lane. At six years old, one doesn't know about the north or south side. These were always picked by mothers who had children in the churchyard and liked to put these first flowers on their graves. Cowslips abounded – we picked them for winemaking. Celandines and buttercups, nettles for nettle beer, hops from the hedge we ate as a vegetable. The new young shoots of hawthorn – why did we call this "bread and cheese"? Marsh Marigolds from the swamps by the stream in Birchwood Close, watercress from the stream down Holywell Lane where the Seven Springs rise (the rise of the river Torne). Luckily, we still have this luxury and many times in Spring my family and I have watercress for tea with egg – a lovely combination. Watercress soup for dinner is delicious and also simple to make.

How sad that so many of our hawthorn hedges are now disappearing. They have been part of the English countryside for generations. During the land enclosure in the 18th. and 19th. centuries many hedges were planted and became a wonderful habitat for wildlife. Trees too were put in – the lovely oaks, beech, ash and elm were interplanted in the hedges and gave shade to horses and cattle and sheep in the heat of the summer sun. Does my memory play tricks or was it always so much sunnier then? Since writing this, farmers and landowners are being encouraged to put hedges back, thank goodness. The summers are becoming summers again.

The woods at Ruddle Mill were full of bluebells, primroses and daffodils and we wandered wherever we pleased. Nobody said us nay. In fact if any farmer had turned us off his land we should have been amazed. No one to harm us as we wandered away from home either on foot, or pony and trap, or horseback, taking picnics of cold tea (no flasks) or home-made ginger beer and parcels of sandwiches. We visited Roche Abbey, Lilly Hall, Stainton, Wilsic – all by crossing the fields and stopping to chat to the farmers and farm men alike.

Saturday mornings there were always queues forming at the Village Pump – with water barrels. Most of the local farmers filled their horse-drawn water-carrying carts and butts there. They then gave the local kids a 1d. to hold the horses whilst the men popped into the pub for a drink, or more than one – drunk in charge of a water-waggon. We used to sit on the orchard wall and watch the procedure – much jostling for position and cheerful banter between them all.

There was a cottage, now demolished, by the dam across the meadows down Holywell Lane, later called Dam Cottage – originally called "Wild Duck Cottage". They had three sons and every time they came to the Village, they brought two two-gallon buckets across the fields on a yoke. These they dropped off at the Village Pump. When one of the lads returned home from the pub or work, he filled these buckets at the pump, put on the yoke and returned home with full buckets. Their mother then was never short of drinking water. Her other water came from the dam.

Mr Pickin of Cedar Farm always loaned a horse to take a water barrel to Moat Hall and Moat Cottage and Wild Duck Cottage by the dam. He of course owned these cottages. Mr Bradbury from Church Lane filled a water container for his houses up Church Lane and left it in the passage for the use of all his tenants. Some farms with wells also filled water carts. After all, the water had to be pulled up by bucket at home. This was tedious, time-consuming and hard work. They always came from Foredoles as their well often ran dry due to the fact they were on top of the hill. We were lucky. Our pump was in the Dairy. The well was covered by stone slabs and was under the floor. It was piped underground to the Fold Yard and the horse- and cow-troughs were pumped full each morning by the cow man – Bob Houghton or Russ Brewster.

In winter we still hear the cry of the foxes. This of course is their mating season. Fox hunting is a matter of great concern for some people. We always had the Grove & Rufford hounds come to the Village before the motorways stopped this. A very sad day. They met at the Plough in Micklebring and Mr. Dick Robinson's at Croft End and the hunting cup was passed round. If mounted, you all got a drink. My brother and I always followed on horseback as they hunted our land. Of course in those days there were no anti-hunt people. If there were, they certainly didn't live here. All the Village loved it. When I had 100 pullets on the point of lay and they were killed one night by a fox, I was happy to hunt him! And so would they be if they'd seen my pullets laid out in the croft and they'd belonged to them. Of course now it's the unspeakable in pursuit of the uneatable. I have never seen a more wonderful sight than hounds in full cry across the fields with huntsmen and horses in pursuit. Foxes seem to be getting more plentiful. In the winter of 1992, two were chasing round our orchard in the snow and mated there. Still a beautiful sight to me when I saw the vixen and her cubs up Hoyle Croft Lane afterwards – I have a great admiration for them.

Hares too were hunted by the beagles and met often in the Village. Beagles of course were followed on foot and good exercise it was too. You just got your breath back when you were off again. The two Mrs. Robinsons (Mrs. Dick and Mrs. Ron) still followed in their late sixties. I often had a struggle to keep up with them and I was in my teens! Mr. Ron. Robinson was Master of the Clayworth Beagles and Brian, his son, was

Whipper-in. We had some wonderful days following them. The Beagles met at the Cottage (Mr. and Mrs. Ron. Robinson's) and later at Elmfield Farm (Mr. and Mrs. Brian Robinson's). The hare is a wonderful animal and often in March from my window I see them, six or seven at a time in the field next door. "Mad as a March Hare" is a very apt expression. They chase round and round and seem to stand up and box.

The cry of the owl in the night is quite eerie. My mother told us that when she first came to Hall Farm and heard the screech of the barn owl, she woke Dad up. She thought the old House was haunted – she was terrified, he was very amused. Winter is hard for owls. Their prey (rats, mice, voles etc.) stay very close to ground in the cold spells. Unlike most birds, owls swallow their prey whole and then disgorge the parts not digested in pellets. Neat little parcels which on examination by experts can reveal what the owl had for dinner. How sad it is that barn owls have decreased so dramatically, due partly to the lack of barns. Owls always nested and lived in our lovely old Tithe Barn – its window was always left open for the owls to live and nest there. The screech of the barn owl was something vividly remembered from my childhood. We always thought: "There goes another mouse." as this was their main diet. Little owls and tawny owls were also very plentiful. When I first came to live at Steetley House we saw these often but we rarely see one now. Only the little owl feeds and flies in the daytime.

Whippet racing was held in the Village field every Sunday morning for many years. Farm lads went out first thing Sunday morning to catch rabbits – they got 6d for each live one. These were released in the field to excite the dogs and make them keen. The whippets were held back by the owners. A rabbit skin was attatched to a tow-line fixed to the rim of the rear wheel of an upturned bicycle some distance away. A man would wind the skin along by furiously turning the pedal! As soon as the rabbit skin got 20 yards in front, the whistle blew and these men literally threw the whippets as far as they could to get a good start. Sometimes they landed on their feet, sometimes not but always got into the race. The shouting could be heard for miles as owners and spectators urged them on. There was betting of course. The field was the one that now runs down to Little London at Maltby – The Foxholes. Then, of course, there were no houses there. This sport was much frowned on by the local vicar but he never managed to stop it.

There used to be horse-racing at Micklebring. It is even mentioned in the school report in the 1800s at Braithwell Church School that "Children were kept off to go racing." We also used to have horse racing in the Village with bookies and tic-tac men. A great night of fun it was. Donkey races too. Up Ashton Lane in Marsh Close.

Down Fishpond Lane at the bottom of Yardley's Braithwell Nursery is a small stream. When I was a child this stream was dammed and used as a sheep wash – all local farmers with sheep used it. The sheep were driven from the Village by the men and a sheep-dog and washed in this stream. They were penned into the corner of the field and one by one driven into the water held down under it and driven out the other side. They were then all driven back to the farm. This spot is still known as the Sheep Wash. This rhyme was written by Tusser in his "June Husbandry"

> *Wash sheep for the better*
> *Where water doth run*
> *And let him go cleanly*
> *And dry in the sun*

Sheep were then dipped at the farm.

There was a lot of cruelty in those days to farm animals. Farmers with little money and few horses would work them almost to death and use a stick if they couldn't get them going on a hill pulling a fully-loaded cart. How sad to see some poor old horse straining away to move a load when really another horse should have been hitched on but they didn't have another horse. It was very much frowned on but very few people intervened. Pigs and cows were often hit with a stick to make them go in the right direction. But most farmers respected their animals and treated them very well – well fed, well groomed and not overworked.

We had a lovely sheep dog called Rex – he came from Mr. Bagshaw of Blyth owner of "Owd Bob". Bob was the dog used in the film called "Owd Bob". We saw it many times. John Loader, Will Fyffe and Margaret Lockwood were the stars. Rex was a direct descendent and lived with us for many years until he was killed in a road accident. We always thought Rex was fit to be in the movies. He was a very handsome dog and so intelligent he hardly needed any training.

CHAPTER 21

Gentlemen of The Road and Don't forget The Ladies!

These tramps usually stayed put in the winter and travelled in Summer – they knew which side their bread was buttered, as the saying goes. Always there were tramps. Calling for a "bit o' sumat, Missis" or: "Have you got a crust, Gaffer?" One, a lady tramp – Lizzie Dripping was always on the scrounge. One morning our cowman, Russ Brewster, getting straw to bed down his cows at dawn – probably only half awake – stabbed the fork in the straw and caught Lizzie. She let out a yell fit to wake the dead. He took fright and ran – straight down the drive and home, Lizzie after him. She wanted to escape my father's wrath – he had warned her about sleeping in the barn and smoking her clay pipe there. The final straw came when he went down the cellar one morning to skim the cream from the milk for the morning cup of tea. Coming back into the kitchen – tea mashed ready for drinking – he heard a commotion outside. He dashed out. The bull was loose, pawing straw up in great flurries in the open yard. It took Dad ages to get him back into his pen. Thankfully, in he went for his tea keeping warm on the hob. There was Lizzie, just sneaking out. She'd drunk all his tea and all his cream – he was furious. He chased her off and she didn't appear again for weeks.

Bill Coggin – was big, had a big moustache and helped with thrashing; he often slept in our chop chamber. He always spent the summer on the road. Paddy lived in Foredoles buildings but wandered into Braithwell. Kingy mostly spent his time at Micklebring; wintered in Spencer's Black Shed. Cambridge known by this name because of his accent. He always wore a bowler hat and lived in a wooden hut by Holywell Springs in the gardens where Lisa Ward & Fred Ward lived in a caravan – this was very cosy and it had a pot-bellied stove. Then they were re-housed in 1937 in the council houses up Ashton Lane; I don't know where he ended up.

Sweedie had a dog called Nell – always at his side. He collected and sold watercress from the spring and always had a bag on his back. This is how he got his name:- Herbert (Spoff) Allison was leaning over his gate one day at Maltkiln Farm when Sweedie came past. "Do you want to earn a Bob or two?" asked Spoff.

"Ai, Gaffer," answered the tramp, "what is it?"

"Go dahn to my field dahn Chapel Lane (Hosswood Lane we called it) and strike them sweedes. I'll get ye a hoe and pay ye when ye've finished 'em." And they settled a price. Off went the tramp. He was back that night for his money. "Nay," says Spoff, "I said I'd pay when ye'd finished."

"But I have finished, Gaffer." "Finished" said Spoff, "there's over a week's work there – how can you be finished?" He'd been to the wrong field and struck all Albert Fidler's cauliflowers – the air was blue and after that he was always called "Sweedie" He lived in Hellaby brickyard in winter and Micklebring in summer where he made a tent of old bags in the bottom on Greave Syke Lane.

Georgie Boy Skinner, another tramp, would call at Moat Hall Cottage where Mr. Frank Crawshaw lived – foreman to Mr. Billy Pickin of Cedar Farm. It would be early November – just when potato-picking had finished and casual labour on farms, which the tramps always helped with, would be over. The Crawshaws were very Christian chapel people and Mrs. Crawshaw, a kind and caring soul, used to save all her husband's old clothes, long thick pants, vests, shirts, sweaters overcoat – in fact a "new" wardrobe, for Georgie Boy. He would fill the copper with cold water from the well, light it and then put it in the wash tub. He'd stand in that in the outhouse and scrub himself down with a scrubbing brush and wash his hair, beard etc.. He'd then don his "new" clothes and burn his old ones in the yard. Mrs. Crawshaw would then give him a hot dinner and a bag of sandwiches and away he'd go to find winter shelter at one of the farms – all set up for the cold weather – with a: "God bless you missis.". "Thank you kindly missis – you'll be rewarded in heaven.".

The people not only worked together on the land but spent all their leisure time together. There were some real characters and a wonderful community spirit, still noticeable in this Village today, where some of the same farmers and farm labourers' families still live and work.

The people with their own bit of land would usually work elsewhere in the day and tend their small acres at night, or at weekends. Their wives would help out with milking or making butter and feeding the stock. The skimmed milk was given to the pigs. Nothing was wasted, all the scraps from the table and the garden going to the pigs. These smallholdings, or homesteads, were handed down from father to son – some owned, some rented – this made them very independent, insular, unlike estates or villages like Stone, Firbeck, Hooton Pagnell, etc., where people were dependent on the Lord of the Manor. This independence can still be seen in the Village today. People from outside used to say, and still do, "You're a bloody independent lot!"

Most cottages in the Village had a pig sty at the bottom of the garden. All the swill was fed to them and they were killed for Christmas. Most people kept their own hens. Some kept ducks and geese but these were dirtier and messed up the yard. Cream was bought straight from the farm and had been hand-skimmed off huge pansions of milk in the cellar – some people made their own butter. All farmers did.

But the agricultural village was a very self-contained community. A village like ours was known as an "open village". Most men were able to hire themselves out and not generally tied to one master. The farm worker who did work for one master often lived in at the farm. He either ate with the family, or in the scullery if there was more than one hired man; and there were always two sets of stairs – back stairs for farm men and front stairs for family. Sometimes these men had a room over the stables.

Many families belonged to clothing clubs 1/- a week kept them in clothes. It was the only way they could afford them and the wife bought household goods this way too. The man came round each week to collect the shilling and delivered the goods at the same time.

Pots were brought round the Village by hawkers. There were small potteries in all areas where there was coal and clay and the hawker fetched panshions (for bread-making), bowls, cups, saucers and teapots and big pint mugs on his horse and cart and sold them round the Village.

The furniture in the houses of the farm labourers was usually very poor – stools, table, Windsor chairs (now making a fortune!) or wooden chairs with horsehair or leather seats. There were rag rugs on the floor and sacks outside and just inside the back door to wipe your feet on.

Many cottages had only two bedrooms. Often father, mother and several children lived there. If you lived in a row of houses, you shared wash-houses and outdoor closets. Otherwise you washed in your own kitchen – no water on tap at all. You fetched it from the Village well or pump if you weren't lucky enough to have a well or pump in your own backyard. I have discovered many wells, some with pumps, in the Village – as the name implies, Braithwell is a Village of Wells. (see list of Wells)

The one place for gossip in a village is the local pub. Any news always seems to come from there and many a scandal originates there. All the farm men with a 1/- in their pocket would spend the evening there but usually Friday and Saturday were their nights there as, on 30/- a week, they hadn't much to spare for entertainment. Many sat all night with just a pint but enjoyed the chatter and companionship.

Many of the old Villagers Flo Tomney, Nance Markham, Annie Dickinson could always tell you when some old dear passed away: "Before she were wed she were so and so." They could also have told of a few skeletons in most of the people's cupboards but, as I've said before, we all have them and so keep our neighbours' secrets to ourselves. Of course between themselves they aired these but never to outsiders.

Before Dad bought our farm in 1938 the front of the house was rented off. Mr. & Mrs. George Wells and Marion (now Byron) lived there. Marion has been my life-long friend and still talks about Mum tapping on the dividing wall and passing a plate of chips or a dish of trifle through the front window to her. We had the big front room on the north side. It was our dining room but was always called the Far Room.

The Wells family had two great misfortunes. Georgie, as we always knew him farmed Ashton Farm. When Marion was born in 1922 they also had a daughter Joan – a beautiful girl who was five and a small son Maurice who was two. Mr Wells took Maurice with him to the field with the horse and cart to help out his wife with the new baby. Sadly, Maurice fell out of the cart onto his head and died. When Joan was eleven she died of meningitis. My mother always talked of it with great sorrow and I'm sure that was one reason she liked to give Marion a treat. She was always very fond of her. Marion (Bub I always called her) and I lived so near to each other it was only natural of course that we spent so much time together and were such friends and, although I was younger that her, I used to bully her into doing things. Jumping off stacks, riding horses bareback, climbing trees, swinging from ropes in the barn: I did the lot and so did she – although she was older than me, she was a timid and quiet child unlike me. Dennis used to dare me to do things – and I was scared but did it. It's only in later years I realised that Bub was much braver than me – although I egged her on she would have done it anyway – probably before me. I was just mouthy and scared.

There was very little time for jollification in a rural village but everybody took time off for farm sales and a great time was had by all. Great excitement in the Village when a farm sale was advertised. Farmers, their wives, sons, daughters, old and young flocked there on the day. Farm machinery, tools, stock all there; furniture, dairy tools, butter churns, 10-gall. milk churns etc. all on display. On a wet day this was a sad sight as somebody's lovely old kitchen table and benches, which had seated 12 for generations and was now too big to go into the new house, was sold under the hammer. Dressers, chests all surplus to requirements. A sad day but if the sun shone and everything made a good price the farmer and his wife went away smiling into their new cottage or smallholding, where they'd keep a few hens and relax for the first time in their lives. The raucous chant from the auctioneer shouting the odds: "Two I'm bid, two I'm bid – who'll make it three?" was understood only by those in the know and absolute gibberish to the uninitiated. Some people never understood at all. I remember one stranger, a woman, saying to me at a sale:

"Did that thing make £3?" – a form I was bidding for at a local sale.

"No," I said "it was 3/-." and proudly carried it home. It was the first farm sale I've ever made a bid at – I was 17 at the time and still have it today, although my brother Derrick once bought a calf by mistake by touching his cap. Luckily Dad was with him to settle the debt. He never did it again.

We used to have magic lantern shows in the old church school in the evenings. Mr. Ted Littlewood, a local Parish Councillor, ran them and I think it was a penny for children, 2d for adults. Great excitement when these were shown about once a month.

As we grew older, we went to Maltby pictures to see Rin-Tin-Tin (an alsatian dog rescuing people) and another picture we saw was "Lassie" (a sheep dog). These were adventure stories shown week by week and stopping at a really exciting time so we all had to go next week. I think it cost 3d. We always walked there and back. I remember the noise in the cinema was horrendous. We all screamed out when Rin Tin Tin was in danger and when the "enemy" was trying to catch Lassie. Mr. Knowles, the cinema manager, used to walk round with a long stick with a pig's bladder tied to the end. If children messed about or talked too loud, he would rattle them with the bladder. We couldn't wait for the next instalment.

PART 3
THE VILLAGESCAPE

CHAPTER 22

Ancient Monuments and Old Buildings

Location on the map is given in brackets.

I couldn't write about my Village, its tales and people, without also telling of the ancient monuments and houses I knew – they were just as much a part of my childhood.

The Village Cross (No. 1)
At the bottom of the Village Street, in the centre of the cross-roads, is the 12th. century Magnesian Limestone Cross. The shaft rises from an octagonal base. Although restored and missing some of its original components, the Braithwell Cross is a good example of an inscribed Standing Cross which, being in its original location, also preserves the mediaeval land surface on which it was set up. Though suffering from the effects of weathering, its inscription is still reasonably preserved and is a rare and interesting example of a public dedication. The square-section magnesian limestone column would originally have supported a further shaft and cross head and the scale suggests that the missing cross shaft was quite slender and may therefore have been made from wood. Whilst the core and foundation stones of the original bottom step still survive, the treads were replaced with Roche Abbey stone in the late 19th century – the later step has a chamfered top edge inscribed: "Erected about 1191. Restored 1887, the jubilee year of Queen Victoria." when coins were found under the foundations.

The Inscription, in old Norman French, around the

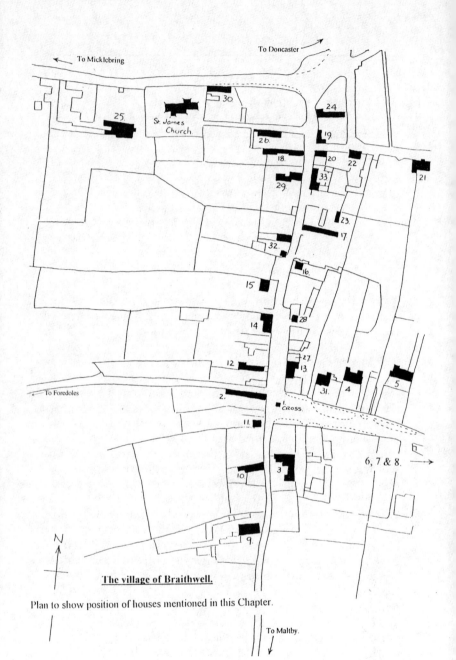

To Micklebring

To Doncaster

To Foredoles

St. James Church

CROSS

The village of Braithwell.

Plan to show position of houses mentioned in this Chapter.

N

To Maltby.

98

chamfered top edge of the socle reads:

"JESY LE FIZ : MAIRIE : PANSE TOOLIERI :
MORROI : QEVVS : PRIE"

and has been translated as:

"Jesus, the son of Mary, remember our King
and deliver him I pray."

The Cross was erected in 1191 (north face, "MCXCI"), according to one legend to commemorate the freeing from bondage of King Richard I. It was set up by a prince who resided in Braithwell when Richard I was a prisoner in Germany. It was said the villagers contributed liberally to the King's Ransom and their loyalty was rewarded with a Charter to hold a Fair on the first Thursday in May annually. This theory is doubted on a number of grounds. Firstly, the Villagers at that time were paying many taxes and most were living in poverty. Secondly, if the cash had to be raised, it would have been in the form of a compulsory tax, not a voluntary donation. Thirdly, it is unlikely that such a collection could have been organised with the castle of Prince John only 5 miles away at Tickhill. John was the youngest son of Henry II but had no love for his brother King Richard, whom he succeded to the Throne.

Whilst the cross was being renovated in 1798 the Surveyor of the Highways made the folllowing note: "To fetching stone for the Cross 4/-." and an entry reading: "For ale for Cross setting up 3/-." A stone mason, I. Coulton, trying to make the lettering more legible, re-cut the stone and lost the original meaning but a copy of it, as it formerly was, may be seen in Gough's edition of "Camden". In Norman French it reads:

Jesu le fiz marie
Pense toi
Le frere no roi
Je vus prie

("Jesus the son of Mary, think upon the brother of our King we beseech you."). It is thought that this reference to the "brother of the King" appertains to Haneline Plantagenet, Earl Warrene, who was a "natural son" of King Henry I and half-brother of Henry II (1154–1189). He was resident at Conisborough Castle.

It has also been said that it is religious in nature and nothing to do with the myths of Richard I's Ransom. Who can tell, such a lot of different things have been written. Irrespective of which story proves to be the correct one, both versions place the date of its construction to the last decade of the twelfth century. It should be noted that a similar Cross was erected in Doncaster by Oti de Tilli, Steward of Conisborough Castle at about the same time.

"7th Day of Dec the year 1652 (Parliamentary Survey)
That there hath bine a markett once in a week kept within the Mannor of ye Brathwell and also a fayre once in the year which hath bine of a long tyme discontiued soo that none can remember but that by tradition they have heard their ancestors say so however the tennants produced certain papers whereby we in it find that in a charter in the 12th. year of the Reiyne of Edward I that he did grant to one Elias de Hindwell a faire and a markett to be kept within the Mannor of Brathwell. The markett to be once every week on Tuesday and the Ffayre to be kept once in a year viz on the vigil of St. Margarett on St Margretts day for six days after."

The earliest mention of this Monument in the Braithwell Parish Records is to be found in the Constable's Accounts for 1782. The Minute simply states:
"Braithwell Old Cross setting up . . . . . . 9s 6d."

In 1953 when the Cross was again renovated and cleaned (Coronation Year), the Parish Council in its wisdom added a new plaque to the structure. My cousin Allen Smith noticed on viewing the new inscription that it referred to Richard III and not Richard I – only a matter of some 280 years difference! He went into the Red Lion across the road and pointed out the error to a member of the Council. Great consternation. A special Meeting was called in a great panic and the stonemasons were hurriedly called back. Carefully they removed two of the "I"s but a discerning visitor can still see the marks today. It would seem that mistakes about the origins of the Cross were not just the prerogative of the Villagers of the latter part of the eighteenth century!! The real story – we'll never know. All we can do is put forward these theories of the historians and speculate. Now take *your* choice. The myth of Richard is still the most exciting to me.

Milestone
Situated at the corner of Ashton House – bottom of Ashton Lane – is probably 18th century and magnesian limestone. A squat square stone pillar with re-cut inscription on side reading

"To Rotherham 8 miles". This stone, well-used as a seat by locals, is known as the "virgin stone". Don't ask me why. I don't think many virgins ever sat here.

Moat Hall (No. 7) Holywell Lane

A ruined mediaeval structure with coursed rubble walls up to waist height with an interesting chamfered ashlar pointed arch to doorway

The Village of Braithwell was granted, with the Manor of Conisborough, to Earl Warren at the Conquest. The Earl granted the church and certain lands to the Priory of Lewes. The monks of Roche Abbey, a Cistercian Monastery three miles south-east of Braithwell, held certain lands here at the time of the Dissolution. In the early 13th. century, the monks were granted land by Thomas, son of Atrop de Braithwell. The monks then had pasture for 120 sheep in Braithwell. Around 1560 was the Dissolution of the Monasteries by Henry VIII. Until then we were a Catholic country. Moat Hall would then no longer be used as a home for elderly monks as it was thought but changed to some other use.

The old Moat Hall has many vicissitudes. Dr. Holt Yates suggests that it was once a chapel, or a hospital for Roche Abbey. The western side (where the fireplace is) would be the dwelling place and the eastern side would have had the altar at that end. Another suggestion was that the monks lived here and gave sustenance to travellers on pilgrimage. Moat Hall's history is very obscure and sketchy. It was surrounded by a moat, now almost completely filled in. Some partly-demolished stone walls still remain, 1' 10" thick. It was altered extensively in the 16th. century, when window cills and mullions were inserted in the south side when the house was turned into a private residence. "Access by drawbridge from the lane where beautiful willows bend gracefully over the water".

After the Dissolution, the house of the Abbot (Moat Hall), with the Belltring Lands (now known as Holywell Close) were let to William Wilson at £1. 6s. 2d per annum. This land adjoins the Holy Well where a chalybeat spring still bubbles at the side of the road. The ruins of Moat Hall, once a rectangular building 69' 9" long by 19' 7" wide has exposed stone slabs showing an old fireplace at the western end of the room. One 12th. century arch only is still in existence. The main entrance was in the centre of the south wall. Dates coincide with Roche

101

Abbey as the same mason's mark appears on the stone.

David Hey's account in "South Yorkshire since A.D. 1000" tells us that John Vyncent "leased the capital messuage called "Le Priorie" in 1427 and goes on to say that he was allowed to build on to the Hall a room to the west with dimensions 32' x 18' – the exact size of the large room at Moat Hall! Could Vyncent's "Over Hall" in reality be Moat Hall? Obviously a person of his prominence and importance would live in an imposing building. With Moat Hall already belonging to the Priory of Lewes, there is good reason for speculation. Then he must have moved to the Manor as we know he went to war from there and was killed in 1460 in the War of the Roses.

When John Vyncent came to live at Braithwell he lived first at what they called "Over Hall" – did he build a room to the west measuring 32' x 18', as David Hey says, or did he build it 'over-all'? The Moat Hall was reputed to be one story originally. Did Overhall mean 'over the lot'? The whole building to the east measures 32' x 18' – who can tell? Quite fascinating and something I am afraid we shall only be able to speculate on. All purely conjecture but how wonderful to have this history in our Village.

Extracts from Doncaster Gazette Article dated September 22 1932

WHERE ATHELSTANE AWOKE IN HIS COFFIN?
A BRAITHWELL LINK WITH IVANHOE?
The Mystery of the Ancient Moat Hall.
WHEN 'HORN MONEY' WAS PAID TO
CONISBROUGH CASTLE

The old Moat Hall at Braithwell, which is chosen as this week's "Ancient Monument" in a series that has aroused a good deal of interest among our readers, has long been a subject of discussion and the source of bewilderment in the ranks of antiquaries. It may be remembered that some months ago a curious cast-iron image was found by the tenant, Mr Cutts, beneath the soil in the garden which adjoins what remains of the old house, and some notes on the place appeared in the "Gazette" at that time. The house stands well back in a field adjoining the road from Braithwell Cross to Lambcote Grange and Maltby, and is opposite the Rectory, which at Braithwell is some distance from the Parish Church.

Writing in the "Doncaster Gazette" over eighty years ago, Mr Charles William Hatfield, whose account of a visit to Braithwell was republished in his "Village Sketches" described the Moat Hall as "a pile of buildings which have been of more note and character than they now possess.". "It is easy," he wrote, "to trace the moat which has encompassed them. On three sides, it is in a perfect condition, and the willow here and there bends gracefully over the water. The access has been by a draw-bridge from the road (Vicar Lane). The venerable looking premises are full of interest though all authentic records connected therewith are lost in oblivion.". Hatfield went on to affirm that although in his time the house had been divided into three tenements, it had been originally one building. One of the tenements was in a capital state of preservation and exhibited "three as perfect Gothic arches as could be wished." The ponderous doorway, with its beautiful arch, opening into the courtyard, was still (in 1849-50) in its primitive condition. On ascending the staircase, with an old oaken balustrade, he was ushered into lofty and commodious room. (Was this Over Hall?). "By some" Hatfield added, "it is presumed that this pile of buildings was formerly a religious house, and was the place of resort for wayfarers on their pilgrimage to the cross" (the old wayside cross at Braithwell). "It is now the property of William Toone, Esq, of Thornhill, near Wakefield, and on applying to that gentleman for information on the subject, he states that he is not in possession of any facts that can dissipate the mist in which it is enveloped."

Since Hatfield's time the Moat Hall property has changed hands and all but one of the 'tenements' to which he refers has been pulled down, leaving a large space without any outer wall on the upper floor of two or three of the tenements into which the building had been divided. Beneath this now unmasked chamber are the three Gothic arches, now built up, but clearly visible from the outside."

There are curious stories told of the Moat Hall and its history. One is that many years ago, the diggers broke through into a long-forgotten cellar, stored full with wine. All Braithwell, it is said, helped in the disposal of the treasure trove! (Pity I wasn't there).

Regarding the suggestion, mentioned by Hatfield and supported by the survival of Gothic pointed arches in thick stone walls, that the Braithwell Moat Hall had an ecclesiastical origin, there is still a belief current in the Village that it was formerly attached in some way to Roche Abbey. That the Abbots of Roche Abbey had property at Braithwell from the thirteenth century to the dissolution of their house is clear from the records of the Abbey.

A very interesting suggestion concerning the Braithwell Moat Hall is made in the course of an article on the 'Ivanhoe' country in South Yorkshire, written many years ago by Dr Holt Yates, of Wickersley, who devoted a good deal of ingenuity as well as scholarly research to identifying the places mentioned by Sir Walter Scott in his famous novel. He accompanied the article with a sketch map, a copy of which was printed in the history of Conisborough Castle edited by the late Mr Henry Ecroyd Smith and published in 1887. Thus Dr. Holt Yates identified Torquilstone Castle with Thorpe Salvin, placed the home of Cedric the Saxon at Whiston, near Rotherham, and so on. Here is what he says about Braithwell :-

"Perhaps the old church or chapel at Braithwell was St. Edmund's, where Athelstane was detained; it has since been converted into a farm house, and now belongs to Mr. Toone and the tenant still pays 26s. per annum to the family of the Duke of Leeds (the proprietor of Conisborough Castle, from which it is distant only two and a quarter miles) as 'Horn Money.' Formerly this chapel or monastery, on payment of this sum, had the privilege of blowing a horn at the castle gates in time of war and of claiming protection for their valuables.

There is a mill, or rather the site of a mill, in a field adjoining, which probably belonged to the monks. The house is called 'Moat Farm,' being surrounded by water.

Readers of "Ivanhoe" will remember the scene at Conisborough Castle in which Athelstane, believed to have been killed in the storming of Torquilstone and to be lying in his coffin in the oratory which is still shown to visitors to Conisborough Keep, broke in on a conference between Cedric and King Richard "..... in the garments of the grave ... pale, haggard, and like something arisen from the dead" and will recall his account of what had befallen him since he was struck down in the Torquilstone fight. We need not follow Athelstane in his lively account of the way in which he discomfited the monks and obtained his freedom. It is, no doubt, a notion likely to find favour with Braithwell folk that such an exciting incident in a great historical tale was enacted within the borders of

104

their Village and in a building some of which is still standing. One does not know, however, on what evidence Dr. Holt Yates based his theory that the old Moat Hall was originally a "church or chapel."

Rotherham Advertiser 26th March 1938

A FIFTEENTH CENTURY BUILDING
Braithwell's Moat Hall Saved From Demolition

"...the site is of great interest as it presents an example of a fortified earthwork..... . It is in fact, a castle without military trimmings......
......point to its erection in the latter half of the 15th. century ..... . It would be the hall of an important landowner."

Extracts from "THE MOAT HALL, BRAITHWELL" by Dorothy Green 1942
The Moat Hall lies on the rear portion of the site and faces almost due south. It was apparently once a rectanular building of approximately 69 feet 9 inches in length and 19 feet 7 inches in width. The main entrance was in the centre of the south

wall and the thirteenth century arch still remains, bearing upon its stones masons' marks identical with those on the west front of the Abbey Church at Roche. This door gives access to a small apartment 17 feet 2 inches by 8 feet, of which the eastern wall was formerly pierced by three arches of an earlier type than the main entrance. These arches are now erected in the garden of Mr. H. Brown of Maltby.

Opposite the main entrance two moulded stones built into the masonry of the wall suggest that formerly a small door pierced the north wall of the building. If so, this was once a small passage dividing the main building into two almost equal portions, the eastern of which has now disappeared.

The western portion of the house has survived fairly well. This is actually one large room 24 feet 3 inches by 17 feet, of which the walls aproximately 1Foot 10 inches thick, still stand to a height of 4 feet. The fireplace stands at the western end of the room and is 5 Feet 5 inches in width. One side still stands to a height of 4 feet. A kitchen range was inserted in the nineteenth century and thus the four-centred arch has been cut away. Some time during the nineteenth century the building had been turned into two cottages and a 4¹/₂ inch brick wall was built across the end of the room to make a small passage in which stood a cottage staircase. Returning to the passage or arcade and approaching the main door from inside the old bolt holes are visible, and also on the wall it is possible to trace the position of the oaken stairs inserted apparently in the sixteenth century. These stairs and the original nail-studded oak door were chopped up a few years ago according to Mr Crawshaw the tenant of Moat Cottage.

The building on the east has disappeared completely, but the footings of the walls still remain and I have been able to trace one wall to its end which gives a room approximately 28 feet by 17 feet. Outside and to the east of the main door is a beautiful well still full of water.

The history of the place is very baffling and is largely built upon conjecture. The Moat Hall was probably never in the possession of the monks of Lewes. The arch bears marks identical to the mason's marks at Roche and the monks of Roche held certain lands at Braithwell at the time of the Dissolution.

The monks paid one quarter of corn yearly to the mill at Conisborough from their lands in Braithwell. After the Dissolution, the land and house of the Abbot, with some property called "Belltring Lands," were let to William Wilson at £1 6s 2d per annum. It is impossible to trace the "Belltring Lands," but an old map of Wm. Fairbank's dated 1768 now in the Central Library, Sheffield, gives "Holywell Closes" as the name of the fields lying on the opposite side of Holywell Lane and adjoining the Holy Well, a chalybeate spring still bubbling up on the roadside. This well is shown on the 1/2500 Ord. Map 290/7, Ed of 1929, which also gives the lands to the East of the Moat Hall as "Austwood Closes."

In 1838 most of the land in Braithwell was owned by the Duke of Leeds and according to White's directory of that year, a Mr. Thomas Toone lived at the Moat Hall. The mill Dr. Yates mentiones *(sic)* was doubtless the "Ruddle Mill," situate on the east side of Austwood Closes. Near this mill a lane runs north called Chapel Hole Lane. In the bankside near this lane is a place marked "Chapel Hole" on the Ord. Map Sheet 290 N.E. Sometime after Dr. Holt Yates wrote his notes the Moat Hall was turned into two cottages, and Mr Crawshaw, the tenant of the Moat Cottage states that he went to a Dame School in the one now in ruins and that the main archway was obscured by a lean-to scullery, the floor of which remains. This scullery had one great merit – it preserved the archway from the weather.

Some little time later Mr Ethert Brand appeared upon the scene and was instantly attracted to this fascinating ruin with its fine main doorway and three arches still standing. He brought Mr. C.M.E. Hadfield to the place, who made a small sketch plan which I now possess and which is of great value to me. Mr Brand persuaded Mr Pickin, the owner, to let him make some excavations. After his death the place was forgotten until Mr. Northend asked me if I knew anything about it. I did not, but I went over and found the old house in a very bad state. Masses of rubble were everywhere, beams lying about, and the cottage staircase leading up to a non-existent first floor. The three arcade arches had been taken away, leaving only the main doorway standing forlorn in the scene of desolation.

I found Mr Himsley, of Maltby, who was deeply interested in the antiquities of the district, and he spent a few months clearing some of the site. Ill-health drove him from the field, but luckily I met Mr. J. F. Thackery, who undertook the task of helping to clear away the rubbish, and under his care the masses of debris were moved and numerous wrought and marked stones saved for future use. Inside the fireplace were found three carved stones, one of which Mr. T. Salvin tells me is part of a traceried window.

The loose and dangerous parts of the walls were levelled to a uniform height of about 4 feet and the old rickety staircase taken away. Today the Moat Hall is once more fit to approach and shows in its old grey walls remains of its former beauty. Much remains to be done, however, and it is my hope that in the coming summer I may find time to do a little work on the vanished eastern portion. I would like to lay bare the plan of this area.

The old house has had many vicissitudes, and Dr. Holt Yates' suggestion that it was formerly a chapel is interesting. Recently I met a member of the R. A. F. who was formerly the sacristan at Downside Abbey. I described the Moat Hall to him and he said that possibly it had once been used as a hospital for the Abbey of Roche and, if so, the western side, where the fireplace is, would be the dwelling-place, and the eastern side, approached through the arches, might have been used as a chapel, with the altar at the east end of the building. This may account for the remains of the traceried window found by Mr. Thackery. Certainly the little Hospital of St. Nicholas recently reported in the Yorkshire Archaelogical (sic) Society's Journal is a rectangular building not unlike the Moat Hall in plan.".

Extracts from Inspector's Report
File AA 21336/1 1993
Category Moated Site National Grid Reference SK 5343 9434
The monument comprises a rectangular island measuring c. 30m by c. 45m surrounded by a 10m wide moat, filled in to the south and east but still waterfilled to the west and north-west. The moat was fed from the south by a now filled-in channel leading from a tributary of Ruddle Dike, a depression shows the position of the south arm of the moat, which is still inclined to marshiness at its western end. In the centre of the island are the ruins of a group of sixteenth century cottages, demolished in the 1940's and found to contain parts of earlier buildings. These included an in situ thirteenth century archway and the remains of "Moat Hall", a fifteenth century timber-framed grange of Lewes Priory leased to John Vincent (sic) of Braithwell in 1427 and known as "Le Priorie". Associated buildings stood outside the moated area and included a tithe barn demolished early this century. The present house is reputed

to have been the dovecot *(sic)* and at least two other barns are referred to in the Lewes Cartulary.

Moat Hall, Braithwell is an important example of a moated site containing in situ foundations of medieval buildings and with ancillary buildings close by. Indeed it is the best-preserved medieval grange site in the county. The building appears to have consisted of a timber-framed first floor hall, with stone walls beneath. The first floor was demolished c. 1930. The surviving ruins are mostly lower courses, in places reconstructed and 'tidied up', but with a good 15th century doorway arch standing intact. Associated buildings appear to have stood to the south, outside the area of the moat. A 'tithe barn' here was demolished early this century. The present house appears to have been a dovecote, and may incorporate medieval work.

From "The Yorkshire Portion of the Lewes Chartulary' C.T. Clay F.S.A. (F. 296)
"Grant by Thomas, prior of the monastery of Lewes, County Sussex, ... to John Vyncent of Brathewell, county York, and Agnes his wife, for John's good service and council to them in their monastery, and for his good counsel to be given to them in the future, of a certain capital messuage of theirs in Brathewell aforesaid, called 'Le Priorie' with two rooms and two barns, one of which was called 'Le Shepecote' and the other 'Le Peyseberne', with all the demesne lands, gardens and meadows pertaining to the said messuage . . . . .

Furhermore John and Agnes or their heirs within the next eight years were to make anew, well and fittingly within the said messuage, a hall with a room at the west and thirty two ft. long and eighteen broad, also a house called Bakehous and another house called Kylnehous with a Maltehouse and a stone well (fontem) for drawing water, at their own cost . . .

(25th April 1427)"
I had tea here often when I was a child with Mr. and Mrs. Crawshaw and Millie, their daughter (now Mrs Roley). Moat Hall was standing as a private dwelling until just before World War II. It slowly went to ruin when the Crawshaws left and were re-housed in the first council houses built in 1937 up Ashton Lane. Mrs. Crawshaw didn't want to leave there, she loved it. Sadly a great deal of the stone was removed then.

Moat Hall had a peculiar old staircase and a very large room at the end. Mrs. Crawshaw used to let it out for weddings etc..

109

What a beautiful set-up. Oh! that there was somewhere like that in this Village now. And what a pity that with hind-sight we, the residents of Braithwell, didn't try to keep this beautiful ancient monument. Unfortunately in my young days there really wasn't a lot of interest shown. Except by Mrs Dorothy Green of Rotherham, an historian – she paid 10/- a year to Mr Pickin (the owner) to stop the remaining arch being demolished in the 1930s! The other three that were there had been taken down. One went to Mr. Humphreys at Lambcote Grange and the other two to Mr. Bown of High Street, Maltby and were erected in his garden. They obviously saw their potential. Lambcote Grange still has theirs erected in the garden wall but the other two seem to have disappeared.

Millie told me that around 1937 her father dug up two bronze images of monks in the garden. They were about 6" to 9" in height. They went to a museum but despite enquiries I can find nothing about them. She also says a young man came to paint a picture of the old Moat Hall – for a museum and again this can't be traced. Mrs. Crawshaw made him tea and cakes during his stay and he painted her a small picture too. Unfortunately this too has been lost.

Moat Cottage (No. 7)
This is 2-storey limestone, built with stone-coped gables and a steep-pitched, slabbed roof. Formerly, the Moat Hall had a coaching house and stables with pigeon cote over which is all now turned into a house called Moat Cottage. It is a small, two-storey limestone cottage with a large single-storey stone extension to form a new sitting room – built in 1966 by Mr. Alan Myers when he bought the house. The monks used to eat the pigeons for food and also had a carp pond – a usual thing in those days to be self-sufficient, with the right to graze a large number of sheep. A lot of food would be taken to them from the local farmers and Villagers as gifts – and a lot of land was owned by them. They had a big stone tithe barn to hold these gifts, to the east of the cottage. I only remember it as a place where farm machinery was stored. In the early 1940s the roof became unsafe and later the walls were lowered and what remains of the barn today has been turned into garages.

Old School House (No. 16)
This has limestone walls and a pantile roof. It is a 2-storey

building with quoins* and a first floor band. There is a plain raised stone door surround. New windows. The south-side elevation has a stone wall-sundial at first floor level. Above the central door is a first-floor stone panel inscribed:

In
Dei Gloriam
Patriae Commodum
Hancce Scholam
Fundavit
Johan Bosvile
1693

which may be translated as:
"John Bosvile founded this school for the good of his country and the glory of God"
and for once we have no difficulty in dating the building!

In the centre of Village on High Street this house was used as a school until the1800s when the church school was built behind it. A Charity Fund taught four children free and 40/- per year was paid to the schoolmaster for instruction. The schoolmaster was Sexton, Parish Clerk, local historian and general letter-writer. His family lived with him at the schoolhouse, the front room was for the school and the family lived in the kitchen and slept upstairs. The kitchen had a stone sink and a pump. An earth closet was in the yard. This was emptied by horse and cart at night and carried to the outskirts of the Village to Birchwood Close which belonged to the church. It was known as the night soil. The Old School building is now owned and used by Darby and Joan Club and the Church School is a doctor's surgery.

Quoins: dressed stones placed at the corner of a wall

CHAPTER 23

My Childhood Home and the Farms and Smallholdings I Knew

Hall Farm, Braithwell
House and Outbuildings
The Northern part of the house is of three storeys, built of coursed limestone rubble, with a hipped Welsh slate roof. The inscription over the central doorway reads:

B

J E G

1771

There are sash windows and the east gable incorporates an internal pigeon cote with brick nests. The Southern portion of the house has a datestone reading:

B

T E

1683

and is of two storeys, with dripmoulds and chamfered stone mullions to the lower storey. String course moulding separates the upper and lower floors.

Chamfered	*an angle – cut off diagonally*
Mullions	*bar dividing window lights*

Key to the Diagram

1a Kitchen	9 Turnip House (with corn chamber above)
1b Sitting Room	10 Cow House
1c Dairy	11 Stone steps to chop chamber
1d Far Room	12 Stables
1e Front Sitting Room	13 Harness Room and chop bin
1f Second Pantry	14 Pig Sties
1g Passage	15 Meal house; Pig Swill Copper
2 Lawn	16 Small Building
3 Back Garden	17 Dog Kennel
4 Coal House	18 Water Tank
5 Outside Closet	19 Bull Pen
6 Drive	20 Duck House
7 Covered yard	21 Turkey Shed
8 Hen House	

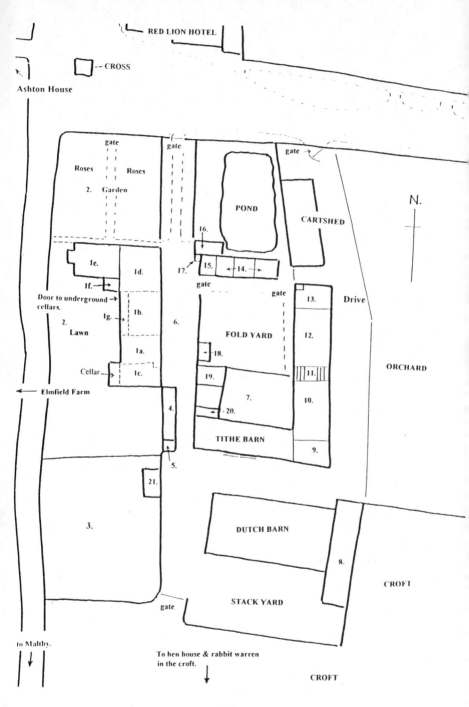

Hall Farm (No. 3)

204 acres with 20 outside acres rented. 70% of the land was south of the farm – easy access without road travel. My father farmed all the land as far as Maltby except for one small field. He did once try to buy this, the narrow field on Maltby Lane on the road side on Dale Hill, owned by Albert Fidler but wasn't successful. He did buy the field which divided our land in 1944 for £80 from Spoff (Herbert) Allison. We still call it Allison's field. The house is reputed first to have been just a crofter's cottage with one room with a well in the corner and a pump on the sink and wooden ladder leading to the loft above. Date unknown but probably 16th century

In 1683 a large kitchen living room was built on to the north of the small existing room and also a sitting room, which was reached by means of a passage. Above were three bedrooms, the larger one being sub-divided by a wooden partition and another small bedroom was on the turn of the stairs. The fireplace was set back and a recess at the side must have been the old bread oven. In my childhood, the farmhouse kitchen/living room was heated by a big black-leaded Yorkshire Range. After many years of nagging by my mother, Dad eventually changed it for a vitreous enamel Yorkshire Range. This had two ovens and was a great luxury to us. When the old stove was taken out, a great deal of plaster fell and a stone arch was revealed in beautiful condition, obviously a part of the original building. Malcolm and I knocked all the old lime from it and it is now a lovely feature of the room. This arch has small lettering dated 1709.

There are underground passages to this farm which lead currently under the house and drive. In 1916, the long passage fell into the cellar and was filled up. Then in 1930 the sitting room floor fell in and this was filled in because of the danger. Nobody was interested in seeing this and my father wanted to get the room back to normal living for his family. How things have changed! People nowadays travel miles to see a little bit of history. Now, only two small chambers remain which can be reached from a door in the passage and down several stone steps. When the sitting room floor caved in, I can remember seeing small cells down below – they each had iron grids and hooks on the wall. If one looks under the window in the drive, one can still see a grid at floor-level which must have been a ventilator for the cellar.

The dining room (far room) had a big cupboard set back into

the wall with shelves. These walls would originally have been the outside wall before the front was added in 1771. Mother kept her home-made wine in here. It was beautifully cool – many a sup we used to have unknown to Mum when a bottle had been opened. In the sitting room again was a big cupboard which went right down below the floor. The draught from it was horrendous so it must have been connected to the outlet from the underground passages.

The back of the farmhouse faces east-west (see drawing). The east kitchen window looked out onto the open yard – the stables and pig styes. Access to the cowhouses was gained through the fold yard. There was a back kitchen which we also used as the dairy and this led to the large cellar which was down five stone steps – quite steep. This was where the pigs were salted. From the living-kitchen up two stone steps, the passage led to the little sitting room on your right. This passage was always rather dark as half the window had been "bricked up" due to the window tax. It became even more spooky further along. Under the stairs on the left was a door which led into the underground cellars. I always swore I heard footsteps coming up the stairs at 2am – I buried my head in the bedclothes. I always dashed past here! – particularly when you'd only got a candle for light. The big dining room at the front we always called the far room. When Dad eventually bought the farm, the house was again made into one. The first time for many years. The door in the far room was knocked through and we had a whole new house. Another big front sitting room, lovely hall and beautiful staircase which led up to two big high bedrooms and then on the third storey – two big attics. Part of the front attic on the north-east is an excellent pigeon cote with the original brick nesting place. This was in use until 1945. When I came out of the W.L.A. with my Land Army friend Lyn we cleaned this out – 200 years of droppings. Quite a job. We lowered the buckets full from three storeys up onto a cart below.

Through a door in the east side down a ladder and into another attic – this led to another ladder and yet another attic. These were very rarely used but the next attic (there were five altogether) was over the back kitchen, again up wooden steps from this kitchen. This was used for storing farm tools, household paint and brushes and lots of other things. There were four bedrooms at the back of the house and two huge bedrooms at the front. Of course no bathroom in those days. During

1697–1851 when the window tax was in operation, one third of the windows were blocked up to avoid this tax but these have since been re-instated.

In 1683, the second part of the building was erected by Thomas Bosvile, Rector of Sandal Parva and Vicar of Braithwell. A more imposing residence was added onto this in 1771 by John Bosvile. Georgian in style, three storeys high and approached by a long drive through the garden, with stone gateposts surmounted by globes, the Bosvile seat in Braithwell was Hall Farm with a commanding position facing north, it views over the Cross and right up the High Street.

Quote from old book (Hatfield Village Sketches, 1849) "To those who have wandered that way and noticed the old stone columns surmounted by globes will recognise the spot which is rendered sacred by the remembrance of the venerated name of Bosvile."

When I first wrote about Hall Farm and its history, there was very little written about it. I borrowed from Ilene Foers (The Rectory) old documents and have quoted from them. Never dreaming of publishing, I never wrote down where all these quotes came from but always understood the Bosviles built and lived in Hall Farm as I have stated. Since writing that, I have had a letter from an Australian lady trying to find out about her family The Birks. Strangely, this name features in our family tree but the most interesting thing was she said her ancestors the Birks built Hall Farm! It is written as follows in "The Chronicle of the Birks Family of Brampton-en-le-Morthen" by Edith Mary Birks in 1912: "Joshua Birks, born 1732. Facing the cross, at a little distance from the road Joshua erected his house, a substantial three-stored *(sic)* building plain almost to ugliness. Over the front door is a stone marked "- – B J&G 1771" (Joshua and Gertrude). "A picture postcard of Braithwell Village gives a good view of the house, and my father said the fine tree almost overshadowing it was planted by his great-grandfather. "He died on September 15th 1810, aged 78. I like to picture him walking about the picturesque villge – practically unaltered since his day – wearing a long-tailed coat, knee-breeches, frilled shirt and high stock.

"In July 1948 Cousin Edith visited the Hall Farm at Braithwell built by Joshua Birks. In addition to the inscription over the front door she found another stone over an old door marked " – - B T.E". She wondered if Joshua had added to a

Derrick, Joyce, Dennis and cousin, Alec
Cooper Smith

Joyce with Topsy

Joyce and her brother Dennis in
fancy dress

The Braithwell Mafia! Bob, Uncle
Harry and Uncle Lal.

Dad, Epe and Crafty with the horse team.

Bob with harvest teas on Dicky Revill Lane.

Harvest tea-time with Jack Kershaw, Harold Smith, Olive Trueman, Dad, Crafty the dog, Dennis, Ivy Smith (behind) Bob Houghton, and Mr. Smith (Ashton Farm).

Derrick with Tommy Boy.

Great Grandfather Richard Dunstan with his second wife outside the Poplars.
Ernest Lawrence is holding the horse.

"Oh, I do like to be beside the seaside." Auntie Flo Tomney (Pear Tree Cottage), Mrs Ted Littlewood (The Poplars), Mrs. Yeomans (The Police House, Doncaster Road) Mrs. Nance Holmes (Rook House Farm) and Auntie Hilda Dunstan (Orchard Farm) enjoying a paddle at Cleethorpes.

Aimée Marshall and Her Girls. *Back Row:* Eva Wadsley (née Davison), Edith Pearson (née Allison), Mrs. Harrison, Carole Johnson (née Byron), Joyce Milnes (née Dunstan), Mrs. Aimée Marshall, Joyce Parkes (née Harrison), Kathleen Leigh (née Davison). *Front Row:* Margaret Stewart, --------------------, Iris Godwin (née Davison).

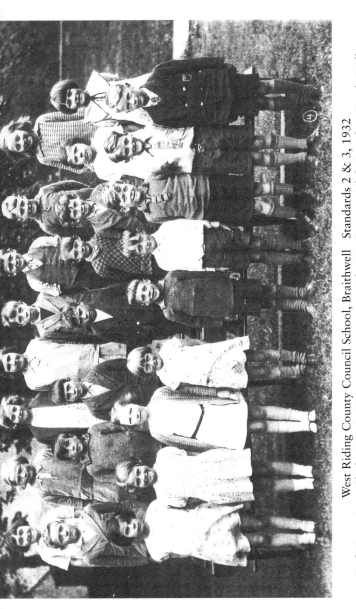

West Riding County Council School, Braithwell Standards 2 & 3, 1932

Back Row: Joan Clark, Winnie Haines, Joyce Dunstan, Chrissie Sargan, Ralph Doughty, Frank Radley, Roy Trueman (Micklebring), Rachel Dunn,

Middle Row: Harry Wadsley (Micklebring), Johnny Green, Jim Earnshaw, Charlie Morgan, Sam Smith, Bunty (George) Cook, Blanche Ashley, Kath Taylor,

Bottom Row: Sheila Stewart, Sheila Brookes, Edith Allison, Alice Farnsworth (Birk Lodge), Tony Trueman (Micklebring), Ken Mollekin, Norman Lucas, Donald Ashley, Ernest Appleyard (Clifton).

Braithwell High Street looking south towards Hall Farm with the Red Lion on the left

Holywell Lane, Braithwell with the pump in the foreground.

Maltkiln Farm and shops on the High Street, Braithwell. Maltkiln farmhouse is the large building on the left facing down the High Street. In front stands a greengrocer's shop and across the road a very small general store. Two doors up on the right is the Post Office, newsagent's and sweetshop.

Braithwell High Street looking north from the village cross.

The Chapel, Austwood Road, Braithwell.

The old blacksmith's shop, Braithwell.

Harehound House, Maltby Lane, home of William and Aimée Marshall decorated for the Coronation, June 1953.

still older Birks' dwelling. In the churchyard were innumerable Birks ancestors."

I can't check on the original Deeds as they were destroyed by a fire, so again we take our choice.

There is a Tithe Barn in the stackyard, on which Tithes were paid until 1936, when they were abolished. It is in an excellent state of preservation and still in use after all these hundreds of years. We celebrated our Silver Wedding there in 1973. It was hosed down and cleaned inside – probably the first time ever. A good time was had by all in a wonderful setting for such an occasion.

The Manor House (No 25) Micklebring Lane

This was formerly the home of all the most notable families of the Village. Local legend ties it to the inscription on the Cross. It is supposed that it was at the Manor that a Prince stayed in the days of King Richard I. Whether true or not, the "old" house certainly dated back to that period. The room he slept in was still called "Prince John's Room" – the brother of Richard I? The first family of note to live here were the Sheffield's. Early records spell the name "Seefeuld" and later "Scheffeld". Within the altar rails of the Church lies the tombstone of Thomas Schefeld who died in 1406.

In 1450 we know that John Vyncent lived there. Before going to battle in the War of the Roses, he planted two white roses in the presence of his household, as a memento of his sincerity and faithful adherence to Richard, Duke of York. He was killed at the Battle of Wakefield in 1460. In 1750 one rose still survived on the east side of the house to perpetuate his memory. His daughter Dorothy married Thomas Waterhouse in 1573 and the Waterhouse's lived there until 1709. It was then sold to the Shepherds and, by marriage, it descended to Mr. Dyson, whose family resided there until the middle 1800s.

The old house was razed to the ground in 1837 with the exception of the two apartments which reputedly had been occupied by the Prince mentioned above. They were left exactly as before and a new Victorian structure was built on to them with stone from the Silverwood quarries, belonging to T. Bosvile of Ravenfield Park. It was designed by J. Weightman of Sheffield. The first stone was laid by Mr. Dyson's mother and he himself laid out beautiful gardens with evergreens and roses. There were also kitchen gardens and a vinery, judiciously laid

117

out and kept in admirable order. Beyond were pasture and meadow lands, in one of which was a rookery preserved with great care – not a gun was allowed to be fired to spoil the magnificent elms.

This quote comes from "Hatfield Village Sketches" 1849 "The private entrance facing the churchyard is through a stone-built portico. To the right is the portion of the old house which was left, the lower apartment of which is approached by the descent of two steps. Here were received, in the days of the troubadours, the free offerings of loyal and devoted people. The homage was cheerfully

performed and the peasants and yeomen vied with each other in generosity and attachment to their Sovereign. In the entrance hall was a beautiful oaken cabinet of olden times. In the drawing room, the ceiling of the old house has adhered to the original style of decoration. The house and grounds afford everything that is to be desired and is a delightful residence for an English country gentleman."

Manor Farm Dovecote (No. 25)
In the stackyard is a fine 17th. century Dovecote with square-opening interior brick nesting holes and rat course. It has rubble walls, a pantile roof edged with stone slates and stone-coped gables. There is a widely-projecting stone band and stone mullioned windows. Some red brick repairs and alterations have been carried out.

Foredoles Farm Marsh Hill – Ashton Lane
This 18th. century farmhouse is cement rendered, 2-storey with Welsh slate roof and sash windows in plain raised surround. Fields to the east and south are called Foredoles Close. Once the largest farm in the Village, Foredoles faces west, overlooking what were the Braithwell Common Fields. My great-grandfather Richard Dunstan came first to Foredoles and farmed here followed by my grandfather. He then moved to Hall Farm. Great-grandfather retired from there to the Poplars, High Street; then he built "The Hawthorns" on Holywell Lane and the houses were known as "Dunstan's Row" until he died.

The farm had a piece of land known as the Bull Piece. He paid £1 a year to the Parish Council for this. I know that this money was paid by Mr. Revitt who farmed Foredoles when I was on the Council but no-one knew its origins. When he left the farm, it was lost. I can only think that it was a piece of land where the bull was kept. Perhaps the bull used by the Village – who knows? There was no artificial insemination in those days. The land had been given to the Village and the farmer had to pay a £1 a year rent. The money did go to the Charities, as shown in the Records. Despite many enquiries, I'm still no wiser. My brother Derrick, Arnold Pawson and Dennis Revitt all think it's the east side of the Public Right of Way. In the early nineteenth century Foredoles Farm was the home of the Amery family. The payment of "Bull Piece Money" is noted in many of the Braithwell Constables' and Churchwardens' yearly accounts. The Charity Commissioners looked into this payment when they met in the Village in 1895. They called it the "Bull Close Charity" and, although identifying the farm, they couldn't accurately locate the field and neither did they give any account of ownership or Benefactor. The money was paid direct to the Constable who used it in performing his Village duties. Those present at the 1895 Meeting were of the opinion that the payment is "probably made in discharge of an obligation upon the owner or occupier of this field to maintain a bull for the use of the Parish."

The spelling of the name appears to have frequently changed. In 1771 it was referred to as Four Doles, in 1817 as Fardells House and on the 1841 O.S. map as Fordoles Head. (1805 Foredeles, 1852 Fourdoles, 1897 Foredoles)

Well House (No. 4) Holywell Lane
This large dwelling was built behind the Village Well and pump by I.S. Thompson in 1784. There is a date panel, over south-facing central front door,

T

IS

1784

which may refer to a rebuilding of an earlier structure. Cement rendered with casement windows and, originally, a Welsh slate roof, which has been replaced with red pantiles.

The "original" John Thompson came from the West Country with his brother. They came to the Village, ex-soldiers, after the war in the time of Queen Elizabeth, 1558 to 1603, looking for somewhere to settle – they came with feathers in their hats ("Red Cochers"), liked what they saw and stayed. He grew to love the Village and his descendants lived here and prospered.

"Time rolled on; generation after generation passed away, sons and sires were gathered to their fathers and a name that was unknown has now become familiar in the whole neighbourhood. The two enterprising men were founders of two families of the Thompsons, which, since that memorable time have extended themselves to no less than 40 branches." They built Well House so that everybody who came for water could see how well their family had done and it was also used as a wayside inn called "The Well".

In 1839 the Thompson family was still in residence and by that time John Thompson was farming in excess of 130 acres. It was turned into two dwellings in 1974 – when I was a child it was a small farm of about 35 acres but is now without land. The only Thompson left in the Village was John Thompson who lived in Forge Cottage. The Thompson who built Well House also owned this cottage and one of the family was the Village blacksmith. Mr. John Thompson and his wife Mary were the last of the original Thompson family to live here. John died in the 1950s, Mary died in the 1960s and the house was then sold.

There are many Thompson graves in the churchyard – on a tablet near the pulpit: "Here lieth interred in this Churchyard, John Thompson (at Well) Yeoman, nephew of Thomas Tompson, who died in October, 1712, aged 90. Also John Thompson, yeoman, second son to the aforesaid John Thompson, who died in October, 1726, aged 72. Also John Thompson, yeoman, son and heir of the late John Thompson, who died in April 1800, aged 89 years." He left James Thompson, his son and heir aged 62, also John Thompson his grandson and heir of the said James Thompson, aged 20. The above James Thompson died Jan 5th. 1829 aged 90 years. Also the above John Thompson died Dec. 25th. 1837 aged 57.".

Cedar Farm (No. 5) Holywell Lane
Stone and with a date panel above the front door facing south

S

J

1687

so there is no dispute about the age. This probably refers to John Shepherd, a yeoman farmer living in the Village at that time. In my school days the owner was William Pickin who also owned Moat Hall, Moat Cottage and Wild Duck Cottage (Dam

Cottage), way over the meadows. It is now whitewashed with some alteration to the frontage. It has an attractive diamond-shaped window over the front door with clover-leaf insert and a Welsh slate roof. Once had tanneries here. Just to the east of the farm adjacent to Holywell Lane is a spring – this once ran through the Village Green. The stream follows the road and then swings north to the Dam. The stream which flows out of the dam becomes the eastern Parish Boundary. In the field next to the farm was a pond, now filled in. This provided plenty of entertainment for the youth of the Village in frosty weather – a good time sliding was had by all!

Elmfield Farm (No. 10)

This house is late 18th. century with a red pantiled roof and sash windows; it is now cement rendered.

When I was a child, it was divided into two parts and the farm workers lived there. Mr. and Mrs. Palmer with their son and daughter Willie and Hilda in the back. Mr. Palmer ran the dairy herd and Willie had the milk round. Mr. and Mrs. Spencer and their son Tommy in the front – he was the horseman. Later it was let to various farmers in the district. The two Mrs. Robinsons owned the farm and in later years, when Mrs. Ron's son Brian came out of the army he lived and farmed there. Now a farm complex on Maltby Lane. It is no longer a working farm, the two outbuildings having been turned into houses.

Fox House Farm (No. 22)

Buildings used as a farm complex. The old farmhouse was demolished in the 1950s and almost completely rebuilt. The barn was made into a house – "Michaelmas Cottage". The slaughterhouse and butcher's shop have been made into two houses. Fox House Farm was formerly the home of the Parkes family. The farming operations have moved from Austwood Lane (Chapel Lane as I knew it) to Ridgewood Farm, Cockhill Field Lane with a new house – an entirely new pig farm owned and operated by Mr. Jim Parkes' grandson John and his family.

121

CHAPTER 24

An Historical Walk up the High Street, West Side, and around the Village

Why the west side? Perhaps because the Great Field ran behind this and it provided easy access to the farm strips before the Inclosure of the Open Fields. The gable ends of most smallholdings faced the street. Again common practice not to take up space on the street – see also Maltkiln Farm, Pear Tree Farm. The main farm houses faced the street – Hall Farm, Orchard Farm, Well House Farm, Cedar Farm, Manor Farm – all but Orchard Farm are built well back from the road. The Village is more haphazard in arrangement than some of the nearby estate villages because its inhabitants were farmers and smallholders.

Harehound House (No. 11) Maltby Lane

18th. or early 19th. century, situated near to the Cross and just over the road from the front garden of my childhood home, Hall Farm. Facade ashlar, roof was Welsh slate at the front and red pantiles rear. A square-fronted stone house with four sash windows with stone cills and lintels, centre door up two stone steps. There was also a small enclosed front garden and a garden to the rear up stone steps.

In the early 1900s, Martha Marshall came from the Plough at Micklebring to live here – it was her family home. Just before 1920, her nephew William came with his wife Aimee to live with them. This was an alehouse until 1920 as the name suggests. When Aimee died the house fell into disrepair. Later due to deterioration the upper storey was demolished. (Originally in my grandfather's day this was also a smallholding).

Ashton House (No. 2)

Situated opposite and to the west of the Cross. One room deep with the chimney opposite the doorway; 2 storeys and an attic with Pantiled roof. The gable end is to the street and drip-mouldings are apparent over modern windows. This is a good example of a 17th. century yeoman farmhouse, now partly pebble-dashed and with a joiner's shop attached. One mullioned window survives in the attic storey. The main room has a beautiful stone arch over the fireplace with salt hole and a bread oven, which has now been exposed and cleaned; not greatly altered. In my grandfather's day this too was a small farm.

In my childhood it was the home and workplace of Mr. & Mrs Lawrence – he followed his father there. Ernest was Village undertaker and a very skilled joiner, turning out many carts, gates and cart wheels – he made the wheels and Mr. Fidler (Blacksmith) made the iron bands. These were then heated to red heat on an open fire and placed over the wooden wheel where they burned into place. Then gallons of cold water were thrown over the lot to cool it down and contract the iron band to make it a tight fit to the wheel. Sisters Ida and Clara also lived in the Village and became Ida Wells (Marion Byron's mother) and Clara Fenn (Dick Fenn's mother). Their younger sister Madge married Colin Wild, a local milkman and lived in "The Bungalow" on Holywell Lane. He was in partnership in the milk business with Billy Pickin of Cedar Farm. His sister was Billy's wife. Ernest Lawrence was a good and careful man. He was a regular attender at church and did lots of carpentry work there, making the altar rails across the width of the chancel in 1932 and also making the altar – the carving was done by a Mr. Scholes. He loved cowboy pictures and went every Saturday night to the pictures, often with my brother Derrick. He was very fond of cake and biscuits and if ever I went and he was having his cup of tea, he always had the biscuit tin by him. Ashton House had a stone staircase and his wife, who was a bit of a tartar, was always nagging him to put in a wooden one. He never did, always pleading too much work to do. Sad that we haven't now got an undertaker in the Village. I was pleased he buried Dad. They were good friends.

Ashton Farm (No. 12)

A two-storey stone farmhouse with a red pantile roof, out-buildings and barn which have been much altered in recent years. Modern windows with cyma recta dripmoulds, windows now put into the north side. There was also a big old barn to the west of the house and an old tannery to the east with a small croft behind and land elsewhere. It once had a Malt House. Inside is beamed and there were no windows to the west, north or east. This was a very common thing in the olden days and can be seen in many cottages. Light was only drawn from one side – the bigger houses had light from all sides.

123

This had about 50 acres which my father bought in the early 1950s to get the land on Maltby Lane when Mr. Cook and his family moved to Rainborough Grange. He then let the house for several years. He sold it in the 1960s to Vincent Hill for £1 800 with the Austwood Field – we always called it "Hosswoods". When Vincent died, my uncle Albert bought the farm house and field and now his grandson Peter lives there.

Marshall's Yard

This farmyard was between Ashton Farm and Orchard Farm, now the car park for the Nursery to Ashton Farm. The small stone cottage in which the owner lived was attached to the Butcher's Arms; the house was pulled down in 1937–8 when the new council houses were built up Ashton Lane. The Marshall's moved up there, much to Bill Marshall's disgust but he continued to run their holding. They had a lovely Jersey cow and they had the field between Springdale Cottage and Birchwood House. If ever we wanted a special treat, (we had cream in plenty at home – we ran a Friesian herd) Mum would let me go up to Marshall's for 3d worth of Jersey cream. Rich and yellow and whipped so easily to fill one of Mum's lovely chocolate cakes for Sunday tea. Bill used the skimmed milk for his pigs and his wife made butter with the rest of the cream

Bill Marshall also worked at the pit. He was messenger to the manager and came round the Village with a lovely pony and trap. He was a real character and every other word was "bugger". In fact he was known as "buggering Bill", even by us children. When it was suggested that the Cross should be moved to allow lorries to get up Ashton Lane more easily, we had a public meeting in the school. Tempers ran high and lots of voices were raised in anger but Bill's voice came above all. He stood up shaking his fist and shouted on the top of his voice: "Ye buggers. What silly bugger wants to move the Cross eh? Leave the bugger where it is. The bugger's been there for hundreds o' years. Bugger ye all. We'd be better to move you buggers from t' Council and put some other more sensible buggers up there." The place was in an uproar. Needless to say, they never did move the Cross and it has never been suggested again. A later newspaper report said that: "Mr. William Marshall, aged 72, resident of Braithwell fired verbal arrows at the Council." – an apt description!

124

Orchard House Farm (No. 14)

An early 17th. century stone house, it has a Pantile roof, has two storeys and to the rear of the house is a wood-mullioned window in the upper storey; outbuildings with a date stone 1688, probably not *in situ*. Now completely restored it was a small farm of about 60 acres farmed by the Hardcastles who had three daughters – Ada, Lucy and Hilda.

Ada married my uncle Frank (father's oldest brother). He worked as a winder at the pit and they also had the fish and chip shop and lived in Cremona Cottage. They had no children. The proprietor of this fish shop always lived in Cremona Cottage behind the shop. Mr. and Mrs. Baker kept it next, after my aunt and uncle. Mr Baker was also a cobbler but was always known a Chippie Baker or Daddy Baker and ran his shoe-repairing business from there also.

Hilda married my father's youngest brother Albert and they farmed Orchard Farm for many years. Uncle Albert also ran a coal business from there – even in those days on a small farm, you had to diversify. They had three children – Mary, Hilda and Joseph. Joe loved to tell tales of Braithwell and talk of the past – particularly when he was ill later in life. He told me many tales.

Lucy Hardcastle married Fred Bailey. Before he married he and his sister, a spinster and a very quiet, prim, plump little woman, kept the shop at No. 27 High Street. It was a general store and still stands out on the causeway to the north of the Old School House. Lucy also did the laying out in the Village. When Fred died, Lucy moved to two rooms in Orchard Farm and turned one into a shop. Her old home of course. She lived there until she died. They had no children.

Cardwell House (No. 15)

This mid-19th century stone-built house middle of High Street, opposite the Butcher's Arms Inn, has a grey slate roof and stands back, facing the Street. Not greatly altered outside. It had 3 acres, kept pigs and a cow and was fairly self-sufficient. There was a substantial pig-sty and run for the pigs attached to the north side of Orchard House Farm as well as a cottage on the south side. The man too kept a pig and also saw to the live-stock at Cardwell House. Hens, geese and ducks would also be kept for eggs for the house and for the pot.

The Woods lived at Cardwell House. They owned Elmfield

Farm. The two daughters later became Mrs. Ron & Mrs. Dick Robinson. Mrs. Ron lived at The Cottage and Mrs. Dick at Croft End. They built their houses on land they owned up Hoyle Croft Lane belonging to Elmfield Farm. These two were very well known Braithwell characters but were born at Ravenfield. I used to love going with mother for tea with them as a child. We always had cucumber, egg or Marmite sandwiches – we never had Marmite at home and it fascinated me! Until they died, I visited regularly and missed them both very much. Mrs. Ron lived to be 95 years of age. Mrs. Dick was very outspoken and if she thought anything was wrong, she said so in no uncertain terms. People like them kept the Village on its toes. How I wish there were more people like them in this Village today – real characters. They ran the Sunday School, the Cubs and they were both great workers for the Church which they loved.

The Foers family lived there next (the daughter married a Mollekin, builders in Maltby) and they built and lived in "The Bungalow" on Holywell Lane, later moving to Scarborough. Their daughters Mary and Norah were great friends of mine as our farm was just over the wall from them. We roamed the fields together.

Butchers Arms Land
The small children's playpark and the car park, opposite the Butcher's Arms, had pig sties all up the north side, attached to the wall round Maltkiln Farm. These were with the Butcher's Arms. This smallholding was run by the Allison's when they ran the pub..

Maltkin Farm (No. 32)
This old stone farmhouse, with buildings, is in the centre of High Street, with pantile roof and its gable end faces the street. Now much altered, as the name denotes it had a Malt House. The small one-storey building at the side of this was once a cottage then a shop, a dairy and now an out-building. This house was completely modernised in 1974 and as the name denotes it was a Malting House many years ago and a small working farm. The small cottage mentioned above which was one-up and one-down, had not yet been turned into a shop in the early 1900s – a man called Jimmy lived there and was quite a character. He came from Norfolk and always thought Yorkshire

folk were a bit "thick" (simple). He told of vegetables they grew in Norfolk – one onion and one carrot from a Norfolk garden would feed a large family for a week. And the turnips! – why, one of them would have fed all Braithwell! And sprouts – as big as banty eggs! A bit of a liar was our Jimmy and you can imagine what the locals thought of him but it never deterred his tales.

Rook House Farm (No. 29) opposite the one-time Village Store
This lovely old house faced south down the Village and had two big south-facing front rooms with ivy climbing all over the frontage. It had a bread oven by the kitchen range, a salt hole to keep salt dry and was a typical Yorkshire Farmstead. It was very picturesque but not, I suppose, to the people who lived there, as it had no mod. cons.. Part of it had once been a butcher's shop: they always called the wash-house "Top Shop."

When they thrashed here at the farm, part of the equipment used to be out on the High Street because the stacks were built in the stack yard and it was too narrow to get the thrasher and engine in. It was quite a manoeuvre and, until the first stack was out of the way, traffic practically came to a halt in High Street. Not that there was much traffic those days and as local farmers knew of this, they went up Cedar Farm track, which brought them out on Austwood Lane and then on to Doncaster or wherever. They used to try not to thrash on market days when more people were out and about to Doncaster or Rotherham. The Holmes family farmed here. Nance Holmes was a widow. Mr. Holmes I don't really remember. She had three children Nora (later Mrs. Grindle), Fred, (husband of Violet) and Marion who married and went to live in Maltby. Fred ran the farm and also worked for the council. These small farms didn't support many. They lived and farmed there with some land around the Village until the house was pulled down in about 1965. A new bungalow is now built on the site – Rook Bungalow.

Pear Tree Farm (No. 18)
A 17th. century stone-built farmhouse with outbuildings attatched. It has a red pantile roof and is two storeys with an attic. The stone-coped gable faces the street and there are Cyma recta dripmoulds to modern casement windows. The small attic window is mullioned and still filled. It has been much altered in the recent years.

The Fidler's lived here. I only vaguely remember old Mr.

Fidler but I understand he was a wonderful blacksmith and worked at the blacksmith's shop where the electricity station is now. He had two daughters, Annie and Mary and one son Albert. He (Albert) continued with the blacksmith's shop. It was a working farm with a small paddock at the back and a few fields in the area. The big field on Long Leys Lane, west side where all the bungalows and houses are, belonged to them and the grass area in front of the school was part of it. The road that goes round the back was cut in years ago and went from Micklebring Lane to Long Leys Lane – the main road to Doncaster went up Austwood Lane and turned left – this part still known as Doncaster Road. Albert Fidler still owned the Lump(ing) in front of the school. This was the soil from the road which had been heaped up years before and grass had grown over it. We played for hours there as children – it was a real children's playground. Then the Doncaster Council wanted to buy it – Albert wanted £50 and would take no less. After much negotiation the deal was done and the Lump(ing) was removed and made flat and re-seeded as Council land – now the grass area in front of the newly-built Birchwood Gardens.

One thing from my childhood I vividly remember is the mule (a cross between a mare and a donkey, neither male nor female) that Albert had. We didn't have any other mules in the area and to see it pulling the cart up the Village street was a sight indeed. Albert was the Chapel Sunday School Superintendent and, in later years, his wife Peggy played the organ at chapel. His sister Annie married Ernest Dickinson, a lovely man and lived at Fox Cottage. Albert had a vegetable round and grew his vegetables down Cockhill Field Lane. The mule pulled the cart and sometimes could be very stubborn, making Albert late home.

North View (No. 26) Church Grove (off High Street)
A 19th century farmhouse in limestone with a Welsh slate roof, the stone house called North View, on the south side of Church Lane (as it was called before it became Church Grove), was another smallholding in my grandfather's time. The stackyard was where the houses are built and also part of the old church-yard to the west was with it as an orchard. This was farmed by the Bradbury's and they sold the land off and just kept the house. Mrs. Bradbury was a real lady and Mum and I used to go for afternoon tea. It was always beautifully served with a white tablecloth with lace edge, beautiful napkins and silver tea

service and the thinnest china cups I have ever seen. I think she must have come from a very well-to-do family. They had a daughter, Marjorie, who married and lived in Maltby and a son, Willie. He left the Village and went to Canada but came back after a few years with a Canadian wife. They were all vegetarians – something we'd never heard of in the Village at that time. One of the farm men said to Dad: "Dus it mee'an the don't ait meyt? (meat)". Dad replied:

"So I understand."

"Ai, well, there's no wonder they're so bloody thin. I should think all't veg. runs right through 'em. Think of all them beans rolling round in yer stomach wi' nowt to elasticate it together. And think on tha doesn't get down-wind o' that lot, gaffer – Poooh!!!" The Bradbury's were my idea of vegetarians for years. Thin and pale with very little energy. When we kids asked what else they ate, they said nuts. We thought this very funny –

"Nuts for dinner – haa! haa!" Poor kids, we really took the mickey. How cruel children can be. Now with friends and relations who are vegetarians, I'm much more careful – although I still don't understand how anybody can make a dinner without starting with meat.

In the Village there are now still seven working farms:

Hall Farm	opposite the Cross
Cedar Farm	Holywell Lane
Orchard Farm	High Street
Ashton Farm	High Street

(These four used to be dairy farms, as were Elmfield and Low farm)

Foredoles Farm	Ashton Lane (Moor Lane)
Manor Farm	Micklebring Lane
Ridgewood Farm	Cockhill Field Lane

Old Rectory (No. 8)

Built in 1847 of stone in Victorian Gothic style and with five beautiful chimneys. The change from the Vicarage to The Rectory happened on December 6th. 1866 and was published in the London Gazette. Mrs. Ilene Foers, who lived here, gave me the following quote from an old book:

"1899: Drive onto Vicarage Lane (now Holywell Lane) and The Rectory stands in three acres of beautiful, well-laid-out garden with lovely and some very old trees including yew, unusual lime, walnut and copper beech."

I always thought the first Rectory was situated near the Church as many old residents called the farm house (which was situated where the new churchyard is) "Church Farm", although it really was Low Farm and belonged to the Earl of Scarbrough. I, along with many others, thought this must at one time have been the Rectory but having seen an old map dated 1839, it shows the rectory as being on the same land as now but with the frontage much nearer to Holywell Lane – in fact just opposite to where the old stables and carriage house used to be. The old outbuildings would be demolished as the vicar no longer had stock and corn etc. as tithes to store, since money was paid instead (1838-40). Perhaps the next Rectory was built on the site of the cowhouses, barn etc. as these would surely be well away from the house – but why so far from the Church? The vicar apparently preferred to remain secluded from his parishioners (especially when there was a diphtheria epidemic – the vicar crossed the fields to the Church so as not to pass through the infected Village). The house was surrounded by trees in open country, away from the Village and 1/4 mile from the church! Remember Holywell Lane was only a cart track then and part of Braithwell Green. In 1765, when the Inclosure of the Commons took place, land was given to the vicar in lieu of "lesser tithes" paid on Common Land. We now have a new Rectory, built in the 1950s which is approached from Micklebring Lane and which is at last in the vicinity of the Church! This land was given by the present Lord Scarbrough.

No 1. Maltby Lane (No. 11)
Was stone but now cement rendered. Two doors used to face north up the street – now changed to face south. High steep-pitched Pantile roof with slabbed eaves and the gable end faces onto Maltby Lane. The core of building could be 17th. century. Once two cottages, my godmother Nurse Mummery lived in one of them.

Club Cottage (No. 6) Holywell Lane
A 17th. century limestone cottage with stone-coped gable facing Holywell Lane. Formerly called "Greenwood Cottage" – obviously derived from its standing on what was then the Braithwell Green. The original wood-built Working Men's Club was in the garden here, hence Club Cottage. A new Club has been erected on what were the allotment gardens. This cottage

faces east and was also called East View – two up and two down. The other side of the pair was called "West View". At the end of West View's garden stood a pigsty and enclosure. West View completely altered but contributes to the Villagescape. Greenwood Cottage was one of the few buildings to be mentioned by name in the 1839 Tithe Award.

Rotherwood (No. 31) Holywell Lane
An attractive old stone house of 18th. or early 19th. century origin. Facade of ashlar. Welsh slate roof with stone-coped side elevation and two storeys, with three sash windows with flat arches. Plain front door surround and the east casement windows are surmounted by dripmoulds. The outside is not greatly altered and there is a small out-house at the back, about 17th. century, reputed to have once been a cottage one-up and one-down.

On the East side of High Street
Lion Cottage (No. 13) Nos. 1 & 2
Two small west-facing 18th. century stone cottages, situated at the bottom of the High Street, with pantiled red rooves, sash windows and now cement rendered. The cottage still retains its original character. Small enclosed garden at rear. As the name denotes, attached to the Red Lion Inn. Stone inside uncovered with the date 1751. John Snipe, the schoolmaster who helped with the Village Inclosure lived here.

Nrs 35, 37 & 39 (No. 17)
Row of three south-facing stone-built cottages. Early 18th. century, possibly with earlier core. Pantile rooves, pebbledashed and with modern windows and gable end to the street. Originally they had a shared wash house and pump with an outside toilet in the gardens to the east.

No 41 (No. 23)
Early 19th. century. As with most of the stone cottages in the Village, this could have been built in the 18th. century. Limestone, ashlar with a red pantile roof it lies behind Rose Cottage.

Once The Village Shop and House (No. 33)
Large plain frontage, age unknown but perhaps of early 19th. century origin. It has a central door and casement windows and there is a mounting block in the yard. Once owned by the Clarkson

family and the building at the back was once a stocking factory. The Clarkson family name crops up in most of the old literature on Braithwell. Charlotte Clarkson was my grandmother.

Fox House Cottage (No. 20)
Small stone cottage facing High Street, gable-end facing north, it lies on the corner of High Street and Austwood Lane. Two rooms upstairs and two downstairs. Once the farm cottage to Fox House Farm. Originally limestone and pantile, it is now rendered and completely renovated.

Nailor's Cottage (No. 19)
Situated north of Austwood Lane facing High Street and opposite Fox House Cottage. It was completely cement rendered but this has been removed from the front elevation and the old stone frontage exposed and repointed. Probably 17th. or early 18th. century, it is likely to have been a single-storey building with an attic and is reputed to have once been a nail-maker's cottage. It has now been completely restored.

Forge Cottage (No. 24)
Probably 17th. or early 18th. century. South-facing with gable end to the street, the original building has been pebble-dashed. Pantile roof with Yorkshire sash windows in the upper storey, this was once a single-storey building with an attic and to the rear was a large open yard and orchard.

CHAPTER 25

Gone But Not Forgotten

Unfortunately, many old houses and shops have been demolished over the years – dates are given.

1934 Cardwell House Cottage off High Street
This was up Cardwell House drive.

1937 Butcher's Arms Cottage off High Street
This was a stone cottage attached to the south wall of the

Butcher's Arms Inn and the stone wall on the north side of the hairdresser's shop was the frontage. The garden of this small dwelling is still there. Mr. Billy Marshall and his wife, daughter Dorothy and son John (always known as Jonka) Marshall lived there. His smallholding was between Orchard Farm and Ashton Farm.

1937 The "Alley Houses" off High Street
Four very small stone cottages three facing south and built onto the south wall of the Village Store, one to the north on the wall of Rose Cottage on the opposite side to the others. I don't suppose any of those living here thought of it as the good old days.

1937 Moat Hall Holywell Lane
In 1934 when I used to visit the Crawshaw's at Moat Hall it was an interesting place. It was reputed to have cellars underneath leading to Roche Abbey and Conisbrough Castle

1950 Manor Farm Cottage Micklebring Lane
A small farm cottage which was on the south side of Micklebring lane and east of the Manor House set back into the wall. The blocked door still remains. The Parkin family lived there. The daughters Alice and Phyllis did the milk round for Mr. Leonard Waterhouse of Low Farm. When it was demolished the family moved to Laughton.

1954 Low Farm up Church Grove facing south
Most Villagers referred to this as "Church Farm". Owned by Lord Scarbrough who gave this land to the Church – the new churchyard and new Rectory are in what were the grounds and fold yard.

1962 Dam Cottage off Holywell Lane
Across the meadows and the dam, this was reached by the gate to Moat Hall, turning right. Known also as "Wild Duck Cottage" this would originally have been the home of the keeper of the dam. The last family to live there were the Dimbleby's.

1967 2 small stone cottages Doncaster Road
On the land where Lansing House is now built, the cottages were demolished after being condemned although the present owner of Lansing House dearly wanted to buy and convert

them at the time. Miss. Little and Mrs. Dent lived there. They were sisters and Miss. Little did tailoring.

1968 Rook House Farm High Street opposite the one-time Village Store

1974 Ruddle Mill House Ruddle Mill Lane
The original House to the Ruddle Mill is now a derelict building by the Mill but a new brick house had been built on land higher up. This was flattened by the quarry owners who bought Ruddle Mill House and land because they didn't want any complaints from the people who would have lived there about noise, dust, traffic etc.. A crying shame to this day. The old mill is now derelict too – sad to see it go, it was part of our heritage.

A lot of these houses were destroyed when the first council houses were built in Ashton Lane in 1937 and people from these were re-housed. These houses really helped the village-scape of Braithwell but the residents were pleased to move to new council houses up Ashton Lane with electric light and hot water on tap and bathrooms. Some people of course moved away from the Village to new jobs. The Bailey's from Cardwell Cottage and the Parkins' from Manor Cottage; the landlords then took the opportunity of knocking them down. The Holmes', the Greens, the Grimwoods, the Pettys, the Lucas', the Wards, the Marshalls, the Franklands – all old Village families moved from old to new accommodation. Some still live here today.

Red Lion and Butcher's Arms
The Old Red Lion and Butcher's Arms were pulled down in the early 1900s to rebuild when the Pit came to Maltby – obviously to accommodate the new people coming to the area. Dominoes darts and cribbage were played there a lot then and are still part of Village life today. It's still a regular night out for some of the locals as it was all those years ago. The Landlord of the Red Lion was Mr. Crowcroft. He owned the field where the allotments were and the new bungalows and Club are. He sold it to the council for allotments. The other land which borders the Rectory with housing (Holywell Crescent) was considered for building the new school in 1926 – he owned this too.

Pinfold (No. 27) north of Lion Cottage, lower High Street, south of The Poplars

Small square grass area with limestone wall round. Used as a pound or pinfold for stray animals. There was a Pound Master (Pinder) who fetched in straying animals, put them in the pound and charged the owners before they could get them out – when the Open Field system was in force, stray animals were a problem and could cause a lot of damage. There was a rope kept there for the Pinder's use called a choke rope. It is mentioned in the Parish Minutes that in the early 1800s: "Mrs Fisher – from Foredoles – hasn't returned it and she must be told to do so." This Pinfold unfortunately has been lost to the Parish.

On the High Street

1. In the middle of the High Street there was a small shop. It stands out on the pavement next to the Darby and Joan house. Miss Bailey lived at no. 27 and ran this very small shop as a general store.

2. Small Building on the west side. In the yard of Maltkiln Farm. This was a greengrocers shop in my childhood but before that had been a house. It was later used as a dairy by Randal Allison who lived at the farm. It is now a storeplace. The shop was first run by Miss Padgett, then the Gooch family.

3. Just a bit higher at No. 29, on the east side, was the Post Office, news agents and sweet shop. Mr. George Brooks had this and he delivered the papers in the Village and in Micklebring and Clifton on his 'bike. His two daughters, Sheila and Catherine were great friends of mine and went to school with us.

4. Higher up the Village at No. 49 on the east side was The Village Store. Then run by Mr Travis and his very pretty wife. They were a kind, mild and gentle couple but had no family and didn't mix much at all in the Village. He was one of the first men in the Village to have a car. A Ford.

5. At the top of the Village on Doncaster Road as now where the Post Office is was another General Store – just remember very few people travelled outside the Village for their groceries etc., so these shops all survived and made a good living. Mrs. Edwards had this shop, followed by Mr & Mrs Goodman (parents of Faith Houghton). He was a local chapel preacher and very good too. This is still going strong

– Post Office, General Store and Newspapers.
6. **Fish & Chip Shop at No. 23** (now the Hairdressers) This is one of the oldest buildings in the Village. It is a "cruck cottage", extremely rare in this area. It was 1-up, 1-down and before it was a hairdresser's, it was the Village fish & chip shop – for a youngster in the 1930s this was the centre of Village life...... ah!....happy days!
7. **Austwood Lane Slaughterhouse & Butcher's Shop** Where the new farm complex is now lived Jim Parkes and family. All the Village people bought meat from him. They had their own slaughterhouse and made sausage, pork pies, savoury duck etc..

Many of the Villagers tell me of working or helping in the slaughterhouse. Beasts were brought in and fastened by a short rope to a hook in the wall. The butcher would then down it with a pole axe (like a sledge hammer with a spike on it) and then cut its throat. There was then beef for all Braithwell. Now, of course, a humane killer is used. In 1933 new rules stated butchers couldn't kill without a licence. Up to that period anybody could kill. A little while later the humane killer became compulsory making the Pole Axe illegal. Very few slaughterhouses now exist outside abbatoirs. Although, luckily, we do have one in nearby Wadworth, run by the Slack brothers and used by local farmers. The Butcher's Shop went too, in 1980, due to supermarkets. The shop and slaughterhouse are now converted to houses.

Ruddle Mill
This old mill at Braithwell was built around 1790. Agreement signed 1792 Millers Book 1804. This mill operated on a simple principle – the water rises at Holywell Spring then runs under the road and across the field to the main dam which is beyond Birkwood Terrace houses. This water was then diverted by a race which ran through the small wood (in my youth full of primroses daffodils and bluebells) where the water flowed through a stone-lined culvert, remains of which can still be seen today, then in a swirling, churning froth to the wheel at Ruddle Mill. Ruddle was still milled there in the 1800s – the red ruddle colour's still on the walls. The water then continued under the road on Ruddle Mill Lane and on down the side of Chapel Hole Lane (Granny Grindle's Lane) into Stainton etc.. In many vil-

lages the miller was not allowed to keep stock – in fact only one cockerel and three hens for his own use. All geese, pigs, ducks etc. were forbidden him because of the chance of cheating with the corn. This old mill in Braithwell was eventually used as a corn mill by all the farmers and was still working in the early 1900s but I don't know when it eventually finished. When it closed, the farmers took their corn to Roche Abbey and it was milled at Brown's Mill Farm, Roche Abbey.

The Ruddle Pit
The mineral called Ruddle, or Raddle, is obtained near Micklebring, a hamlet in the parish of Braithwell, near Doncaster. A shaft is sunk of about twenty-three feet in depth, and five in diameter, which passes through strata of limestone and gritstone, and immediately under this last the ruddle is imbedded universally in clay, which is three feet thick above and below the vein. It lies nearly horizontal, and is generally about nine inches in thickness. The miner in working sits down and uses a short sharp axe, similar to that of the lead miner. He excavates to the distance of about four yards from the centre of the shaft; but, as the clay cannot be easily supported, as soon as he has reached this distance, a new shaft is sunk near to the other. The ruddle was carried from Micklebring in carts to a mill (Ruddle Mill, Braithwell), where it is ground to a powder; then mixed with water and ground afresh, and afterwards let off into a reservoir, where the ruddle subsides, and the water is evaporated. It is afterwards cut into small squares, packed up in casks, and sent to Hull and London, from the port at Bawtry (this gives some idea of the date!), whence it is exported for polishing spectacle lenses to Holland and America. I understand ruddle is found in only one other place near Bristol, very near the surface, which injures the more expensive preparation of it here. This substance is used by carpenters for marking their timber and for Ruddling sheep, colouring tiles and doorsteps and windowsills. Tups are raddled on the chest. When the ewe has been served, the raddle is left on her rump showing that she is hopefully in lamb. Ruddle was also used in the manufacture of paint used for the painting of carts and waggons. A substitute was later found and the pits closed in the early part of the first World War. Many fields in the area are called Ruddle Pit Shut – obviously all at one time used for the purpose of mining Ruddle, or Raddle as it was known locally.

A book on the Ruddle Pit has been written by Mr. Douglas Haigh of Maltby.

Advertised in 1894: "Corn Mill for Sale, Still in Operation". Doncaster Gazette 13th. November 1812
.   RUDDLE MILL – RUDDLE LANE
   Colour Mill and Manufactory. To be let . . . newly erected stone building now used as a colour mill for grinding red ochre or ruddle, plentifully supplied with water . . . . situated at Braithwell . . . . with all neccessary *(sic)* and convenient machinery, outbuildings and appurtenances thereto . . . . now in the occupation of Messrs Gleadall and Co..

The Mineral is procured near to the manufactroy *(sic)* and a plentiful supply may be had at a price to be agreed on. The mineral is only to be found near the manufactory and at one other place in England. Enquiries to Messrs Gleadall and Co, Micklebring

❧

CHAPTER 26

When I see a little church, I always call and visit
So when I'm carried in the Lord won't say: "Who is it?"

The Church of St. James
There have been many alterations to the church. The only original part is the carved tympanum over the south-facing door. The original shape of the Cross was lost when the tower was moved to the west end of the church in the 15th. century.

It is said that the marerial for building the church was left overnight, ready to start, on the south side of the Village. This was on the corner of Holywell Lane by The Hawthorns – almost equal distance between Moat Hall and Lambcote Grange. Next day these materials, to the amazement of the men, had moved to the top of the Village *so* there they built it – where the church stands today. In the place where the materials had been left, a spring gushed up. Still there today and known as the Holywell "Spring."

Taken from Listed Buildings, 1960s
DESCRIPTION   REMARKS
1. Church   St. James. Late 12th. or early 13th. century
             14th. century aisle, perpendicular west tower
             Late Norman south doorway with carved
             tympanum
             1828 south porch with wall sundial
             1845 chancel rebuilt by the 8th. Earl of
             Scarbrough
             Monuments, early panels let into pulpit

Notes from Braithwell Parish Register 1559 to 1774
1619 Dec 21st
Anne Daughter of Edwarde Cuttenfurthaie alias Sheephearde
(Did the people of Braithwell find it a strange name to pro-
nounce and make up their own name? It sounds strongly like a
Breweller's way to me – or was he a bit thick?)

1632/33 Jan 29th
John son of Marie Fretwell begotten upon her bie Daniell
Grotte – gent

1635 August 12th
John the bastarde of Marie Poole – the nominated father
Vincent Waterhouse (Why are these two boys' fathers described
so differently – did one confess & one not?)

In Charles II's reign it was considered fashionable to be
dressed in ornamental linen shrouds. In the interest of the
woollen trade, which was declining, this was forbidden and in
1666 woollen shrouds were the order by law. Before burial, a
certificate was issued saying this law had been complied with
and two witnesses had to sign the register to certify same –
sometimes just a 'X' beside the witness' name as most people
couldn't read or write – often the women who laid out the body.
Many instances of this are in the church registers of our Village.
It was also the custom for a virgin's coffin to be preceded by
two maidens in white – carrying a round wooden willow hoop
completely covered by a garland of fresh flowers made into a
ring with a white glove in the centre. This was hung up in
church and left until it decayed. Sometimes the age and initials
of the girl were on a paper amongst the flowers. In later years

paper flowers were substituted.

There was an old belief that the east side was God's side, the south the side of the spirits made just, the west the man's side and the north where you didn't get buried if you could help it.

"A tenier of all ye glebe lands, tithes, stipendiary payments, ye other ecclasiastical *(sic)* dues and profits, whatsoever, belonging to ye vicarage of Braithwell in ye years 1746, comprises a vicarage house containing three layes of buildings, one stable and cow house, four layes, one garden orchard and croft, one acre, all ye tythes of Braywell and Mickelbring except corn tythes, all manner of tythes in the hamlet of Bramley. Marriages publishing one shilling, consummating and registering 2 shillings and sixpence, married with liecnce 10 shillings, Burials in ye quire within ye rails, 13.4d without ye rails 10/-d. and on any other parts 6/8d. Burials in churchyard 1/-; if covered with stone and lettered 3/4d. Register and bookkeeping five shillings, a copy making and sending to York one shilling. Holds one shilling, pigeons in hand or to ye value of ye coat mortuaries; all persons in ye parish dying worth 40 pounds clear when their debts are paid 10/-; if thirty pounds 3/6d. Wool in hand, Lambs in kind or sheep in lamb, ye common lands, ye enclosed, according to value. Churchings, one shilling.".

It was always the custom in this Village that after the birth of a baby the mother was "churched". This was a form of cleansing, I always understood. This service took place as soon as possible after the birth of the child. Even when my son David was born in 1959, this was still the practice in this Village. When I returned from hospital, I had to visit the church on my way home and say a prayer of thanks. Otherwise my mother and her friends wouldn't have liked me to visit their homes with my son. Later I went through the churching service from the prayer book.

May the 30th 1746 A Bill of Charges for going to York with the Man who Broke in the Church and Stole the Silver Chalice

Paid Joseph Newton for ale	0	3	6
Paid att (sic) Doncaster Turnpike	0	0	8
Paid att Wentbridge for ale	0	0	8
Paid att Ferrybridge where we lay att night	0	8	9
Att the Turnpike att Ferrybridge	0	0	3
Att another Turnpike	0	0	3

Att Tadcaster for Ale and Turnpike	0	0	9
Att York Castle a receipt and ale	0	0	10
Where we put up or horses and baited[1]	0	3	9
Where we lay att night at Sherborne as we came back	0	5(7?)	6
Ferry bridge turnpike as we came back	0	0	3
Where we baited as we came back att the Red house	0	3	9
Doncaster Turnpike as we came back	0	0	3
For ale when we tooke *(sic)* the Man and had him in Hold att John Jacksons	0	4	6
For G^{eo}: Thompson for going to York with the Mann for 3 daies*(sic)*	0	3	0
Robert Rogers Ditto	0	3	0
Myself for going to York Ditto	0	0	3
For one of Robert Rogers Horses and 2 of my own 4 shillings a piece	0	12	6*(sic)*
For a Dormant Warrant	0	2	0
For his Mittimap Makeing *(sic)*	0	3(?)	0
[1] ate, fed	2	15	1

If this chalice was returned as seems likely, where is it now? Our chalice is of much later date.

Copy of Terrier dated 15th June 1786 (Old Rectory, Holywell Lane)

The vicarage house consisteth of 3 bays of Building which contain 4 low rooms namely the House, the Hall, the Parlour and the back kitchen, over the house Hall and Parlour are three chambers and two garrets and over the back kitchen is another chamber the whole house is built with slate and tile.

The outhouses are one stable consisting of one bay of Building with a hay chamber over it. One Barn, one Cowhouse and some small outhousing. The barns and stable are built with lime and stone and covered with Tile, the Cow house is built with lime and stone and covered with thatch.

The Glebelands are one church yard which is fenced by a wall and contains by estimation one acre more or less. One garden, orchard croft and Foldstead or yard adjoining the vicarage mentioned orchard and croft all which said several parcels of ground together except the churchyard are bounded on the east and North by the High Rd on the West and South by the ground of Joshua Birks.

Rectory 1843

Mortgage for building the New Rectory was £800. "This money to be laid out and expended in re-building the parsonage house and other necessary offices upon the Glebe Land belonging to the Church." The Rectory was started in 1843 and finished in 1845 for the Rev Robert Cope Wolfe. He was vicar for eight years and died here in 1851. In church the Lectern was a gift from Miss Wolfe in 1885 in memory of her brother Robert.

Copy of Terrier dated 19th May 1857 (New Rectory, Holywell Lane)

The vicarage house consists of three bays of buildings with seven low rooms viz. Dining room and drawing room, Library, two kitchens, the Hall and Pantry. Over the these are six chambers. The pantry, hall and kitchens are floored with flags. The other low rooms are floored with deal boards and ceiled with lath and plaster.

The chambers are floored with deal boards and ceiled with laths and lime. Over the chamber are two garrets with boarded floors and covered with slate.

The outhouses Are one stable with hay chamber over it which is 17' square without the walls built with stone and lime and covered with tiles, one carriage house in length 31ft, in breadth 10ft without the walls covered with tiles and built with stone and lime.

Micklebring Oct. 30. 1866
To the Right Honourable the Earl of Scarbro'
My Lord

I beg most respectfully to inform Your Lordship that the Stove put into the Chancel of Braithwell Church by Your Lordship's late Agent (M^{srs} Etkison?) is worn out and entirely useless, and the old Air Flue in the body of the Church is in the same state. We propose to have two new stoves to heat the whole Church in lieu of the old Flue &^{tc} – and as the parishoners are very poor having most of them lost their cattle by the Rinderpest we find it impossible to raise the money by a Church Plate; we therefore propose to raise 15£ by Subscription for the purpose; and we most humbly ask Your Lordship either to put us a small Stove into the Church or to give us a subscripn.

towards the purchase of the two hoping Your Lordship will take the necessity of the case as a sufficient reason for troubling Your Lordship,

I remain your

Lordship's humble and obedient

Servant EDWARD SPENCER

Churchwarden

Things never change – text of letter to Lord Scarbrough 1869:

Braithwell

March 5/69

Dear Sir/

I am equally surprised with the Earl of Scarbrough at the insignificant sums which the inhabitants of Braithwell offer to the House of God, partly no doubt owing to the influence of Methodism. His Lordship's £5- which he has kindly promised for which in the name of the Committee I thank him, Giving(?) some £4- to the parish are approached only by a few shillings by some whose Church Rates was more than £2- Such however seems to be the working of the Voluntary System. It is my intention as his Lordship suggests to apply to other owners of property in the Township.

I presume his Lordship intends the Donation he has kindly promised to be an Annual Subscription as the wants of the parish Church will yearly be the same. I am dear Sir/

Yours faithfully

JAMES REECE

A vicar of note at Braithwell was Christopher Hodgson. He became vicar in 1871 and continued until 1891. His son wrote the book "The Happy Cricketer" which, of course, is about cricket but tells a lot about Braithwell and the Rectory and tells of the cricket field which was where the playing field is now – this seems very strange because it has been on several different fields in the intervening years.

In 1896 the church was in debt for £200. They held a cake and apron stall on November 25th. and 26th. from 2pm – 10pm. Refreshments were served and teas were 1/- each.

Presumably all the Village ladies made cakes and aprons for sale. The school of course was closed for this – the usual procedure when money needed raising.

In 1897 organ blower got   10/- a year (50p)
In 1898 communion wine cost   8/9d
In 1899 Mr. Harper was organist at £5 per annum

In 1897 Lord Scarbrough received a request from the Rev. Seed to provide money for a Village Tea to commemorate the Diamond Jubilee of Queen Victoria. Lord Scarbrough replied he thought the Village could provide their own tea. (I should think so too cheeky beggars). He commemorated this Jubilee by restoring the chancel in the church.

In the early 1900s the Scarbrough's sent a cheque for £5 every year:-

£1 for the Sunday School
£1 for choir children
£3 for the sick and poor

In 1905 the Rev. Seed again wrote to the Scarbrough estate asking for money for the poor. A husband had left his wife and three children and gone abroad. She was destitute and quite a lady – he said. He needed 5/- to give her as all the available charity money had been given out to the poor and needy. Lord Scarbrough again obliged.

The "new" churchyard was extended in 1908 – this is the land down the steps opposite the church door. The land for this was bought from Mr. Bradbury and Mrs. Ward Fox. Mr Bradbury lived up Church Lane at North View and Mrs. Ward Fox owned Pear Tree Farm. Several parishioners gave donations towards this as the church hadn't the money to buy it. I presume they were threatened with nowhere to be buried if they didn't comply. The contributions ranged from £6 to 1/-.

I am pleased to say my grandfather gave a guinea (£1 – 1s – 0d) and now rests in that part of the churchyard. The monies came to £69 – 8s – 6d.

1910 The communion rails from church were sold for £2. Mr. Seed was the vicar here at the time.

In **1935** Church Army missionaries came to the Village. We youngsters really enjoyed their stay here and we became really keen on religion. They were two bright and keen young men. They had a caravan parked in the drive or the old Church

144

School House (where the doctors' surgery is now). We visited them and learnt songs, poems and prayers. One of the poems was:

Jesus is the sunshine of my heart
Jesus is the sunshine of my heart
Joy and peace eternal he does impart
Jesus is the sunshine of my heart

We sang "Tell me the story of Jesus." and "Gentle Jesus Meek and Mild.".

On Sundays, children attended either church or chapel. I always attended both – my father was a Methodist and my mother C. of E. I always thought I had the best of both worlds. Two lots of trips to the seaside, two Easter and Harvest Teas, Chapel School Anniversary and Church Flower Service and both Harvest Festivals – keeping a foot in both camps!

The Law in early times meant Church Law, Church Charity. Poor law meant helping the poor through the church, schooling was church schooling. The church and vicar took first place in the Village and Village life revolved round them.

The church Bells – the voice of the Village heralding services, weddings, funerals and, years ago, mid-day – for farm workers to return home for dinner. Also for a death at whatever time of day or night. The ringing of the bell for a death was supposed in Pagan times to help the souls of the dead to heaven and drive away the devil. Pagan customs were hard to abandon. Death bells were rung nine times for a man, six for a woman and three for a child. It was always said in our Village if a woman died: "If it (the churchyard) opens for a she, it opens for three." How often have we seen this – Pagan too I suppose, or superstition – but still we have seen it happen here.

George Jackson, the Village bell-ringer was fetched from the Butcher's Arms one cold winter night to ring the passing bell six times – as he rang, he saw a vision of the old lady who had died standing in the church doorway. He was so frightened he hung onto the bell in sheer terror. As it clanged loud and clear on the frosty air, the fellow revellers coming from the pub dashed up to see what was amiss. Poor old George was white as the ghost himself and they had to take him home and lock up the church. He never rang the passing bell again late at night. This custom still went on for may years but only in the day-time. In 1892 it was 6/6d per quarter for ringing the bells at lunch time. At one period, the headmaster did it – he often trained one of the elder boys to do the job. I don't know if he shared the money. This still happened up until the second world war.

Another custom – brides used to have flowers strewn in their path as they walked to church and they always went up Church Lane (not Grove then), as there were no cars to block the way of the horse and trap. The last time this happened was for Mr. Dyson's daughter from the Manor in the late 1800s she would of course come through the side gate from the Manor directly into the churchyard.

Many of the church customs came from Pagan days – Harvest Festival for instance. The Harvest was gathered in and a corn dolly was made and brought home on the last load. Then there was Harvest Supper – feasting and drinking in the farm barn. It was decided by the church authorities to turn this festivity into a Harvest Festival in church. They still had the harvest supper but it was after the church service and not after the last load of corn – no drinking either.

No work was ever done on farms on Sundays. Farmers wouldn't allow their animals and men to work. Only when the tractors came did they succumb to the necessity of getting in the hay and the harvest on the Lord's Day – and this was wartime that brought the change, when more home-grown food was needed. A cowman, horseman and shepherd, of course, had to work Sundays with their stock to feed and cows to milk. When a shepherd died, they always put some sheep's wool in his hand to show the Lord why he hadn't always attended church so regularly.

We always had a flower festival at church in July. We took flowers either in bunches or baskets. It was a great day for the children – new dresses, and shoes. It was always a hot day, as I remember. We sang children's hymns – "Gentle Jesus, meek and mild" "There's a friend for little children" "Loving Shepherd of thy sheep". We all loved it and looked forward to it for weeks.

The Bosviles

In the middle of the aisle is a flat Tombstone in good state of preservation bearing the following inscription, translated from the Latin:

"Here lies Thomas Bosvile son of Jasper Bosvile of Stainton (Gent) who was buried April 15th 1631 likewise his son & heir Thomas Bosvile buried February 6th 1665 Likewise

146

Thos. Bosvile his son & heir vicar of this church for 36 years buried Mar 1st 1673 in the 62nd year of his age all hoping for a better resurrection. This monument for his father's sake & memory has been set up by Thos. Bosvile his heir & successor this Thomas having for 38 yrs served the parish as its faithful pastor here fell asleep with his father this May 24th 1711 leaving 10 surviving children. Beside him lies the body of his beloved wife Elizabeth who died Aug 10th 1719 in her 72nd year.".

Thomas Bosvile 1644–1711

Thomas Bosvile Junior was vicar of Braithwell from September 1674 to May 1711. He married Elizabeth Hatfield on July 13th. 1669. They had 12 children – 10 survived him.

1	Thomas (junior)	Baptised April 22nd 1670
2	Alexander	March 26th 1672
3	Jasper	July 2nd 1674 born 17th June
4	Margaret	August 24th 1676 born August 4th
5	John	August 13th 1678 born July 28th betwixt 7 and 8 at night
6	Elizabeth	June 22nd 1680 born June 4th
7	Nicholas	August 30th 1682 born August 23rd 3 or 4 minutes past noon
8 &9	Hugo & Anthony (twins)	May 15th 1684 (Anthony died)
10	Rhoda	July 17th 1686 died Sept 16th. 1686
11	Antonia	December 22nd 1687
12	Alicia	July 1st 1690 born June 13th.

John Guy

Also, at the western end of Church yard, is the grave of John Guy

> "If you question who here doth lie
> I answer the body of the noted John Guy
> Born 1704
> Died 1789"

said to be as odd a fish as ever lived. He was Sexton of Braithwell for many years. Soldier and general good fellow is how he is described. He enrolled in the army and served against Charles Edward Stuart. When he went to war with Gen. Wade in 1744, he hid his money under a rock at Chapel Holes. When he returned his money was still there. He often related tales of war and was very popular.

147

Quote from "Hatfield Village Sketches" 1849

"Not being content with the simple answer to the question given by the survivors, we found out, as we had anticipated from enquiry, that John Guy was an odd a fish as ever lived. To whom dame fortune had not been liberal with her gifts, and stern necessity compelled him to join the encampment at Wheatley Hills of six thousand English and German troops, under the command of Field Marshall Wade in 1744. He protested, but there was no alternative, he must go, and act against the Chevalier of the Scottish Rebellion. He pleaded time, and a momentary absence, on his promise of returning was granted. He set to work immediately and scraped up all the gns. shillings and pence even to a farthing, he had in world, in order to secret *(sic)* them in the cleft of a rock, known as Chapel Holes, a spot cordoning on the Parish of Braithwell, as subsequently transfixed on return. Nothing daunted he walked to Doncaster, escorted by the Redcoats, and found the town was all alive with noise and bustle, and as the sound of the drums, beating, for recruits, fell on his ears, he flattered himself he was on the road to fame. Shortly afterwards he was conducted before the chief magistrate, Richard Whitake, Esq. and was formally enrolled into His Majesty's Service. To describe his vicissitudes and the life of real enjoyment of Guy, who was the very soul of fun, would be more than our limits allow, suffice to say that on the 21st. of October, he left Doncaster en route to Newcastle with the British and Dutch Infantry.

The march inspired him with great determination to do honour to the reign of King George Second, but his sojourn at that enterprising shipping place was only for a short duration, as the approach of Prince Charles' army into England caused General Wade again to advance into Yorkshire, in consequence of a report that the Highlanders were moving into Derbyshire, He was at Wheatley on the 4th and marching towards Doncaster on the 5th. The alarm turned out to be a mere ruse of the enemy, but Wade, nevertheless, took his position in the very centre of the County. On the 12th of December, Guy formed one of the body of horse which General Wade sent to reinforce the Ducke *(sic)* of Cumberland, advancing over Clanchstone edge, to intercept the retiring host. They

148

however, only reached Preston several hours after it had been evacuated, but it was in time to see the closing scene of the venerable Gardiner – a man who, perhaps combined in his single character, all the attributes which steel has give a Christian soldier. He was then placed in the ranks under General Hawley, and was present at the remarkable battle of Falkirk. This constituted the epoch of his life, and was in his afterdays, the chief topic of his conversation, for it brought out his intrepidility and boldness. If there is any reliance to be placed on his version of the matter, he was as valiant as most of them in the battlefield, and it was only by dint of courage that he escaped from the merciless hands of the Highlanders. He described it as being fought under extraordinary dense mist and that they could hardly distinguish one object from another. The issue of that battle is so well known as to require no further observation. It was however, fully retrieved at the battle of Culloden. This single victory, which showed the emptiness of the expressions of the chivalrous Prince Charles "In a few days" said he at the commencement of the campaign "With a few friends I have I will raise the Royal Standard and proclaim that Charles Stuart has come over to claim the crown of his ancestors, to win it, or to perish in the attempt", – was achieved on the 16th of April at the cost of more than 3 000 of the most valiant men Scotland ever produced. But to return to Guy, on his return John, as may be imagined, who was no little elated with his own valour, and told romantic tales of his Scottish enemies, frequently said – "Dang it, they fought like tigers".

Guy, after all was a great man on his day, and at the village festival was looked upon as a star of the first magnitude. On his return, his first object was Chapel Holes Rocks, and there to his great delight found all as safe as he had left it. In addition to his exploits in Scotland, he had attained considerable notoriety as Parish Sexton, and during the period that he held that situation, like all the rest of mortals, John was frequently crossed in his temper, and when beaten in argument and his metal fairly aroused, he generally turned round and with a sneer said "Some day or other before I die, I shall have you in my Park".

He was the last Sexton for the Parish of Braithwell, as the duties of that office were combined with Parish Clerk.

The best that can be said of John Guy the Sexton is that he was an honest man and never nursed revenge, though to be sure he had a warm temperament."

There was always a Garden Party at the Rectory in summer and a lovely day it was with sideshows and a pig for a prize at either darts or bowls. In later years, this was held at Croft End, Hoyle Croft Lane – home of Mr. and Mrs. Richard Robinson.

Harvest Festival was also a big occasion for the Church and Harvest Supper was held in the Old School, which was a church school. Here we had dances, whist drives etc.. It was a sad day when it had to be sold as the land was given to the Village and the Village people told me they raised the money to extend it. When the church commissioners decided to sell it, the money went to them. We fought to change this but we lost the battle – and the money!

Each year two Churchwardens were chosen and they were sworn in on Easter Tuesday. One was the Vicar's Warden and the other the People's Warden. They had many duties and these often overlapped those of both the Overseers of the Poor and the Village Constable. Nevertheless, their main duty was the upkeep of the Church and its property. Their accounts are brief, repetitive and in many cases just state the amount paid and to whom but, occasionally, they throw an interesting light upon life in the Village at that time.

From 1717 to 1734 the accounts are kept in the Township Accounts Book which also houses the Vestry Minutes. In 1717 we learn of a new south window being purchased:

"21ft. of square glass   12s. 0d.
  16 ft. leaded and 8ft. more of new glass   7s. 4d."

In 1721 two new north windows were purchased at a cost of 17s. 8d. – the Church windows, according to the accounts, seem to have been in almost constant repair!

An idea of the cost of printed books is given when, in 1719, it was reported that a "Church Common Prayer Book" was purchased for 14s. 0d. and in 1792 there is a note of a new Church Bible being bought for 5 guineas.

The accounts for 1724 detail the costs for the painting of the "King's Arms" (which still hangs in the Church):
"Pd. to James Winder, painter, for drawing ye
    Kings Arms   £4. 7s. 6d.
to joiner for Church door, Kings Arms,

| Communion rails & floor laying | 2. 9s. 5d. |
| for beam supporting Kings Arms and fetching | 7s. 2d." |

As well as the Kings Arms there must have been other "boards" on the Church wall:

19th. October 1771:

"paid for ale and setting Commandments up ..... for taking
Commandments down and putting up on Church   2s. 9d.
..... for cleaning they Commandments mending
them ...... finding board and a quart of oyl to oyl them
...... and the Coat of Arms oyling   9s. 6d."

(A bill from Richard Gleadhill).

As mentioned in the constable's reports, the Church bells were used to celebrate events of national importance:

13th. May 1794 ".... paid for ringing at the
Duke of York's victory over the Republicans   3s. 0d."

8th. October 1797 "... paid to ringers for victory over the Duch"

Bells and bell ropes were in constant need of repair and replacement. An interesting entry in 1748 tells of the bells being re-hung:

".... paid for men to help take the bells down
 and put up again   2s. 0d.
 .... to ale for their drinkins ... 17 quarts   3s. 4d.

On February 12th. 1820 the entry reads:

".. for anging little bell   3s. 6d.
 .. for ale when hanging little bell   3s. 6d."

Perhaps if we provided ale now we should get more help in church!

George III's illness caused concern and an entry for 6th. June 1830 simply says: "paid postage for prayer for the King 1s. 6d."

The records show that on 21st. May 1831, the Vestry celebrated the Coronation of the new King (George IV) "to ale, spirits, and tobacco at the King's proclamation £1.7s.6d."

The inside of the Church must have been whitewashed regularly. There are numerous entries which deal with loads of lime. In 1787 and entry reads:

".... a sack of lime to whitewash the Church   1s. 0d.
 .... Church whitewashing .. ale at same time   £1. 2s. 6d."

In 1830 comes the last of the entries. It is a large bill for stoves to provide heating for the Church. The Bill is from G. & J. Lee of Rotherham:

2 Church stoves	4.	0.	0.
Cast metal pipes	7.	8.	4.
Fitting & labour	3.	12.	6.
Total cost	15.	0.	10.

The Terrier was an inventory of all church lands and possessions and it was written annually and presented at the Bishop's (or his representative's) annual "visitation". The Churchwardens' accounts show that in the 1780s the schoolmaster was given 10s. 6d. for writing the document. Needless to say, the Churchwardens took this annual inspection very seriously and the accounts show that the guest was treated well. One example (of three in existence) of a bill submitted by a local innkeeper:

"Visitation Bill 1813 ... to William Jackson, Churchwarden

To eating	£1. 15s. 0d.
To malt, liquor & tobacco	7s. 6d.
To horses, hay and corn	4s. 4d.
To wine etc.	£1. 13s. 6d.
To servants	5s. 0d.
	£4. 5s. 4d."

As part of his visitation in 1743, Archbishop Herring sent out a questionnaire to each Parish. These are to be found in a bound volume at the Borthwick Institute, York.

Sample questions (of 11):

1. What numbers of families have you in your Parish? Of these, how many are dissenters? And of what sort are they?

Ans. Families – fifty two. Dissenters – not one!

7. Do you know any who come to Church in your Parish who are not Baptised? Or, that being Baptised and of competent age are unconfirmed?

Ans. I know not of any unbaptised person who comes to Church, nor any of a competent age unconfirmed

9. How often do you catechise in your Church? Do your Parishoners *(sic)* duly send their children and servants who have not learned their catechism to be instructed by you?

Ans. I catechise in the Lenten season, sometimes of a year. Parishoners *(sic)* duly send their children, but their servants seldom give me ye opportunity.

11. Do you give open and timely warning of the Sacrement

(sic) before it is administered? Do your Parishoners send in their names to you as required? Have you refused the Sacrement to anyone? For what reason, and how has the person so refused behaved himself since then?

Ans. I give open and timely warning of the Sacrament before it is administered. But none send in their names except at the first time of ye receiving it, and I have not yet refused Sacrament to anyone above the age of sixteen.

In one of the earliest balance sheets (1735) the entry reads: "...paid for perambulation 11s. 0d." In 1742 we find that payments were made to "Richard Lockwood for bread and ale for perambulation 9s. 0d." There were also payments made to J. Jackson, Mary Pool and Mary Thompson. This practice took the form of annually walking around the boundaries of the Parish and it appears to have turned into something of an outing for all those concerned!

❧

CHAPTER 27

CHAPEL

Methodist Chapel Austwood Lane
Built in 1799 it is Ashlar with a hipped Welsh slate roof. Single storey, two round-headed windows. Steps up to the doorway with rusticated surround. Later lean-to added with 1 window. Now a house – Austwood Hall.

> *Cold water that comes from*
> *The well is my drink*
> *The healthiest purest*
> *And sweetest, I think*
>
> *It never makes drunkards,*
> *It never brings woe*
> *So I praise it and drink it*
> *Wherever I go.*

The Chapel was built on land belonging to John Hawke. It was opened with a committee of trustees and these trustees were voted in every few years as some died and some wanted to retire due to age. The chapel was tiered and quite unusual as there were very few tiered chapels in the country.

There had been a preaching house in Braithwell from 1790. The members used to meet in private houses then at Elmhurst (High Street) in a stable building (at the end of Church Grove) called "Ebeneezer Chapel". This was a regular meeting place until the chapel was built "to promote Methodism as laid down by the Rev. John Wesley in order that they may preach God's Holy word.". John Wesley preached in Bramley Chapel in 1786 and some of the Village people went to hear him and this must have fired the members to build their own chapel. In 1846 it was found necessary to enlarge it two yards each way and pews were put in – seating for 150 persons and the best congregation in the neighbourhood. A small sunday school was held on the premises.

Most Sundays I went with my sister Audrey to chapel. Then sometimes with my sister Doris to church. I preferred chapel. I always loved singing and they really sang and, as the preachers were usually lay preachers, their sermons were more down-to-earth and I understood them. Chapel always had lay preachers. My grandfather, Robert Laughton Dunstan, was one and jolly good most of them were. Members of the congregation said a prayer. A lot of chapel preachers were all hell fire and damnation and this fascinated me. Also, people in the congregation prayed out loud. Mr Bentley from Micklebring always said:

"God bless oor (our) Sarah Jane	(his eldest daughter)
Oor Bonnie Matt (Martha)	(his youngest daughter)
And oor Will	(his son)
Let the sweat of oor broo	(our brow)
Gree-ess (grease) oor plooshares	(ploughshares)
And mak em run ee-asy	make them run easy
	Lord Amen"

They used to call out people to be saved. I was always very embarrassed by this. The parson asked people to come out to the front to be saved – sometimes somebody got up and went forward. I used to be so embarrassed and hoped none of my family would ever do that. And when they preached of Hell, I was always a bit worried, thinking of my misdeeds and whether I might end up there – the thought of burning by fire terrified me – I shall never be cremated, I've told my family.

Every Sunday the preachers came to each chapel member's

154

home in turn for tea – after the afternoon service and before the evening one started at 6pm.. Although only ordinary men, they really "had fire in their bellies", as was the common expression. The minister, who was responsible for several chapels, only came occasionally to preach – he came to give the sacrament, so of course we never got to know him as we did the local church vicar.

On the chapel wall, on either side of the widow and in large letters, was written:

"KING OF KINGS and LORD OF LORDS"

A big pot-bellied stove was at the bottom of the tiered seats on the right hand side and in winter worshippers went early to get near to this on the front seat. It was a big round iron affair which was rather temperamental depending on the way of the wind. Some poor beggar had to go in first thing Sunday morning and get this going with sticks and paper and love – no swearing!!

Ernest Dickinson of Fox House Cottage is the man I remember most lighting the Chapel stove. He was a very Christian man and helped out many people in the Village. He was dearly loved and was married to Annie Fiddler (the blacksmith family). He nursed her for many years – she suffered with rheumatoid arthritis and was bedfast the last few years of her life. He had to turn her often day and night to prevent bedsores. She was a regular chapelgoer until this illness. I called to see her often and one day called in and said: "Now Annie how are you today?" She replied: "Bloody awful." There was a stunned silence from me and she said: "What's the matter? Haven't you ever heard anybody swear before?" "Yes but I never thought to hear you of all people." She replied: "Lass, if you had this you'd swear. Forgive me, it's one of my bad days." Poor Annie. No help then for rheumatoid arthritis. Luckily now there are pain killers available but still no cure – we live in hope for the near future.

Sarah Jane and Martha Bentley were sisters. They were really good members of Braithwell Chapel when I was a young girl, We children were very impressed for they always put a 10/- note in the collection plate and on special occasions £1. This was a lot of money in the 1930s. They had lived at Hall Farm Micklebring all their lives and worked on the farm. This is the farm my uncle Harold (Lal) worked on and lived in as a young man. Sunday was a roast beef day. A stone of beef, two inches

of lean and the rest fat. I can't believe that this is bad for you –
they lived to a ripe old age – Yorkshire pudding to start of
course. Lots of potatoes and veg.. Apple pie to follow. Tea was
bread and fat bacon (as every other day was jam) but on
Sunday, and only Sunday, they had a cake. This was the diet for
farm men, the same on most farms. There at least was plenty of
home-made bread and butter. Their father Billy Bentley and
brother David ran the farm and the sisters helped out at busy
times with hay-making and harvest (they always wore cotton
pinafores with harding (sacking) aprons over the top) and of
course did the butter-making and the dairy. They were two
lovely old ladies and very much respected. They retired to a
bungalow up Doncaster Road when their brother married and
are buried in the churchyard.

Village outings in these days depended on the church and
chapel. Usually it was a trip to Roche Abbey or Clumber Park
– stamps were given for attendance at Sunday School and then
if enough stamps were in your book the seaside trips were open
to you.

Easter was always a special time. We always sang "There is
a green hill far away" and "Christ the Lord is Risen Today,
Halleluja" and "Jesus loves me, this I know". There was an old
organ which had to be pumped by one of the boy members. A
hard job for any youngster on such a special service. Easter
Monday was a special tea – ham sandwiches, cakes, buns, jel-
lies, blancmange, trifle etc. provided by the lady members.
There were often five or six sittings. People walked from
Conisbrough and Edlington with children in prams for this special day. Auntie Hilda Dunstan, Auntie Ada Dunstan or Mum
Mrs Poppy Dunstan would boil a whole ham in their copper at
home for this day.

The chapel also had a Whit. Monday Pie Supper. All the
ladies of the chapel made pies – big tables were put up in the
Chapel sunday school room. They seemed to serve dozens of
people. I don't know how they kept it hot. Whilst you were
waiting for your turn we played on the cricket field. The bigger
boys played cricket and others watched. We played tig and
shuttle cock and sometimes played in Chapel Lane at hop-
scotch. There was no traffic then. Then you'd be called in and
asked your preference. Meat and potato, steak and kidney, rabbit pie. My mother always made rabbit as we had a warren in
our croft and dad would go out a few days before with his gun

and come back with about a dozen rabbits. He'd skin them, clean them and chop them into joints and Mum would make these huge rabbit pies. I'm not sure how much we paid but I think it was 1/- for adults and 6d for children. I do know it made quite a lot of money for the chapel funds. The school room was at one time used for the infants school. The older children went to the old church school in High Street.

The Chapel always had an Anniversary on the first Sunday in July and we always sang:

> *"Oh gather the flowers together*
> *And place them near the shrine*
> *In the midst of his wondrous glory*
> *And the radiance so divine."*

This Anniversary was a lovely affair for children. A stage was built in tiers and we sat on this platform one row above the next. For a child who liked singing, this was a joy and how we did enjoy this. We had a choirmaster Mr. Jacques. He was very strict but fair. He was also a local preacher but he loved his music and passed onto us this love. You stood up on this stage to say your piece. I always thought I was much nearer heaven as to a small child 8' to 10' up in the air seemed very high.

CHAPTER 28

SCHOOL

The following account of this school, and the donations to it, is extracted from the old parish register:

"John Bosvile, of Wardsend, tanner, (in the parish of Ecclesfield) founded the school and endowed it very plentifully, but by fraud and mismanagement of some persons it is reduced to forty shillings and – due from John Thompson, of the Well, at present; and whose bond for the money lies in the present vicar's hands, given by John Gleadhall. "The said John Bosvile gave also the sum of forty pounds to the poor of Braithwell, payable at present

157

from the above said John Thompson, and his bond lies in the present vicar's hands; which said forty pounds were expended in suit with one Rawson.

"Anthony Bosvile, mercer, in London, gave five pounds to the school, which sum was laid out in land for a garden on the back side of the said school, &c.as appears in another part of this register.

"Mr. Philip Waterhouse gave twenty shillings and — to the poor: ten shillings due on St. Thomas' Day, and ten shillings at St. James', arising from some land in the parish of Conisbrough (Cow Close), enjoyed by Mr. Henry Flower, and now paid by his widow Flower.

"To the forty shillings above named, given by John Gleadhall, for the teaching of four poor children, (as appears by the will in this register) he gave twenty pounds more to the vicar and the poor, which was laid out in house and land, viz. The house adjoining to the school on the south side, and three half acres of field land, occupied at present by Thomas Hasley."

John Snipe was Schoolmaster and Clerk to the Village of Braithwell when there was no Parish Council and it only had Village Meetings and school was the first Church School.

He was involved with the Inclosure Act as he had the local knowledge. He lived for may years at Lion Cottage – next to the Red Lion and his name is carved on a stone on the wall of the cottage inside. He was born in February 1786 and died December 28th. 1860. He was the son of a carpenter, John Snipe.

Feb	1814	John	s of John & Hannah Snipe	Wheelwright
Mar	1816	William	s of John & Hannah Snipe	Wheelwright
April	1818	Mary	d of John & Hannah Snipe	Wheelwright

(Did he change occupations here? I really don't know – in 1820 he was a schoolmaster)

July	1820	James	s of John & Hannah Snipe	Schoolmaster
Aug	1823	Francis	s of	ditto	ditto
Feb	1826	George	s of	ditto	ditto
Sept	1828	Hannah	d of	ditto	ditto
Jan	1831	Sarah	d of	ditto	Schoolmaster & Parish Clerk
Mar	1835	James	s of	ditto	ditto

An account for Braithwell Parish from 1821 to 1834 included the following:-

Writing letters for: John Wilkinson   6d. (2½p)
                      & Jim Hollingsworth 6d.

(They presumably couldn't write but why did the Parish pay?)

Filling military papers up   2s. 6d.(12½p)
Making jury list   2s. 6d.
Making list to elect new overseer for highways 1s. 0d.(5p)

John Snipe did rent charges, tithes and maps for the Inclosure Act – he did the 1839 maps – owners, tenants, acreage etc., showing all the small fields – a marvellous achievement – and worked out Small Tithes in money paid to the church and Great Tithes to Lord Scarbrough instead of Tithes in Kind (corn, hay, sheep etc.).

He received his appointment, as the successor to Mr. Joseph Johnson in 1820, from the vicar and pairshioners. His emoluments consisted of two and a half acres of grass land which was purchased by the churchwardens by a donation from the Rev. Thomas Bosvile of Ravenfield Park. It is rather remarkable that there formerly existed in this field an extensive mound and a corresponding one in the adjoining close – the traditional belief is that the tournament was held here. For many years both the mounds have been removed and there are no traces left to point out the boundaries of this chivalrous encounter of gallant knights who entered the lists for combat. They were subsequently appropriated for the use of the bow and the target. The foot road from Braithwell to Stainton runs across the fields and adjoins Lambcote Grange.

The Town School

"The school at Braithwell founded by Mr. John Bosvile was enlarged last year at the expense of the residents of the Parish. There is a garden adjoining the school which was purchased with £5 given by Mr Anthony Bosvile.

"In 1818 the Rev. Thomas Bosvile of Ravenfield Park gave £250 for the Benefit of the Town School of which the sum of £121 – 16s – 0d was laid out in the purchase of a close at Maltby called Lower Aldersick containing 3acres 1rood 23perches and the sum of £128 – 4s – 0d the remainder in the purchase of a close at Braithwell called Near Birkwood Close containing 2acres 2roods 8perches.".

"The school building was stated to have been built 24 years

ago (1872) by voluntary subscription aided by a grant of £10 from the National Society on the garden bought with £5 given by Anthony Bosvile. The old school, formerly known as the Town School, is now occupied as the Master's House."

Education in Braithwell was first at the Old School House, built in 1693 by John Bosvile to educate the poor in Braithwell. Several Heads came and went. They lived upstairs with the family and in the big living kitchen at the back. The big room was used as a school. Then in 1872 when the School House was too small, a new church school was built behind this and the children moved there when education was given to more children.

The Rev. Christopher Hodgson lived in the new Rectory, built in 1845. He came in 1871 and had three children – Master Arthur, Master Ernest and Miss Emily – they helped with the school work as it was a church school. Ernest wrote "The Happy Cricketer" about Braithwell and cricket. Mrs. Hodgson, the Vicar's wife, helped with the sewing.

In 1872 it was decreed that the head or principal teacher must enter into the log book all facts concerning the school – i.e. progress, cautions, illnesses, absenteeism etc.. At this time the headmster's salary was £12 -10s – 0d a quarter.

Interesting excerpts taken from the School Logbook
1872 February 29th. Headteacher Mr. Varah wrote: "Made fair progress this week. Arithmetic. Working hard for the Inspection. The past year has been one of trials and disappointments, but by the blessing of Almighty God, we have a brighter prospect for the future. I pray that God will give me grace, to discharge my duty faithfully, honestly, and fearlessly, in the midst of a crooked and perverse generation.".
May 3rd. The headmaster, George Goodwin writes: "Several cases in which Parents have kept their children away from school to gather cowslips." (Obviously for the making of wine. My mother made this every year when I was a child in the 1930s. We always went to help her gather them. You needed buckets full.).

They seem to have changed heads very often – in February it was Mr Varah, then George Goodwin started April 15th. 1872 and left July 19th. 1872. Mrs. Parkin started August 1st. 1872 and left November 22nd. 1872. Henry Windle started December 30th. 1872 and left August 22nd. 1873. They didn't last very long – four in eighteen months!

October 18th. the cost of education went up viz.: 6d, 4d and 3d in lieu of 4d, 3d and 2d.

November 18th. the vicar Rev. Chris Hodgson had an argument with the head Mrs. Parkin re the school and money etc..

November 22nd. The Rev. closed the school (such was the power of the vicar). Mrs. Parkin left.

1873 Marshall & Peace, stonemasons in Braithwell, did alterations to the school

March 28th. there were 50 pupils at school: 27 girls and 23 boys. The schoolmaster rang the church bell at mid-day for 6/6d a quarter. (The ringing of the bell carried on until the 1930s and called all the farm labourers home to dinner.).

May 9th. the records tell us several children were kept away for "Tenting" This meant looking after the animals grazing, usually in the lanes, and watching they didn't stray.

Always in July the school had poor attendance – the children were hay-making. Lots of children had ringworms caught from the calves. In September, gleaning in the harvest fields kept children off school – comment from the School Inspector was always: "Attendance poor" (so prevalent in country schools).

July 21st. to July 28th. Feast Week Second week in August, they always had a half-day holiday on the Wednesday as the Sunday School treat.

Sept 29th. Attendance small. Gleaning not yet finished which prevents several children from attending school.

Oct 27th. Rev Chris Hodgson wrote: "Mrs. Burton elected headmistress Nov. 3rd 1873. Mrs. George Watson sent Jane Watson with a message to say she was to be "Free" (not to be paid for), that Mr. John Thomas Thompson said so. I sent her back to say that the election of free scholars rested with the rector and that she must apply to him if she desired Jane to be free. She returned answer that Mr. Hodgson must mind his own business. This led to an interview where Mrs. G. Watson said that Mr. J.T. Thompson and his father both said: "Jane was to be free." On our way from school, Mr. J.T. Thompson insulted both myself and my son."

1877 April 27th. 4 children admitted from the "new houses".(I wonder where these were?)

In 1879 they did not break up until September 20th.. When they returned on November 1st., the harvest was not all in even then and some children stayed off school to finish it.

In the 1800s the church school always closed for: Shrove

Tuesday (½ day), the choir trip, children's concert, the Sunday School Trip, the Sunday School Outing (either Roche Abbey or more often tea in the Rectory Garden) and Feast Week.

1886 May 10th. one headmistress had to teach six different standards. This had been so for about 3 years – always asking for a monitor but never getting anybody. There were between 41 and 57 children in school. Attendance down often due to weather (children from outlying farms and villages) and epidemics.

1887 May 21st. a Club Feast is mentioned on Ascension Days – (was this the Working Men's Club which used to be a wooden hut next to Johnson's "Club Cottage" on Holywell Lane?). "The Ash Grove" was sung in school. (We always sang this and "The Farmer's Boy." in J. J. Fox's day.).

Due to the long distances children walked to school – i.e. Clifton, Stainton, Micklebring, Birk Lodge, Foredoles – if the weather was bad it cut the attendance by 1/3rd.. My father born 1884 started school there at three years old in 1887. He walked from Foredoles Farm – a long walk for a three-year-old with his elder brother Frank who was six. His brother Albert wasn't born until 1890.

In 1889 parents here were still paying for education yet 1877 free education came in. Children left school at 12, or before if they had passed the IVth. Standard and had a job to go to.

1889–1892 Charles Briscoe – Head.

1890 Mrs Burton the past headmistress (November 1873, to March 1889) of Braithwell C. of E. School started a Dame School in 1890. Several children left the C.of E. to attend it. (I think this was at the Moat Hall.).

In 1891 education in Braithwell became free – the 4d a week which was hard for a labouring family to find ceased. Some did get free education through a Trust – yet the free education act came in 1877. They were all taught the Ten Commandments, The Lord's Prayer, all tables up to 12 times, Spelling and reading. The vicar played a big part in the education and took R.I..

1891 April Rev. Hodgson. School closed for jumble sales (3 days).(Also closed for socials, teas and concerts, as this was the only place to hold them.).

1893 October 23rd. William Marshall punished for using bad language. (This must be our "Buggering Bill" – he started early!).

1894 January to December Head – C. Heitman.

1895 January 14th. N. W. Harper head.

1896 On November 13th. Friday a great stable fire raged at Bentley's Farm Micklebring

In 1899, for the sewing class:

1 y(ard) of flannel was	1s – 0 1/2d
1 yd calico	3 1/2d
sheet pins	1d
reel cotton	1d

1900 E. W. Pearson head.

The school could no longer cope and a building fund was started in the Village. The school was enlarged in 1901 and it opened again on 1st. April. Another classroom and various offices were built on.

1901 A new extension was proposed – new classroom and "offices" (toilets).

The adoption of a voluntary rate was proposed and the election of Representative Managers. No further grants could be paid by the Board of Education as long as the school exists in its present form.

1903 Nov 17th. Headteacher Mr. E. W. Pearson. "Nearly half the school late through playing foxhounds. As this is not the first time and as I threatened to use the cane the last time it occurred, all the boys in the upper Standard (9) received 1 stroke each on the palm of the hand.".

1904 Jan. 14th. In the afternoooon the boys drew on paper from memory a sketch of the Braithwell Dam.

1905 Feb. 14th. The assistant teacher uncertificated Miss Little had her salary increased by £1 to £20 per annum.

Aug. 31st. E. W. Pearson left.

From Sept. 4th. 1905 to Dec. 21st. 1906 Three temporary Head Teachers.

1907 Jan. 7th. Isabella Atkinson took charge.

1908 It is mentioned on May 14th. 1908 as being Empire Day – friends and parents visit, School-children sing National Anthem and Empire Hymn and Song. Each child received two oranges and a bun.

Whitsuntide holiday was one day – Whit. Monday.

Every year horse-racing was held at Micklebring and some children were absent from school for this. Several children also attended Doncaster Races in September, with parents and with permission given from school.

1915 September 17th. The Penny Bank was opened in connection with the school – this still continued until the school closed in 1994. Deposits from one penny upwards were received and interest was allowed at 2½d per annum.

1916 Sept. 26th. The attendance at school fell this morning to 103. A great number of children were late coming into school owing to the fact that there was a Zeppelin scare last night and everyone (adults and children) spent all night in the lanes.

1916 December 21st. A Roll of Honour subscribed for by the children was unveiled by Mrs. Reasby Spencer (mother of Geoffrey and Gertrude the wife of a School Manager). Fred Thompson killed and Sgt. Birks Steers (my mother's cousin) had gained the Military Medal.

1917 January 10th. As the choir boys were requested to sing at a wedding in the morning the school closed .

February 5th. Extremely cold in school at 7 minutes to 9, thermometer registered 26°. Written work out of the question as children cannot hold their pens.

Miss Sheldon as Temporary Cerificated Assistant Mistress £2 – 0s – 6d per week.

Miss W. M. Doers Temporary Supplementary Teacher 19/6d.

Feb 27th. Mr. Rawlinson left for military service. Miss. Mary Howard became headmistress. 32 lbs chestnuts collected by children and sent to Director of Propellant Supplies.

131 on roll.

April 2nd. Heavy snowstorm – only 45 attended school due to the fact that children come from Clifton and outlying farms and from Micklebring

April 16th. Notice was given that in order that the farmers might have the benefit of the school in the evening, for a meeting, school closed early.

Children applied after 12 years of age for exemption forms to leave school (called a Certificate of Attendance) and be employed on farms.

July 23rd. Feast Monday. A cricket match was played and the children were released early from school

December 7th. 149 on roll

In school, the Catechism had to be committed to memory, singing was always commented on.

During 1918 the school was closed for seven weeks due to an epidemic. This happened very often for influenza, measles, diphtheria, scarlet fever and whooping cough – from 1870 to 1920 the school closed often – sometimes for several weeks. It was then disinfected and cleaned throughout before re-opening. Infection seemed to spread like wildfire.

1918 On St. George's day, April 23rd.
Flags were sold in aid of wounded horses by the children 12/6d was forwarded to the R.S.P.C.A.

After 1914 – 1918 war Armistice Day and Ascension Day were holidays

1919 April 11th. There were 150 children on roll, the highest ever recorded. At one time in 1920 the head, Mr. Rawlinson, who had been at the school for seven years, was teaching 77 children – 49 in second class, 28 infants. 150 on roll and room for only 90 pupils! The infants were transferred to the Chapel School Room in Austwood Lane as there was no room in the school for them.

Up to the 1920s school holidays were decided by the farmers. Summer holidays always called Harvest Holiday and if harvest was early, holidays were early and vice verca. A holiday for potato-picking, turnip singling etc.. All these jobs were done by school children at a cheap rate – making extra money for the families.

Ring worms, head lice and worms were very common in schoolchildren. Hair was cut off if you had ringworms and treated with a tar ointment. A cap made of white muslin was worn to stop infecting others so they could not be touched so spreading the ringworms. These usually came from calves. Hair was treated with paraffin for hair lice and a derbac comb (extremely fine with long sharp teeth) was pulled through the hair. These small lice then dropped onto a newspaper held on mother's knee and were crushed. Worms were treated by medicine and a liquorice-like tablet covered in small coloured sweets which you chewed.

After any epidemic, the school was thoroughly cleaned walls and floors, desks and chairs all washed down with disinfectant but several times mention is made of the terrible state of the closets, which were obviously in a very unsatisfactory condition. Several pupils died of diphtheria, whooping cough and scarlet fever. The school closed whilst the head and staff and children followed the funeral. For some reason, the toilets were always called "offices" and for a long time the same entrance was used for boys and girls.

1920 The chapel schoolroom was used for infants due to over-crowding at Church School – the rent of 5/- per week hadn't been paid.

October a potato-picking holiday. If potato-picking wasn't finished, children stayed off school.

1921 The school was closed from November 15th. to Dec.12th. for influenza epidemic. The head was himself teaching 72 children.

1922 A boy George Clapham was killed in the Village on December 1922. He was run over by a horse and cart. All children and teachers went to the funeral.

1923 January 22nd. The divisional clerk visited the old church school and took Mr. Rawlinson the headmaster to inspect certain proposed sites for a new school.

1923 The Chapel schoolroom was used for the infants as too many pupils were using the old schoolhouse. This continued for several years but in 1925 àgain the rent of 5/- per week had not been paid by the C. of E. to the Chapel for several weeks.

An extension had again to be built and land was sought from Mr. Durrant of Rotherwood and Mr. H. Hall of Pear Tree Cottage next door – part of his orchard.

Mr. Hall was offered £21. 17s. 6d. for his plot of 175 sq. yds.
Mr. Durrant was offered £64. 5s. 0d. for his plot of 514 sq.yds.

Mr. Hall refused. He wanted £50. He said he may want to return to Braithwell and didn't want to lose his orchard. They offered £40 but he refused.

April Mr. Colin S. Rawlinson – head, resigned

May 16th. Mr. Stirrup the new head teacher started May 1st. and formed a cricket team and cricket was played on land belonging to Mr. Crowcroft (the landlord of the Red Lion) adjoining the allotments.

September 28th School closed for mumps until October 15th.. Ringworm very prevalent in school. Caps and ringworm ointment supplied to the school.

The school closed often for epidemics. There's really no wonder as when children arrived wet through, there was nowhere to dry clothes – they sat in wet shoes and clothes and top coats were put on again wet. Often the temperature in the shool, heated only by open fire, was almost on freezing and the children couldn't hold their pencils to write.

1923 Scavenging contract for school Mr. F. E. Holmes.

1924 the Church school was rented out at 4/6d per week for dancing classes. Mr Ernest Pawson (uncle Ernest), with horse and cart, carted and levelled ashesfor the drive at 6/6d per load

A report was always entered in the log book re. Religious

Instruction and was tested as follows: Old Testament, New Testament, Catechism, Prayer Book, Scripture, Hymns and Collects. When tests were taken in school, always the scriptures were the most important thing tested.

1924 From September a record of temperature had to be kept and cards were distributed to each class.

1925 January 10th Infants transferred back from Wesleyan School Room to Church School as rent not paid.

It was decided to build a new school. Mr. Crowcroft's land on Holywell Lane (where the new Club is) was looked at but they decided to build on High Land at the top of the Village belonging to Mr Mottram. This land was then bought and a new school completed and opened on 1st. February, 1928.

1927 Jan Miss Lilywhite taking an exam at Portsmouth. (She taught me at the new school and for many more years.).

Report by H.M.I. Received 1928 (Inspected on 15th to 18th November, 1927) The work of the school is carried on under conditions of unusual difficulty. The premises are old and badly ventilated and Standards I to VII have to be taught by two teachers in one undivided classroom. The infants room is over-crowded.

CHAPTER 29

Old Yorkshire Sayings,
Recipes and Childhood Games

You ought to have red hair and a title	*too clever*
Tha's full of wind and piss	*full of talk*
A bellowing cow soon forgets its calf	*those who make most noise crying forget quickest*
Scrattin' abaht	
R.A.O.B.	*ragged arsed old bugger*

Folks are like hosses – breeding will tell
You're that sharp you must have come out of a knife box
Your eyes are bigger than your belly
Tha's better to keep a week than a fortneet

Them as eats most puddin' gets most
   mait *(Yorkshire pudding to start the meal)*

We're throng *very busy*
She'll go round and round 'till she
   ends in a cow flop *waiting for the right fellow to come along*

Where there's muck there's money
He is as crooked as a tup's horn
He's as fat as butter
He's taken t' hig *offence*
He's got t' hump on
I says nowt to nobody about nowt
Clever clogs *think you're clever*
Marry in Lent, live to repent
Marry in haste, repent at leisure
Tha' does rattle on *talk a lot*
In a muck sweat (He's wer in a
   muck sweat) *scared to death*
Dressed up like a dog's dinner
He's that mean he'd skin a louse
It's better to wear out than rust out
All about sumat and nowt
Tha' not framin' (Tha not framin' reight)
Yer've med yer bed, yer mun lie on it
Tha's soft as barm *old name for yeast*
He's only halfpenny to a shilling *half daft*
Tha' like a fart in a cullinder (who can't get out for holes)
Dressed up to 't nines
Whole bag o' mashings
Stop whittling *stop worrying (or nagging)*

Ars tha blowin?
I can't mak heead nor tail on it *don't understand*
Clean up thi trough *eat up*
Beer in, wits out
Tha's like a man wi' no arms
There's nowt so queer as folk
If you soled your boots with a woman's tongue, it would
   nivver wear art (out)
Smooth as a babbie's bum
Straight as a dog's hind leg

As bent as a butcher's hook
As fit as a butcher's dog
Living o'er 't brush
Soft as a brush
Tarred wi 't same brush   *with the*
Can't make a silk purse out o' a sow's ear
Dry as a boo-en   *bone*
Puts lead in yer pencil   *your*
One more potato than a pig
Every little helps, said the old woman
    when she peed into the sea
He's a real turnup hee – ad   *he's dim*
    (turnip head)
Tha's ree-al gormless
By gum – he's reight badly (poorly)
Tha's a daft ha-porth (h'aporth) (silly)

boz eyed	*unable to see properly*
mash 't tea	*make tea and allow to brew*
come a purler	*fall down*
nesh	*feels the cold*
rooring	*crying*
manking abaht	*acting daft*
wittling	*moaning on about something*
wagging it	*taking time off*
mardy	*sulking*
sideling away	*moving away from someone*
udging up	*getting nearer to someone*
lading can	*can for taking water from boiler at side of fire*
fettling	*cleaning*
gi' o'er	*stop it*
lakin'	*not working, playing*
knockin up	*rousing, usually for work, by rapping on a window*
knockin off	*finishing work*
gawping	*looking on with mouth open*
knockin on	*working well*
cadging	*begging*
coil 'oil	*coal house/shed*
mucking abaht	*messing about*
clout	*hit (usually around the head)*

clot	*fool*
spice	*sweets*
clamming	*leaving a bird or animal 24hrs. without food before killing – this leaves the stomach and bowel clear*
Skep	*large round metal container with handles – used to carry feed for the animals*
Clarts	*clods, of earth usually*
Clarty	*sticky*
Fodder	*hay or straw for animal feed*
Truss	*hay cut from a stack by a hay knife*
Staddle Stones	*stones used as a foundation for a stack*
Chop	*oat straw chopped into small peices for horse feed*
Balk	*untitled boundary strip*
Gysting	*feeding animals on somebody else's land for payment*
Beast Gate (or Cattle Gate)	*the right to graze sheep or cows on land which goes with the house*
Four Crop Rotation	*Wheat, turnips, barley, clover*
Skiggs	*open fields or strips*
Gore	*a triangular piece of land*
Furrow	*a long straight cut in the ground made by a plough*
Furlong	*a measure of length – 220yds*
	a subdivision in an open field – all running the same way
Chain	*farm measurement of 22yds*
Headland	*land at the end of the furrow left for the plough to turn*
Ains	*'whiskers' on barley*
Gleaning	*clearing a field of dropped grain*
Chaff	*the husk of the corn – removed when thrashed*

MEASUREMENTS FOR LAND
Length

5½	yards	= 1 rod, pole or perch
4	rods, poles or perches	= 1 chain (66') (or 22x)
10	chains	= 1 furlong
8	furlongs	= 1 mile

Area

1 furlong x 1 chain	= 1 acre
1 acre	= 4840 sq yds
1 rood	= 1210 sq yds
1 square perch	= 30.25 sq yds (1/40th of a rood)

SEVEN RECIPES FROM GRANDMA CHARLOTTE DUNSTAN

RASPBERRY FLAT

This was one of my mother's specials and was often taken to the Mother's Union and The Bright Hour, both of which my mother attended religiously. The flat was cut up into triangular shapes. The outside edges which of course had less jam in, were all cut off and left at home for the men. My uncles always used to say: "Oh! She must a' gone to 't women's gossip and left us 't "goorings" to eat." (The Gorings were the awkward corners in fields, or land left, where the plough couldn't reach.).

1 lb flour, ¼ lb butter, ¼ lb lard, 2 tsp baking powder, ½ tsp salt, 2 eggs mixed with a little milk.

Rub fat into sieved flour and baking powder. Add eggs and milk and mix. Roll out half the pastry. Spread on a flat baking sheet and cover in Raspberry jam. Roll other half and put on top. Bake in a hot oven for 20 mins. When cold, cut into triangles and sprinkle with icing sugar.

PARKIN

This was a great favourite with my father but he didn't like oatmeal in it.

½b white flour, ½ lb brown flour, ½ lb treacle (golden syrup), 3 oz lard, 3 oz butter, 1 tsp. bicarbonate of soda, 2 tsps ginger, good pinch salt, 1 large egg, 6 oz brown sugar, ¼ pt milk

Melt treacle, sugar, fat and milk in pan. Allow to cool and add rest of ingredients. Put in a 12" square tin and bake for 1½ hrs. in a slow oven

Once, when Mum was making this, somebody came to the door. Dad nipped up from his chair and popped in another great dollop of treacle – he loved sticky parkin – and put back the lid. When baked, it went right down in the middle – Mum was very put out – never knew what Dad had done but he said it was the best parkin he'd ever tasted.

171

The following two were not only made at Christmas but every time anybody dropped a basket of eggs. Or if a nest was found on the stacks and they were of indeterminate age – we always broke eggs separately into a cup first!

LEMON CURD

¼ lb butter, 1 lb sugar, 6 eggs, rind & juice of 4 lemons
Grate lemon rind thinly and squeeze out juice. Put butter, sugar, juice and grated rind in basin over a pan of hot water. Stir until it melts. Add beaten eggs, stir until thick – coats back of a spoon. Put through sieve and pot whilst hot.

MAYONNAISE – for salmon

Always eaten with fresh salmon. Nobody in our house would eat salmon if we hadn't any of this,
4 oz butter, 2 tbsp castor sugar, ½ tsp mustard (dry), 8 tbs wine vinegar, a good pinch of salt, 4 eggs
Put all ingredients but eggs in basin over hot water. When melted, add beaten eggs. Stir until thick. Pot whilst hot in screw-top jars.

MINCEMEAT

In my father's young days, this really meant minced meat. Often lights from the killed beasts were used
2 lbs apples, 1½ lbs brown sugar, ½ lb suet (from the butcher, of course and grated), **1 lb stoned raisins** (this was my job to stone the raisins), **1 lb currants, 1 lb sultanas** (these all had to be cleaned in a tea towel), **¼ mixed peel** (this was either made from fruit and sugar or bought in), **½ an orange and ½ lemon** (sugared and cut up), **juice and grated rind of an orange, juice and rind of a lemon and grated nutmeg, 1 tsp salt, 4 tbs rum.** (My uncles used to try to slop more rum in when Mum was down the cellar).
Mince apples. Add all other ingredients. Leave in a big bowl for 48 hrs. to swell. Put into pots and pour a drop of rum over the top of each jar, seal. Many people use brandy but we always preferred rum.

QUINCE JELLY

4 lb quince, 6pts water, sugar
Wash and cut up quince, simmer in covered pan until tender (about 1 hour). Strain through jelly bag or muslin cloth. Next

day add 1 lb sugar to 1 pint juice. Simmer juice then add sugar, stir until dissolved. Boil rapidly until setting point (usually 15 – 20 mins.). Put in hot jars and seal.

Quince and apple   can be made in the same way – 2lb quince and 2 lb apples (washed and cut up – no need to peel or take out pips).

Crab apple   exactly the same

HORSERADISH SAUCE
20tbs grated horseradish, 8tbs wine vinegar or white vinegar, large can evaporated milk (far superior to cream – keeps much better), **2 – 6 tbs sugar** (depending on taste).

Grate horseradish, add vinegar and sugar and milk. Mix well and serve.

This freezes well and I provide nearly half the local Village with it. Don't forget – it makes your eyes run making it and eating it but beef without horseradish is like lamb without mint sauce or pork without apple sauce – they're made for each other!

> *We had whips and tops and marbles*
> *Kick-can and hopscotch too*
> *We played them all on the Village Street*
> *No cars to bother you.*

Kick Can
An empty can was kicked by one member who was chosen by saying a rhyme and pointing to each person in turn and the last word picked out the one who was "on". "One potato, two potato, 3 potato four, five potato six potato seven potato more – ON!" All the others hid. The one "on" had to find the rest. When he did so, he had to run back and touch the can. If the other person reached it first, he kicked it again and the game started over again. These rhymes were also used to start other games.

Hopscotch
A flat piece of stone was kicked whilst hopping on one leg on a marked-out chalk pattern of numbers on the floor.

Snobs
Five small stones (or regular, cube-shaped "snobs" if bought)

were put in the hand. These were tossed in the air and caught on the back of the hand. After three goes, you counted up and your opponents had a turn to see who won.

Skipping
Rhymes – "Hot Cross Buns, Hot Cross Buns, One-a-penny, two-a-penny, Hot Cross Buns" and
One fine day in the middle of the night
Two dead men got up to fight
One blind man to see fair play
Two dumb men to shout "Hooray!"

OR as kids we said:-
One fine day in the middle of the night
Three old Tom cats started to fight
One had a fiddle and one had a drum
And one had a pancake stuck to his bum

Leap Frog

Hoops
Bowling (rhymes with "howling") a wooden hoop (or a bike wheel or inner tube) which was kept rolling along the road by tapping with the hand or a stick

Hide-and-seek
Rhyme as for Kick Can.

Shuttlecocks & Battledore
A small raquet like a tennis raquet and a shuttle – a cork piece with feathers in it. This was knocked backwards and forwards, usually over a rope like a tennis net.

Two-ball
Played against a wall with two balls being thrown and caught, or with a bat.

Kites
We flew these, usually home-made with (brown) paper and a garden cane – one long spine and one short cross—piece. Tail was made from tightly rolled strips of paper.

Whip & Top

Always started on Shrove Tuesday. All the tops were different and painted to make them look good when spinning. There were window-breakers, big bens, monkey, etc.. A thin piece of round wood 18" long with a boot lace or string (not as good!)attached. This was wound roung the top, flicked to unwind it and start the top spinning – it was then kept going by hitting it at the bottom with the lace.

Marbles

Statues

Pulling children by hand and they have to stand where they end up very still – like statues. First to move is 'on' next time.

Conkers October

Peggy

This was a game that was played all the time. A piece of shaped wood, placed on the edge of a brick, was hit into the air (by striking downwards on it with a stick) and hit as far as possible with the stick. Each taking a turn (distance measured by 'strides').

Sports days at school were exciting times for us – three-legged race, sack race, egg and spoon, potato race, obstacle race, as well as 100yds. running races. We loved it all. I never remember anybody who didn't want to take part. Even if you weren't a good runner you had a real chance with the races of chance – dropping your egg and having to start from the beginning made lots of good runners come last. And sack races were really a matter of luck – we always had plenty of hessian sacks to practise with. We used to hold sports days up in the cricket field, which at that time belonged to Hall Farm and was up Maltby Lane, just beyond Hoyle Croft Lane and on the opposite side. Of course these fields were much smaller and surrounded by hedges then. We only had to nip up the croft, cross Jenny Field and we were there. The sports were held in the evening after tea so that all the parents could attend. And a good turn out it was too. Sweets and ice cream on sale, pop too, with Aunt Lucy Bailey dispensing same. How did they keep the ice cream frozen on those hot sunny evenings? No electricity then.

CHANGES

Cart horses aren't used any more
Pigs stand in tethers without straw
Now battery hens just scream and caw
Oh now the farm's so different

Big Shire horses warm and soft
Corn was thrashed and stored in loft
Pigs all day dug up the croft
Oh now the farm's so different

The hens went clucking round the stack
The chickens rode on the sheep's back
The smell of horses and their tack
Oh now the farm's so different

The changes I have seen alas
Have very quickly come to pass
No longer moonpennies in the grass
Oh on the farm it's different

I have lived in and loved this Village all my life and up to eleven years of age I really knew nothing else. Then I took the 11+ for the Grammar School and to my great delight and amazement I passed. From then on my life changed considerably. In a much larger and different environment, I learned there was more in life than farming. I owe a great debt of gratitude to Maltby Grammar School and Mr. Rush, the then Headmaster. I was so happy there and had some wonderful teachers, particularly Miss Manton my English teacher. They all wrote on my reports without fail: "Could do better and talks too much and is often late." If they were here now, they'd probably say exactly the same but I have done my best over the past thirty years to write things as I remember them in my life from being born to twelve years old – but I still talk too much and I'm always late when I arrive at church. They all say: "We can start now – she's here." I have told some of the tales that I remember – many I shall remember later. Some I remembered but are best forgotten and these are all secrets I shall keep to myself.

PART 4
THE HISTORY OF BRAITHWELL

CHAPTER 30

The Inclosures and their Effects on Village Life

Candlemass

> *If February brings no rain,*
> *'Tis neither good for grass nor grain*
> *If Candlemas brings clouds and rain*
> *Winter will not come again*

Dates to know

Candlemas Day	February 2nd.	Old Candlemas was 11 days earlier
St Gregory's Day	12th. March	
Lammas Day	August 1st.	

These dates were used when commons were divided and in private possession from February (or March) to August, then it was thrown open for general use. It was closed (Hained) at Candlemas in the succeeding year.

From Braithwell Enclosure of Commons 1763
It was enclosed under the George III act for dividing and inclosing certain common pasture, fields and waste ground in the Parish of Braithwell in the County of York. The award starts with a recital of the terms of the Act before proceeding to the terms of the Act itself.

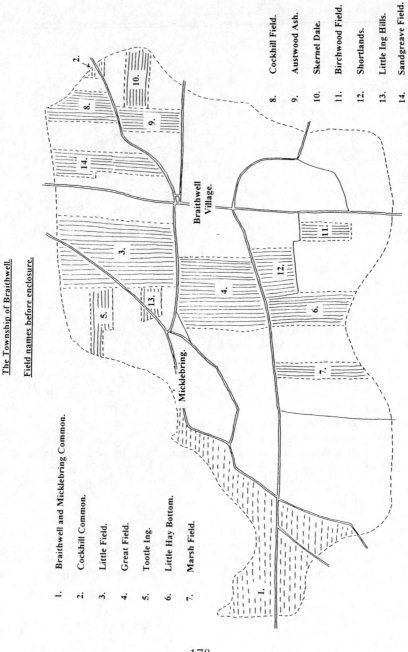

The Township of Braithwell.

Field names before enclosure.

1. Braithwell and Micklebring Common.
2. Cockhill Common.
3. Little Field.
4. Great Field.
5. Tootle Ing.
6. Little Hay Bottom.
7. Marsh Field.

8. Cockhill Field.
9. Austwood Ash.
10. Skernel Dale.
11. Birchwood Field.
12. Shortlands.
13. Little Ing Hills.
14. Sandgreave Field.

Braithwell Village.

Micklebring.

Description of the Commons
Two open and unenclosed common pastures – "Braithwell and Micklebring Common, and Cockhill Common" – are the ones dealt with. There was also Braithwell Green "a small piece or parcel of waste ground". They were said to be "in the Parish of Braithwell in the Manor of Conisboro." The size was said to be estimated at 200 acres but a survey established 167 acres and 35 perches (including 14 acres, 1 rood, 5 perches for roads).

The Act and Award
The award document included an interesting piece of information – there were already 637acres and 18 perches of land enclosed by consent before 1765! This would appear to be more than $1/3$ of the Parish! The Act claimed that the unenclosed land was "inconvenient, largely useless and incapable of improvement". It was decided that a meeting be held to decide on enclosure and that notice should be given in the Parish Church at least 10 days before the date. The enclosure award had to be made before 25.03.1766

Terms of Reference
The land was to be shared between those holding common rights in proportion to those rights. The Commissioners were to have regard to the quality as well as the quantity of land and its convenience to dwelling houses. The Duke of Leeds was to have "one sixteenth in quantity as well as quality and was to retain mineral rights". Of the remainder, half was to go to people having houses and half to owners of land having common rights. The twenty-year rule was to apply to recent enclosures. The yearly value was to be calculated on the 1764 rates. The Vicarage was estimated at £24 per annum. A proportion of land was to be allocated to Rev. J. Turner in respect of the Vicarage house, in proportion to the houses of the other proprietors. The Duke of Leeds' Right of Soil, and all other Rights of Common were to cease but "the Earl of Scarbrough can continue to enjoy tithes".

When the Braithwell Common (see map) was enclosed in 1765 the vicar of Braithwell, received an allotment of 4 acres 3 roods and 35 perches in lieu of Small Tithes. The word "Allotment" came from the days of the Inclosure Act when the village labourer was allotted a small piece of land to cultivate for food. Previously they had a strip of land in a field. Fences around plots had to be made within twelve months. The cost of fencing was estimated at 40 shillings per acre. The expenses of this fencing were to be "borne by the owners, occupiers and proprietors". This was as well as the costs for "obtaining and passing the Act, surveying, dividing and allotting the land" – all except the Vicar!! His holding was to be fenced at no cost to himself. "The Vicarage is to be inclosed with a ring fence in a substantial manner, with quicksets and guarded with ditches, posts and rails". Openings are to be left in the enclosed plots for twelve months to allow passage of cattle carts and carriages through in order "to complete the Award". This was then part of Braithwell Village Green. The Pump was also on the Village Green and the dyke which now runs down the side of Cedar Farm field and past Moat Hall was on the Green as well – the dirt lane, Holywell Lane (then known as Green Lane), ran through it and led to Stainton. Maltby Back Lane was the only road to Maltby.

In our Village, Braithwell Common was enclosed. Some land was enclosed by common consent when Villagers got together prior to this and decided between themselves. The Common ran from Micklebring to Ravenfield to the west of the Parish and covered 167acres and 18 perches (see map). It was used by the Villagers – here a cow, sheep, or geese could be grazed. Each farm or holding would have grazing rights for so many animals depending on the size of the holding. The Poor Lands were also used for grazing. These lands are still known by that name and rented out to local farmers. These rents still go to the Charities money; used in this parish today.

There was provision in the Award for Highways to be built or improved. It was specifically stated that the road between Moor Lane End and Ravenfield Lane should be 60ft. between ditches and it would be called Rotherham Road Lane. Another one was to run from Back Lane, Micklebring, to join Rotherham Road – this was to be called Cownhill Lane. The road running from Moor Lane End to Hellaby was to be called Hellaby Lane.

Low Farm 1845

Thomas Gandy Remarks

This farm for the most part is held in Common with other lands, it consists of about 70 Acres comprised in 20 pieces

180

scattered over almost every part of the parish, so that without the aid of a horse, the Tenant could scarcely see them all in one day_ Lands under such circumstances are if held together farmed under the greatest possible disadvantage _ Every endeavor should be made to obtain an Enclosure of these open fields and in the event of a failure through the obstinacy of any particular individual or otherwise, it wold be well to let the Lands off in parcels to the adjoining Occupiers in preference to keeping up a set of Farm buildings for them. By this method doubtless a great increase of Rent might be obtained over the present proceeds. It is presumed nearly £100 a year might be realized in lieu of the £58. now paid _ The Farm House and Buildings situate near the Church in the Village might be profitably converted and altho' they have recently been put into tenantable repair for the occupation, it would be well otherwise to dispose of them if from any cause and enclosure cannot be obtained."

Braithwell Inclosure 1857

Before the enclosure act a field was worked by the Village community. Each man or family had a strip, or several strips – scattered about, not in one piece and not fenced. This was a sad waste of land and resources as at the end of the season this land was thrown open for common grazing – and imagine the trouble that caused in a village!!!

Most strips of land farmed by labourer or landowner would be a furlong long and one chain broad (220yds by 22yds) – one acre (4840 sq yds) but sometimes only half this or less. If you had ten strips (10 acres) these would all be separate pieces of land. Neither sensible nor economical as with a balk (a strip of land or grass) to separate these, they would be difficult to cultivate and keep free of weeds – remember there were no sprays. It all had to be hand weeded – very labour-intensive.

There were many good reasons for enclosure. The weeds from a man's plot who didn't tend it well would ruin his neighbour's crops who was a good farmer. There must have been many rows. The waste of land where the balks divided the strips. Then when the area was opened up after harvest, the cattle and sheep would mix – scab would be prevalent in sheep and ringworm in calves. These diseases would spread like wildfire.

The crops for the strips had to be decided at a Village meeting when all interested parties would attend. What noisy, awful meetings these must have been with the large land-owners often having their agents there as Ward Fox and Nicholson didn't live in the Village and agents controlled their land – intelligent men who the poor farm labourer had to battle against. Two-thirds of the people had to agree and then it was passed for the following year's cropping.

The enclosure was really a necessity but the farm labourer and small farmer lost out on this, as the bigger farmers and landowners were the only ones with the money to enclose the land with hedges, so these men lost their land. They then had to hire themselves out to the bigger farmers and lost their independence, which most of them never regained. In the 1800s people were waking up to the fact that the poor farm labourers should not be deposessed of their lands as their cows sheep and pigs and their independence went and they were totally dependent on the farmers.

In 1803 Lord Scarbrough had a letter from thirteen small landowners in the Village saying they didn't want to be enclosed.

May it pleas your Lordship
We have an Objection to a general In Closer of the Town fields of Braithwell as Witness our hands This 30 day of September 1803.

James Thompson   William Dungworth
Robert Thompson
John Hicks
Ricd Thompson
William Thompson
thos Sibury
Wm Fidler
Richard Smith
William Ardron
Thomas Wild
Matthew Wild
Tomas Wild

Braithwell
Freeholders that
oppose the Inclosure

Cry of the Farm Labourer in the 1800s

When plenty smiles – alas she smiles for few
And those who eat not, yet behold her store
Are those same men who dig the ground for more
So wealth about them makes them doubly poor

I have a picture in my mind of our community of smallholders – a few acres of land, a cow, a few sheep – a pig in the pigsty by the cottage. It was said if it was made sure that a labourer had a garden and land, he could work on it in the evening and weekends rather than go to the alehouse. The small farmer was a farmer some days on his own land and a farm labourer on the others – he often married the servant from the big house almost always a local girl. Men and women who have to work in the fields are resigned to the peace of nature. They're not used to discontent. They are patient and kindly. This was always obvious to me even as a child. They always had time for you. Show you how to milk, how to hoe, how to recognise birds and wild flowers, how to enjoy country life.

In 1814 a 4lb loaf cost 10d
In 1815 a 4lb loaf cost 1s. 2d
Yet a man's wage remained at 8 shillings a week

When the farm labourer's land was snatched from him, it destroyed his economic independence. It made him just a wage-earner. He also lost his status in the Village. The Villagers used to say this rhyme about the loss of the common rights:

The law arrests the man or woman
Who steals the goose from off the common
But leaves the greater rascal loose
Who steals the common from the goose

There was then a fair number of country clergy ready to supplement their modest income by any honest means. In those days the country parson had a very practical knowledge of farming – he actually farmed his glebe and collected his tithes in kind. A tithe was paid by all parishioners to maintain their parish vicar from the fruits of their labour – corn, hay, wool etc..

Unfortunately the big problem that affected the farm labourer in his fight to keep his land was – making his voice heard above all the bigger farmers. If he did and managed to keep his land his joy was short-lived – he had to fence it. This was essential and most of them found this impossible due to cost. So often after winning his rights he still had to give it up. There must have been many unhappy people in this Village in the mid 1800s. They were trapped by circumstances beyond their control. Before 1774 any wealthy landowner could make a claim through parliament for land to be enclosed – get it passed without the poorer owner knowing until it was a fait accompli . After that year, it was ruled that a notice had to be displayed in the church porch for three Sundays running before any move could be made and smaller holders had a chance to put their case.

"It seemed that by notice it was expedient to "divide and enclose the open and common arable fields and open and common meadows and pasture land or fields and untitled strips and Balks appertaining to or belonging within the township and Parish of Braithwell aforesaid pursuant to the Provision of an Act of Parliament of the Sixth and Seventh years of the Reign of His majesty King William the Fourth and as notice under the hands of the said John Thompson, William Wild, Thomas Toone and William Wasteneys Toone four persons being proprietors entitled to said lands intended to be divided and enclosed on Wednesday 30th. May 1855 at 11 o'clock in the forenoon for the purpose of taking into consideration the expediency of enclosing these lands was duly affixed to the principal outer church door of the Parish of Braithwell advertised in the Sheffield & Rotherham Independent and the Sheffield Times newspapers circulating in the county of York more than 14 days prior to such day of meeting."

"George Kay – of the Red Lion – Meeting on August 29th 1855 re. enclosure act for the Parish of Braithwell
Present were: George Dyson Simpson as the attorney
John Thompson, Samuel Vickers, Thomas Toone, Thomas Vickers, George Nicholson, Robert Thompson, George Godber, George Godber the Younger, George Pearson

Nicholson, John Milward, William Wild, Mathew Waterhouse Roberts, Thomas Wright Watson (Agent to Ed. Ward Fox) and George Pearson Nicholson – attorney for Edmund Denison, William Wasteneys Toone, Martha Wilson, Jane Snipe, Ely Snipe, Margaret Wild, William Wild and Joseph Roberts, being persons interested in open and common arable fields and pasture lands within the Parish of Braithwell.".

Villagers then lost their rights to till small pieces of land. Life became very hard and the Villagers who had eked out a living on a small plot, perhaps also doing a little thrashing or harvesting, now had to find employment. The farmers with large acreage quickly took advantage of this and with so much labour on the market wages were poor – if one man refused a job because of poor pay, there was always some poor wretch with many mouths to feed eager to take it on. This caused great unrest and eventually led to the farm labourers' uprising and many were transported before, eventually, unions came to farming.

I have a copy of a tithe map from 1839, copied by my cousin Allen Smith, drawn up by John Snipe – schoolmaster and Parish Clerk – of all the land in Braithwell Parish before it was enclosed and showing all the field names. It also has information re. acreage, crops, Tithes to the church and Tithes to Lord Scarbrough. This was when tithes on land (corn, sheep, hay etc.) were commuted to tithes in money; John Snipe worked all this out. He must have been a very clever fellow. We were one of the very last Villages to be enclosed.

In 1855 George Dyson Simpson was appointed commissioner to the enclosure of the fields. Henry Ellison of Stone was appointed Surveyor.

It seems to me that all the work had already been done in 1839 by John Snipe.

Braithwell Parish had	1,920	acres of which:
	1,368	were arable
and	502	meadowland
with	8	woodland
and	42	waste & roads

The Commissioners who drew up the plans and enclosed the land, as well as their fees, also got their refreshment paid for at the local inn. Usually, the price was between £1 and £2 for three. Villagers complained this was excessive as, of course, they ultimately paid it but of course nobody took any notice (as they still don't with Borough Council expenses).

The Inclosure Act of Braithwell (1857) is a substantial calf-bound volume the skins of parchment folded in the middle to give folios 2' x 1'6" – this contains a large-scale colour plan of land enclosed – 492 acres, 3 roods, 4 perches.

FIELDS IN INCLOSURE ACT

Field Names

Alder Holt	
Ash Holt	
Austwood Ash Field Lane	between Austwood Lane and Cockhill
Austwood Closes	(also between Austwood Lane & Holywell Lane, Hosswoods or Horsewoods)
Batty Close	
Batty Holt	
Birchwood Closes	between Fishpond Lane & Birchwood La.
Birchwood Close	between Holywell Lane and Maltby Lane
Birkett	from Hoyle Croft/Haids Lane
Black Hills Holt	
Bog Close	
Broad Ings	
Calf Crof	The Bungalow, Holywell Lane, is here
Chapel Holes	bottom of Chapel Holes Lane
Church Croft	
Clay Croft	
Clifsty Close	
Cockhill Field	left hand side, just past first bends
Cow Close	Conisbrough
Cownhill Close	Micklebring
Crag Close	
Dale Hill	up Maltby Lane
Dawsons	second down north side Cockhill Field Lane
Far Nursery	
Folly Field	
Foredoles Close	next Foredoles Farm
Fox Holes	second field down Birchwood Lane
Graftswell Close	

Great Field	between Ashton Lane and Micklebring Lane
Grime Riddings	
Home Close	
Hoyle Croft Close	off Hoyle Croft Lane
Hudson's Flat	
Lawton Crag	opposite "The Cottage" and "Croft End", south of Hoyle Croft Lane
Limekiln Close	
Little Field	between Doncaster Road and Micklebring Lane
Little Ings	behind Little Field, nearer Micklebring
Little Hay Bottom	off Ashton Lane beyond Short Lands
Longleys Field	Doncaster Road
Marsh Field	beyond Little Hay Bottom (Ashton Lane to Maltby)
Marsh Hill Close	between Little Hay Bottom and Marsh Field
Near Nursery	
Nethershut Close	
Parson Close	in the old rectory grounds, Holywell Lane
Pearson's Fog	west side of Maltby Lane
Pippin Croft	
Poor Lands	Ashton Lane
Ruddlepit Close	Micklebring opposite Ruddlepit Field where quarry was
Rudddlepit Shut Close	back lane from Ashton Lane to Micklebring Lane
Sandgreave Field	first down Cockhill Field Lane on left hand side
Short Lands	Ashton Lane, first field past Fieldhouses
Skernel Dale	off Austwood Ash, long narrow field running towards Stainton
Three Islands	now with houses built on at Dale Hill
Towfield Gardens	Towfield Bungalow, Maltby Lane
Tootle Ings	behind Little Ing Hills
Top Croft	
Well Close	behind Well House
Yew Tree Close	where tree is, Parish Boundary Doncaster Road

CHAPTER 31

The Township of Braithwell, The Tithe Award
1838–1840

Before the 1830s, the Tithe was traditionally a payment to the 'lay Rector' of one tenth of the produce 'that came from, or was nourished by the earth.' It was paid in kind, and was difficult to calculate and collect.

Tithes have been collected from the early Middle ages onwards. To begin with, this was in the form of a grant of a proportion of all the goods produced. This went to the Church and it was at first a voluntary contribution. In late Saxon times it became a compulsory tithe, the proceeds going to the poor of the village, the Priest to supplement his small stipend and some went towards the upkeep of the Church. Tithes were the cornerstone of Church income.

Monasteries received a sizeable proportion of Tithes as they flourished and were endowed but an act of 1391 made 'Vicarial upkeep' compulsory and binding upon all receivers of the Tithe. With the dissolution of the monasteries, their lands and rights of tithe passed to the Crown and this was later granted for favours rendered, or sold outright to administrators, notables and Court favourites. In this way for the first time, the tithes became private property. In the case of Braithwell, the 1763 Inclosure Act names the Duke of Leeds as the 'owner of the soil and mineral rights' and Richard, Earl of Scarbrough, as Impropriator and Lay Rector. By 1838, little had changed and it was stated the Earl of Scarbrough was receiver on the Great Tithes and the Vicar, Charles Augustus Stuart was in receipt of the Vicarial or Small Tithes.

Great Tithes were levied on crops of corn, hay and also wood. The Small Tithes were the rest – usually wool, small livestock and garden produce – items which were a great deal harder to assess and collect than those going to the Impropriator! Each vicarage had an original endowment which stated precisely which Rights of Tithe were attached.

As previously stated, the Church needed Tithes in order for the Priest to carry on his duties in the Parish. Many livings were poorly paid and the priest needed the income from the tithes to survive. Because of the difficulty of collection, many attempts were made to tighten up procedures. In some instances, 'moduses' were being paid (a small customary payment made in lieu of a full demand agreed by consent often many years previously). These no longer reflected the present value of the tithe and so the parson was losing out. There were only two in Braithwell at the time:

Plot 87 belonging to Rev. G. Rollinson (Chapel Hole)

Plot 88 belonging to Robert Thompson (Crag Close)

These do not seem to have caused the Commissioner problems as they did in other parishes and they are dealt with in detail in the Award.

The Tithe was a tax on productivity, not on acreage. The Church welcomed this . . . the more the produce, the greater the Tithe to be collected! In many cases the collection of the Tithe led to disputes, in some cases turning the Vicar against the parishioners. Another cause of concern for the Church authorities. Many clergy were forced to accept less than they were due, rather than stir up trouble in the Parish. The poem below puts the case well:

> The Priest he merry is, and blithe
> Three quarters of the year,
> But oh! it cuts him like a scythe
> When Tithing time comes near.
>
> For then the farmers come ... jog, jog.
> Along the murky road
> Each heart as heavy as a log
> To make their payments good.
>
> Now all unwelcome at this gates
> The clumsy swains alight
> With rueful faces and bald pates.
> He trembles at the sight.
>
> And well he may, for well he knows
> Each bumpkin of the clan
> Instead of paying what he owes,
> Will cheat him if he can!
>
> *William Cowper*

In 1834 and 1835 Bills were introduced into Parliament for the commutation of Tithes from a payment in kind to a cash settlement but these failed to become law. This was possibly due to the fact that with the widespread enclosures having taken place, land was now more productive and so greater tithes were to be had! Finally a Bill was passed and the Commutation of Tithes in England and Wales became a reality.

Before 1836 there had been a number of voluntary agreements. The Act did not put a stop to this, in fact they were encouraged. The ways in which a voluntary agreement could be initiated were similar the those stipulated for enclosures. One quarter of the owners of lands subject to Tithes could call a meeting to discuss the matter. At this meeting, if two thirds of the landowners and tithe owners (by value) agreed on the process being started, it became binding on all to accept the change. They could appoint an Assessor to apportion the new charges – usually a respected member of the community – in the case of Braithwell, John Snipe, the schoolmaster. The Braithwell Meeting was held on 15th. November, 1837.

Living locally in the school house, and knowing personally all the owners and tenant farmers, Snipe had an unenviable task. Overnight he became the taxation officer! His task was to get all to agree to the values he apportioned, bearing in mind the acreage, quality of the land and the amounts in kind paid previously. On agreement, the sum was sub-divided amongst the landowners according to the size of their various plots. In order to comply with the terms of the Act, he had to convert all in order to arrive at the number of bushels of cereal crops grown in the village in the previous year. It becomes obvious that this is the way John Snipe went about the process when one studies the figures on the document. They are as follows:

Crop	Price per bushel	No. of bushels
Wheat	7s. – 0¼d	433.94659
Barley	3s. – 11½d	769.68421
Oats	2s. – 9d	1107.87879

(If one multiplies the number of bushels by the price per bushel, the answer in each case comes to £152. 6s. 8d.).

It became general practice that in voluntary agreements, the receipts for produce grown over the past seven years was not necessary, provided that agreement did not seem to injure either party.

No Great Tithes were imposed on houses and orchards and former Common Land, enclosed in 1765, did not pay Small

Tithes because of a grant of land given to the vicar in lieu of them at the time. No Tithes were imposed on woodland or waste.

The Assistant Commissioners were supposed to conduct their own survey to check on the local results and the Work of the Assessor but in effect in many cases this did not take place – out of over 2,200 voluntary agreements, only 17 were disputed! Some maps were found to be very inaccurate. This was not the case in Braithwell. The map appears to have been well-surveyed and excellently produced. No detailed work on the Parish of Braithwell could have been produced without first having studied the Tithe Map. With the enclosure of the Open Fields not having taken place until 1858, the Tithe Map shows the position of all the strips in detail, as well as giving all the local names.

The Award is written on 26 large sheets of Vellum. The first three pages give a brief written account of the distribution. Then follow pages of detailed figures showing the Tithe allocation to each of the 647 designated plots. The final three pages contain a summary, showing the amount of Tithe paid by each landowner. One copy of the Award complete with map is to be found in the Doncaster Archives and the other copy is in the Borthwick Institute, York.

❧

CHAPTER 32

The Clarkson Family of Braithwell

William and Anne Clarkson had eleven children. They were:- Mark, Benjamin, Elizabeth, George Joseph, Martha, Mary Anne, (Charlotte), Jane, Rachael, Ada and Bosdin J. Charlotte Clarkson, born 1848, married Robert Laughton Dunstan – she was his second wife and my step-grandmother. Hence my interest in the Clarkson family.

Indenture   January 5th. 1764   Mark Clarkson
This Indenture   made this
...*Fifth* ... Day of ... *January* ... in the Fourth year in the Reign of our Sovereign Lord George the Third, by the Grace of God, of Great Britain, France and Ireland, King, Defender of the

Faith, etc. And in the year of our LORD ... *One Thousand Seven Hundred and Sixty Four* .... Between ..... *Thomas Scales*..... *of the Township of....Brierley* ..... *in the Parish of Felkirk*...... *in the County of York*..... *Linnen (sic) Weaver*......of the one part...... and *Mark Clarkson*..... *of Brierley*..... aforesaid..... of the other part: Witnesseth, that the said..... *Mark Clarkson*..... hath of his own Free Will, and with the consent of... *Bryan Clarkson*.... *his Father*...... Put and Bound himself Apprentice to and with the said..... *Thomas Scales*...... and with him after the manner of an Apprentice to Dwell, Remain and serve from the Day of the Date of these Presents..... for, during, and until the Term of Seven Years thence next Following be fully completed and Ended. During all which Term, the said Apprentice his said Master well and faithfully shall serve, his Secrets shall keep, his lawful Commands shall do, Fornication or Adultery shall not commit, Hurt or Damage to his said Master shall not do, or Consent to be done, but to his Power shall Let it, and forthwith his said Master thereof warn: Taverns or Ale-Houses he shall not Haunt or Frequent, unless it be about his Master's Business to be done: At Dice, Cards, Tables, Bowls, or any other unlawful Games he shall not Play: The Goods of his said Master shall not Waste nor them Lend, or give, to any Person without his Master's Licence: Matrimony within the said Term shall not contract nor from his Master's Service at any Time absent himself; but as a true and Faithful Apprentice shall order and behave himself towards his said Master and all in Words as in Deeds during the said Term: And a true and just Account in all his said Master's Goods, Chattles, and Money committed to his Charge, or which shall come to his hands, Dutifully he shall give at all times when thereunto required by his said Master his Executors, Administrators or Assigns. And the said... *Thomas Scales*.... for himself, his Executors, Administrators, and Assigns, doth Covenant, Promise, and Grant by these Presents, to and with the said... *Mark Clarkson*... the said Apprentice, That he the said... *Thomas Scales*,... his Executors, Administrators or Assigns shall and will Teach, Learn, and inform him the said Apprentice, or cause him to be Taught, Learned, and Informed in the Trade, Art and Occupation of... *Linnen (sic) Weaver*..... which the said Master now useth, after the best manner of Knowledge that he or they may or can, with all Circumstances thereunto belonging: And also shall find, and provide to and for him the said

Apprentice sufficient and enough of Meat, Drink, Washing and Lodging for and during the said Term and also well and truly pay his said Apprentice Sixteen pence yearly as and for his Apprentice Wages, and also permit Supper and allow unto his said Apprentice two weeks Schooling yearly at a proper time for Schooling during the said Term............... And for the true Performance of All and Singular the Covenants and Agreements aforesaid, each of the Parties aforesaid doth bind himself unto the other firmly by these Presents. In Witness whereof, the Parties above named to these present Indentures ???erchangeably have set their Hands and Seals the Day and Year above written

Sealed & Delivered (being first duty stamped)
in the presence of us
   his
Bryan Clarkson   Lyndley William Atkin   Thos. Scales
mark   Mark Clarkson
                       (This was an earlier Mark)

Mark Clarkson 1835–1905
Painter and Decorator
(Charlotte's brother)
Mark, the oldest son of William and Ann Clarkson, was born in Braithwell in 1835, and in the census of 1851, when he was 15 years old, was listed as a Framework knitter. It is also known that he shared his brother Benjamin's musical talents. Some eight years later, Mark was presented with a Bible by .... "The Wesleyan Methodist Society of Braithwell in recognition of his services as organist." Mark was then 33 and must have been playing the organ for a good many years to have merited such a gift.

Mark received no mention in the 1861 census but was back in Braithwell in 1871 when he was listed as a Painter. On the next occasion he is again given as a painter and living at Number 24. Presumably Mark married after the 1851 census and lived out of the Village, possibly in Tickhill, since he married Emma Kemp of that place. It is interesting to find that Emma Kemp's father, John, had married a Mary Tasker at Felkirk in 1833, just 100 years after Mark's great great grandfather Bryan had married Mary Marsden in the same place. It would appear that there were still close ties between the Clarksons in both villages.

It is known that Mark started his 'Painting, Paper Hanging & Decorating' business in 1868. At this time, he lived in the front part of the *Old Hall* opposite the Red Lion Hotel. Paint, which was sold by the pound, was mixed and prepared on the third floor – paint can still be seen there on the attic floor – the family living in the rooms below and part of the ground floor. The account book started in 1877 records long hours of work for an amazingly low return. Small as they appear today, some accounts were outstanding for over twelve months and some were never settled. One customer must have been declared bankrupt since the ledger shows a receipt of only a few shillings in the pound. A cryptic note in the margin calculates the difference as ".... dead loss".

Cottages, halls and, occasionally, mansions were decorated by Mark:

1st Feb 1877. "To Mrs Hartshorn, Maltby. For rubbing down sitting room, canvassing, papering, painting and varnishing, 4/11d."

April 1877. "To Mrs Woodyeare, Crookhill Hall. *(now demolished)* For papering servant's bedroom, maid's bedroom, housekeeper's bedroom, butler's bedroom. (37 rolls of paper). Also papering gun room, housekeeper's room, Mrs Woodyeare's room and dressing room. (57 rolls of paper). To white-washing ceilings, varnishing, and best flour paste. £13 : 13 : 3½d."

April 1887 "To Earl Scarborough *(sic)*, Sandbeck Hall. To distempering ceilings in dining room, inner hall, billiard room, tea room, corridor, blue lace room, boudoir, the Earl's bedroom and dressing room, bath room, chapel staircase, housemaid's bedroom and sitting room. Painting dining room, blue lace room, shutters, chapel staircase. Papering housemaid's bedroom and sitting room, cook's sitting room. All materials and time. £20 : 9 : 9½d."

It is clear that Mark's work was of a good standard and he was quite prepared to give a complete service. (The ledger shows that he clipped horses and even shook carpets). His business was conducted from Braithwell and Conisbrough. He left a son Robert John who was to carry on the business and a daughter, Constance Ada.

Benjamin Clarkson (1838 – ????) Organist

The following account of Benjamin Clarkson, born in Braithwell (1838), is condensed from a reprint of The Doncaster Gazette 1849–50. The original account, written in the flowery journalese of that period, may be read from the Gazette reprint called "Village Sketches".

* * * * * * * * * * * * * * * * * *

Ann Clarkson, Ben's mother, told the reporter that her son had, from a very early age, shown great interest in his father's violin. William Clarkson had accompanied his wife Ann's lullabies on this "well toned" instrument and that must have been the reason for the fascination.

Ben was given an old instrument to play with and Mr. Dyson, then living at the Manor House, later presented him with a harpsichord. Ben persevered on this instrument to such an extent that, at seven years of age, ".... he produced with beautiful effect, to use the expressive phrase of Billy Mason, a tune which is known by the term "Balance a Straw", in imitation of Tickhill chimes.".

Benjamin continued to play the harpsichord and with such success, that Mr. Dyson allowed him to play the organ at the Manor House and two weeks later engaged Mr. Mason, a music teacher of Whiston, to give him music lessons.

These lessons continued for the next two years until Ben was nine years of age. It seems that Mr. Dyson then, ".... set on foot a subscription for the purchase of a pianoforte." In a very short space of time, the sum was obtained; and this instrument now forms the principle *(sic)* piece of furniture in the house of the humble stocking manufacturer."

The account goes on to say that, at eight years of age, Ben conducted the Church Choir at Braithwell until his appointment as organist of the Parish Church of Tickhill. Ben was then in his 12th year.

The reporter states that these details were provided by Ann and William, the parents of Ben, and that they were very anxious ".... that he should not be led astray with those vicious habits as is too often the case with those who have some ability in pleasing the ear of the public at the village festivals."

A programme of Vocal & Instrumental Music given in the Recreation Hall (The Granby Saloon), on Tuesday 7th. February 1860, lists several pianoforte solos given by 'Master B. Clarkson'. The same programme shows that Ben's brother

'Mister Mark' sang three bass solos. Since Mark Clarkson would have then been 24 years old and his brother only two years younger, it is difficult to see why Ben should have been titled 'Master' and Mark 'Mister'. (Perhaps it was the nineteenth-century custom that 'Mister' was only reserved for the oldest son).

George Joseph Clarkson (1844–1915)

In a book written by Randolph, son of Christopher Hodgson, the first incumbent of Braithwell after the Benefice was declared a Rectory on 18th. December, 1866, George Joseph Clarkson is mentioned several times.

The book is called "The Happy Cricketer" and describes the state of cricket generally and, in particular, the performance of the Braithwell team. It recalls a concert of 1878 in aid of Braithwell Cricket Club (BCC) at which Joseph was to have sung comic songs. Joseph was a Methodist and heir to his Uncle James, a pillar of that persuasion. He stopped his nephew's participation since the way to Heaven wasn't via the singing of comic songs. At this concert, Joe's brothers, Mark and Ben, participated .... they were Anglicans!

Randolph talks much of Joe or "our Joa" as the family called him. A champion cricketer who he obviously had deep affection for. He also talks of taking a short cut up past Cedar Farm on the farm track onto Chapel Lane (Austwood Lane) then up Doncaster Road to the cricket field. The farmer told him he was trespassing and frightened Randolf so he then climbed the wall opposite the rectory and crossed the meadow there until one day the bull was loose and it chased him. This terrified him and he decided the High Street was safer. Anyway he found that by calling at the shop in High Street (the tailor's shop), where the Colbecks lived (an old Braithwell family), he could see when the team came out of the Butcher's Arms and proceeded up the street to the field, bearing a green chest with the initials B.C.C. painted white on the lid. This contained the bats, stumps, balls, pads, bails etc. all on their way to the Village Cricket Match. He followed with much pride. Joe Clarkson was captain but there was a superstition in Braithwell that "silver always fell tails" so Joe used a penny.

How very strange that Randolph's cricket field in the late 1870s is the same one that is now our Village playing field acquired in the late 1970s. He talks of entering from Doncaster

196

Road and Micklebring Lane as we do now.

Randolph Hodgson, himself a cricketer of no mean ability, thought very highly of Joe's prowess with the bat and ball. So much so, that he was sure that Joe (and his nephew William) should have played for Yorkshire had circumstances allowed them to practice and play more often. The Braithwell team of those days must have been quite formidable opponents, giving good account of themselves when playing teams which included County players.

The census returns for 1841 show the Clarkson family to have been concerned with the production of hosiery and other items made on knitting machines. Joseph's great-grandfather, Mark, had been apprenticed to a linen weaver of Felkirk in 1764 and it would appear that this relative brought his knowledge of weaving/knitting to the Village when he married Elizabeth Amery (of Stainton) in 1777 and settled in Braithwell. Just when the frames were acquired isn't known but seven members of the family, as well as other Villagers, gave their occupation as either weavers or frameworkers in 1841. Mr. Harold Clarkson (great nephew of Joseph and now living in Braithwell) thinks that there were about twelve knitting frames housed in a building to the rear of Clarkson's shop (later the Village Store), on the main street opposite Rook Cottage.

Randolph Hodgson's book tells us that Clarkson's shop sold "....groceries, sweets, ironmongery, hardware, patent medicines, tobacco, but above all hosiery, which the family manufactured." Joseph's sisters Ada, Martha and Rachael worked at the looms and produced socks, stockings, vests, pants and underwear generally.

Joseph became manager of the family business sometime between 1861 and 1871 but in 1878 he was forced out of business by the bigger and more sophisticated power looms. Only good quality had enabled him to hold out for so long against the cheaper articles being mass-produced. Just what happened to the knitting frames isn't known but, fortunately, Joseph gave one to the local museum and this is presently housed at Cusworth Hall Museum, together with other relics of a bygone age.

George Joseph Clarkson Died September 3rd. 1915 aged 71. His grave is in the east side of Braithwell Churchyard.

Also Charlotte, the beloved wife of Robert Laughton Dunstan and sister of the above, died July 30th. 1919 aged 71.

Her gravestone bears the legend:

> *"She did what she could*
> *Womanly sweet in all her ways*
> *Slow to condemn*
> *And swift to praise."*

Also Frederic James Clarkson Died July 16th 1920 aged 35

CHAPTER 33

Settlement Orders, Agreements and Old Press Cuttings

Settlement Orders

A legal right to poor relief only arises out of a settled place of abode – The Poor Law Act 1601. A person was recognised as being legally a settled inhabitant of a Parish after a month's abode. Records of removal only begin in 1691. The Act was repealed in 1834 but the principle remained substantially in force until 1876. Anyone entering a township and occupying a tenement worth less than £10 per annum might within the next 40 days be removed by the Overseers of the Poor. He would then be escorted by the Constable along the route back to the place where he was considered legally settled. Overseers tried to get rid of women pregnant with bastards as they became a drain on the Parish.

WEST-RIDING   To the Churchwardens and
    Of   To wit   Overseers of the Poor of the
YORKSHIRE   Township of *Braithwell* _____
       _____in the said Riding,
and to the Churchwardens and Overseers of the Poor of the Township of *Maltby* _____in the said Riding, and to each and every of them.

Whereas Complaint hath been this Day made unto Us, two of his Majesty's Justices of the Peace in and for the said Riding

198

(one being of the Quorum) by the said Churchwardens and Overseers of the Poor of *The Township of Braithwell* ____ aforesaid, That *George Jackson Labourer Hannah his wife and Richard their Son about Twenty Three weeks old*_____ have come to inhabit in the said *Township* of *Braithwell*_____ not having gained a legal Settlement there, not produced any Certificate owning *themselves* _____ to be settled elsewhere, and that the said *George Jackson Hannah his wife and Richard their son are* _____ likely to be chargeable to the said Township of *Braithwell* _____ WE do therefore, upon due Examination of the Premisses *(sic)*, taken before Us, upon Oath, adjudge the same to be true. And we do likewise adjudge the last Place of the lawful Settlement of the said *George Jackson Hannah his Wife and Richard their Son* _____to be in the said Township of *Maltby* ____

These are therefore in his Majesty's Name to require You the said Churchwardens and Overseers of the Poor of *Braithwell*_____ aforesaid, or some, or one of You, to convey the said *George Jackson Hannah his wife and Richard their son*____ from and out of the said *Township* _____ of *Braithwell* to *the Township of Maltby*_____ aforesaid, and *Them* _____ to deliver to the Churchwardens and Overseers of the Poor there, or to some, or one of them, together with this our Order, or a true Copy thereof, who are hereby required to take caree and provide for *Them__* as the Law directs, GIVEN under our Hands and Seals, this *20th*____ Day of *April*_____1782.

ROB^t ATHORPE ATHORPE
?? FRANK

An Agreement
Between Mr Fiddler*(sic)* of Braithwell, in the parish of Braithwell, in the West Riding of the County of York, on the one part. And the Revd. W. Seed, Rector of Braithwell of the said Parish and County. Mr. John Thomas Waterhouse, Churchwarden of Braithwell in the parish and county aforesaid. And Mr. Henry Hall, Churchwarden, of the said Parish and County:- the Schoolmanagers of the Braithwell National School on the other part. That is to say Mr Fiddler agrees to take; – and the Said Schoolmanagers agree, to Let: the Field situate in the aforesaid parish and County; and known by the name of

Birchwood Close; on the following Conditions, VIZ. The rent to be Three pounds five shillings per annum. The first moiety to be paid on the third day of August in each year. and the second moiety on the third day of February in each year. The said Tenant to pay all Tithe Rent Charge, Rates and Taxes; which shall be Chargeable on the said Field And to keep the gates and Fences in good and Tenantable repair. and when the said field shall be mown for hay: the said tenant agrees to put upon the field aforesaid not less than six Cartloads of good Farm Yard manure per acre. The tenane (sic) to expire at Candlemas day on twelve month's notice being given from either side.

As witness our hands this 26th. of February in the year of our Lord 1900.

WILLIAM SEED.	Rector
HENRY HALL	Churchwardens
	and
JNO. WATERHOUSE	School Managers
ARTHUR FIDLER *(sic)*	Tenant.

The Yorkshire Journal and Doncaster Advertiser, 24 May 1788
To be sold . . . at Braithwell . . . [the] late estate of Samuel Parkin deceased; all that copyhold* messuage or tenement . . . now in the occupation of Widow Parkin, together with the old-accustomed grocer's shop and warehouses, barns, stables, cow-house, garden and croft adjoining with about thirty acres of freehold land, three acres and a half of which is in the open field and the remainder in five several closes lying near the town.

The house may be entered upon at pleasure, the land at Candlemas next.

Also to be sold: a quantity of dry seasoned wood for the use of carpenters, consisting of yew rollers and gate posts, naves, posts and rails . . .

> *Copyhold of Land:* Tenancy of land under the Lord of the Manor recorded on official Roll and a copy given to the tenant.

The Yorkshire Journal and Doncaster Advertiser, 31 May 1788
John Robinson, Braithwell, Linen draper and grocer.
Returns his most sincere thanks to his friends and customers in general for all past favours and hopes for a continuance of their future favours. Begs leave at the same time to inform them that

he is removed to a new erection in Braithwell . . . where it will be his constant study to merit their approbation.

John Hawkes, mentioned in this newspaper cutting, was an Attorney at Law living in Braithwell. There is mention of a daughter being born to him and his wife on 23rd. October, 1792. Later, two more daughters and a son. He is mentioned in the book "Records of Methodism" in Braithwell as erecting a building upon copyhold land for the Methodist cause. His brother William farmed at Fordoles and was a Trustee of the chapel but we have no indication as to where John Hawkes lived.

Auction sale of epistle to John

Mr. John Hawkes of Braithwell, near Doncaster, was entrusted with a very special mission by his American clergyman friend, Mr. Parker Hall. Mr. Hall asked him to inquire into the character of a self-styled preacher who was believed to have one wife in England and another in America. Mr. Hall must have had to wait a fair time for his information, however. He wrote his letter on September 15, but it didn't arrive until March 4 the following year. That was in 1803

Auction

The letter, sent from Rhode Island, is expected to fetch at least £40, at a Stanley Gibbons' stamp auction, in London next week. It is well-preserved and bears markings that show it was landed at Dover, and that the Post Office charged Mr. Hawkes three shillings and sixpence for carrying it from Dover to Doncaster. There is no record of Mr. Hawkes' reactions as he read the letter asking him to "inquire respecting the character of one Francis Tomson, who says he was born in Scotchland *(sic)*, but brought up in England; who professes to have a call to preach .... says he has administered ordnances amongst the Methodists. "He has a wife in Philadelphia, and, it is confidently reported, one in England" (More frustratingly, there is no record of his reply).

Doncaster Gazette, 15 July 1814

(Napoleon had surrendered to the allies and had been sent to the island of Elba. Peace was celebrated in every town and village, including Braithwell.)

201

On Wednesday all the women and children sat down to tea near the cross, a band of music playing all the time. The tables were decorated with garlands and laurel, and flags were hung out of houses nearby. On Friday upwards of a hundred and thiry men with a considerable number of women and children were regaled at the cross with plenty of roast beef, plum pudding and good ale. The tables were covered with clean cloths and again decorated with garlands and laurel. A procession with flags flying and garlands borne by young women dressed in white, with a good band of music playing "God Save the King" and "Rule Britannia" etc. paraded the village and the adjoiniung (sic) hamlet of Micklebring .....an effigy of Bonaparte was placed on an ass, escorted by a number of boys.....

Doncaster Gazette and Nottingham & Lincoln Gazette, 15th. October, 1819

In the afternoon of Sunday, 3rd. October, when the whole family were attending the Methodist Chapel, the dwelling house of Francis *Westby* of Braithwell . . . . tailor was broken into and robbed of £10. 5s. 0d. in local notes and some silver. The thieves intended to take away a quantity of cloth but it is supposed they were alarmed; on the family returning from the Chapel an active hue and cry was raised but without success. (This house was No. 27 High Street.)

Doncaster Gazette 22 Sep 1820

Braithwell; to be let by auction at the Red Lion 3 October 1820 at 3pm; Several closes of land now in possession of John Snipe.

Cockhill close	8 acres
dto	4 acres
Wass close or Cockhill Dale close	7 acres
In the Great Field	2 acres

Doncaster Gazette 6 October 1820.

Inquest on the Rev. J. Thompson of Braithwell, found dead on road leading to his house. Verdict: "Found dead."

Doncaster Gazette, 3 March 1826

Auction by Mr Auckland of Braithwell
A dwelling house, cottage, malt house, malt chamber, pump of good water and other conveniences, stable, cowhouse, orchard

and part of foldstead and croft adjoining . . . . a desirable situation for a maltster.

And a barn with stable, the rest of the foldstead and croft, capable of being converted into a very good homestead.

Both fronting the town street,

Both copyhold, held of the Manor of Conisbrough, the fine small and certain. Now in the occupation of William Mason and William Lee respectively.

To view, apply to Mr. Wild, Braithwell, or Mr Holdworth, Braithwell.

(This must be Maltkiln Farm, High Street.)

From the "Doncaster, Nottingham and Lincoln Gazette" June 15th., 1832

Education

Braithwell Vicarage

The Rev. H. Ellershaw receives into his house the limited number of SIX YOUNG MEN whom he undertakes to board and instruct in the various branches of Classical, Mathematical and Commercial education.

The situation of Braithwell Vicarage is healthy and retired; and Mr. Ellershaw pledges himself to pay the strictest attention to the religious and moral conduct, the domestic comfort and the literary improvement of every young gentleman entrusted to his care.

No day pupils are admitted

N.B. Terms, which are liberal, and references to clergymen and others of the first respectability, may be had on application, either personally, or by letter post paid

Braithwell, near Bawtry
June 6th., 1832

(This would be the old Vicarage).

Henry Ellershaw came to Braithwell as a Curate and lived at the Rectory. He left in January 1834. Charles Augustus Stewart was vicar but lived outside the Parish.

Doncaster, Nottingham and Lincoln Gazette June 22nd., 1832

Sale by Mr. Ben Badger

Holly House

To be sold by auction by Mr. Ben Badger

At the house of MR. SELBY, the Red Lion Inn in Braithwell .... on Friday the 29th. of June precisely at five o'clock ....

203

The following VALUABLE FREEHOLD ESTATE
late the property of Mr. Thomas Mawe deceased, consisting of:
All that newly-erected substantially-built . . . . DWELLING
HOUSE called Holly House, situate in the parish of Braithwell
. . . . adjoining the road leading from Rotherham to that place,
with the stables yard, garden and appurtenances and the following closes of land, lying in a ring fence adjoining the homestead as the same were in the possession of Thomas Mawe
deceased . . . . five pieces of land amounting to 16 acres, 3
roods, 9 perches.) . . . .

This house was east of Silverthorpe, Ravenfield Common.
(now demolished)

May 17th., 1833
There cannot be adduced a stronger proof of the healthy state
of Braithwell . . . . than this fact, that there are at present living
(there) nine persons whose united ages amount to 726 years . . .

CHAPTER 34

Ephemera

1. 17th. June, 1690 Sibilla Sheppard (nee Oldom) died at 100
   years old
2. Window Tax
   The Window tax was introduced in 1695 and many
   houses in the Village had windows blocked up – the tax
   was not repealed until 1851. Dairies were free from this
   tax and a sign DAIRY had to be put above the door.
3. In 1710 in this Village:
   lodgings were 3d a night and supper 2d
   Carrying a man on horseback 1/- (it doesn't say
   how far!!)
   A coffin was 4/-
   A burial was 3/-
   A house for rent from £2 to £5 per annum
   Beef and mutton   2d. per lb
   Veal   ½d   (one half penny)
   Butter   4d. a lb

4. In 1780 of ten people who died, nine died of fever. Many in the late 1700s died of consumption, paralysis and convulsions. Many people over 65 who died were put in the Register as "natural decay".

5. Pheasants are not natives of Britain. The Duke of Marlborough brought eggs back from his travels abroad and used broody hens to hatch them on his estate at Blenheim in 1787. This was soon taken up by others.

6. An 18th. Century Farrier's Bill

OSFOADA (Home for a day)	4s 6d
AFOTHOS (Hay for the horse)	2s 6d
ASHUINOFIM (A shoeing of him)	2s 0d
ATEKINIMUMAGEN (A taking him home again)	1s 0d
	Total 10s 0d

1s (one shilling) in those days is equivalent to £7-30 today.

7. In the 1800s all householders had to give six days a year in keeping parish roads repaired and worked under an overseer whose job it was to see the job done correctly. This finished in 1835 with the Highways Act.

8. In 1810 in a Braithwell field (Chapel Holes) was dug up a small sepulchral urn; and in a pit near it twenty-two human skulls supposed, by Mr. Beckwith the antiquarian, to be the remains of some of the Roman soldiers who were slain when fighting with the Brigantes. The ashes of one of the generals he supposes to have been contained in the urn. A few Roman coins have also been found at various times in the above field. In the mid-1900s skeletons were found here.

9. Barbed wire came from America in 1870. We cannot imagine how difficult it must have been without this deterrent to animals straying – that is why they had to be watched all the time (tented) before 1870.

10. Bird scaring was a job done by children who took time off school – they could be employed for a few pence a week. It was a lonely old job. They shouted and waved but also used a wooden clapper made of three pieces of wood

banged together – very much like a football clapper (rattle) in use today.

11. Harvesting and hay-making time brought in some extra money for the farm labourer who was always struggling to keep his head above water. The main thing he always bought with this extra money was a good stout pair of boots for winter – absolutely essential to anyone working on the land.

12. A corn dolly was plaited from the last sheaf of corn and carted home – this is an omen for a good harvest next year and really a pagan custom – a continuity link and seems to be connected with an old fertility cult.

13. The bay in all barns, large or small, is always the same – a perch (16½ ft.) the distance needed to keep four oxen – a plough team. A bay is the distance between each roof truss.

14. Stone was quarried from the quarry above Field Houses in 1893 for the restoration of St. James' Church at Braithwell.

15. Birkwood Terrace ("The Seven Houses" as it is known in the Village) was commissioned by Robert John Clarkson of Conisbrough. They were started in 1905 and completed in 1906 by Robinsons of Denaby. They were built for £560 for the seven – £80 each (how different things were then!). They were painted by R.J. Clarkson for £8 per house – inside and out. The woodwork was all done by the local joiner and undertaker, Mr Lawrence. In 1993 one of the middle houses sold for £34 000. There would be no brick buildings here until the early 1900s.

16. In 1906 Common Close and Braithwell Close were sold to Railway.

17. 1907 Great-grandfather left Foredoles.

18. On 20th June 1921 Thomas Edwards of London House (could this be the Post Office?), who must have been a ten-ant of Lord Scarbrough's was asking if his pump could be repaired. It was fastened to a wall in the passage. Lord Scarbrough paid 10/- per annum for water from a neigh-bouring pump for his two cottages on Doncaster Road (Nrs. 14 & 16).

19. A letter from Fanny Hill to Lord Scarbrough asks him to remove an Elm tree overhanging her property. She had just bought the cottage and chapel at the end of Church Lane . This also proves this building was still known as the Ebeneezer Chapel in the early 1900s (plaque still attached

to gable) even though the chapel in Austwood Lane had been built for over 100 years.

20. During the miners' strike of 1926 coal was mined at Micklebring to a depth of 50' opposite Malt Kiln Farm – hence Coal Pit Lane.

21. In 1926 our Dutch barn burnt down. Gertie Beavers of High Street was playing with my brother Derrick, who was seven and some friends in the croft. They lit a fire to cook potatoes and sparks went on the stack. All the top went up and the pillars were very badly charred. This was re-erected and the charred pillars were used again to re-erect it. Also some of the charred timber was used to build a hen-house.

22. 1st. February 1928 the New School opened

23. Water was piped to the Village from Austerfield artesian wells in 1929 but not everybody got water on tap because of the cost.

24. Sewage was laid on in the Village in 1931 but some houses didn't get water closets until the 1960s

25. Electricity came in 1933/4 (Street Lights – April 6th.). Due to cost, lots of Village people didn't get this until the later 1930s and most people only after the war.

26. The first council houses in Braithwell were built in Ashton Lane 1937. These housed people from the Alley when the houses were condemned and from caravans and wooden buildings around the Village.

27. My father bought our Farm as a sitting tenant in 1938.

28. In 1940 our first tractor was a Fordson. It cost £164 and the registration was BDT 905 (DT being Doncaster).

29. The Ashton Lane stone quarry closed in 1946. John Swift's father worked at this quarry. He made pig troughs, stone sinks, staddle stones etc.. In 1978 a firm tried to re-open this quarry but at a public meeting, when I was Chairman of the Parish Council, we got it stopped. We all breathed a sigh of relief. Fancy having a quarry up there as well as down Ruddle Mill Lane.

30. New Club built 1947

31. Council Houses, Holywell Lane, started 1957

32. Cedar Farm sold for £11,000 in 1960

33. Ruddle Mill – with house still standing – sold for £8,000 in 1961

34. 24th May 1965 at 6.30pm the Children's Play Area opened

32. 1982 Playing Field opened
33. 31st. August, 1994 School Closed. Sad Day
34. **Wells and Ponds in Braithwell in the Early 1900's**

Ashton Lane

1. Field Houses At the back, about 6ft. from the back door. This had a stone surround and a bucket which was hauled up by manpower
2. Ashton Farm · · · · High Street · · in the yard
3. Ashton House · · · · High Street · · in the yard
4. Hillcroft House · · · · Ashton Lane · · in the yard
5. Hall Farm · · · · Maltby Lane · · back kitchen, with pump
6. Elmfield Farm · · · · Maltby Lane · · in the yard
7. Tofields Bungalow · · · · Maltby Lane · · in the yard, on the corner

Holywell Lane

8. The Bungalow · · · · by the wall separating it from Hall Farm, pump is still there
9. Village Pump · · · · in front of Well House – now reinstated
10. Well House · · · · well in the yard
11. Cedar Farm · · · · pump in the kitchen, well in the yard
12. Moat Hall · · · · still in the grounds
13. Birkwood Terrace · · · · a pump in the back yard behind No. 4; removed to Village well, served all 7 houses
14. Springdale Cottage back kitchen – pump
15. The Holy Well · · · · the spring was across the road from Birchwood house. All the houses down there used this water. This spring bubbled up from a hole in the ground.

Doncaster Road

16. Longleys (now Lansing House) · · · · Served 2 cottages now demolished.
   No. 1 & No. 2 · · · · Michael Haynes opened up the well there.
17. Post Office · · · · In yard

High Street

18. Known as "Bill Marshall's Yard" between Ashton Farm and Orchard Farm, just over the wall. This well

208

	was there until 1984 – bucket used to pull up water
19. Maltkiln Farm	in yard
20. & 21. Cardwell House	1 in kitchen, 1 on south side of house
22. Rook House (now a bungalow)	in yard
23. Pear Tree Farm	in yard
24. Elmhirst	in the yard at the back
25. Forge Cottage	in yard
26. 3 cottages off High Street (35, 37 and 39)	in yard – centre of village, 1 pump served 3
27. The Village Store	in the yard at the back
28. & 29. The Butcher's Arms Inn	pump in the kitchen, wells in the yard
30. The Poplars	in the yard, served the two houses
31. The Red Lion	in the yard
32. Cremona Cottage, Pear Tree Cottage, Butcher's Arms Cottage Cremona Villa and the cottage now a hairdresser's	in front of pub wall in the yard to serve all these four
33. Down Cockhill Lane	south side, there was a well
34. & 35. Manor House	1 in the yard, 1 in the kitchen with pump

Church Grove

36. Northfield	once a farm, in the yard
37. Low Farm	now demolished – in the yard

Holy Well, Braithwell (SK 5340 9383) 6½ miles east of Rotherham

This is one of only two "holy well" place-names in South Yorkshire marked on current O.S. 2½" (1 : 25 000) maps.

The well must have once been an important feature, as shown by a siting legend which links it with Braithwell Church but any significance which it once had is now lost on residents and visitors alike, who are far more likely to stop and admire Braithwell's Village Pump which was restored in the mid -1980s as part of a community programme. The holy well, meanwhile,

209

lies enveloped in an untidy pond, overlooked, yet an obvious candidate for restoration.

There were 5 ponds in the Village:
The Spring, Holywell Lane
Where we played leaping from stepping stone to stone and at Easter rolled hard-boiled eggs down the bank and into the water.

The Pond at Foredoles. At the top of the hill
Is real red clay and obviously has traces of Ruddle from the ruddle pits in the area – which were mined at Micklebring Back Lane.

Ruddle Mill Dam. Across the meadows down Holywell Lane
This fed the Ruddle Mill at Ruddle Mill Lane, Braithwell. We visited this often on our walks across the fields. Lots of wildlife – ducks, water hens, etc.

Pickins Pond, Cedar Farm. In the field opposite the Club entrance
This we skated on in winter – skating meaning sliding – we never had skates.

Dunstan's Pond. Going up the drive of Hall Farm
This pond was between the cart shed and the house drive and Holywell Lane (see farm map). The horses drank here and there was a direct entrance from the fold yard. It froze in winter too but Pickin's Pond always froze first as it was more exposed to the elements. This one was enclosed.

CHAPTER 35

Braithwell Census and Occupations
and where they lived

1801   331
1811   396
1821   438
1831   455

1841	447 221 females (95 under 20) 226 males (116 under 20)
1851	493
1861	422
1871	372
1881	362 reductions due perhaps to Inclosure
1891	357 when many would lose their living
1901	345
1911	480 increase perhaps due to Maltby pit opening
1921	699
1931	687
1941	not done due to war
1951	691
1961	848
1971	927
1981	1023
1991	1013

Occupations – Braithwell 1841 Census

John Snipe	Teacher of Free School Schoolmaster
Charles Colbeck	Tailor
James Thompson	Butcher
William Snipe	Wheelwright
Samuel Snipe	Apprentice Wheelwright
William Markham	Horse Breaker
George Hall	Farmer
Charles Hall	Framework Knitter
George Hicks	Victualler (Red Lion)
John Pearce	Clothier
William Thompson	Farmer
John Deakin	Farmer
William Law	Farmer (Foredoles)
Joseph Clarkson	Framework Knitter
Mark Beighton	Farmer
Robert Thompson Gent.	Farmer
Thomas Spittlehouse	Shoemaker
William Nortron	Shoemaker
Robert Dawson	Shoemaker/Journeyman
James Clarkson	Framework Knitter
Thomas Gandy	Farmer
George Satterfit	Farmer
William Greensmith	Farmer
John Thompson	Blacksmith (Lived at Well House)

Ann Mason	Publican (vict.) Butcher's Arms
James Thompson	Blacksmith (Forge Cottage)
Thomas Kay	Butcher
Elizabeth Westron	Milliner
Sarah Nettleship	Milliner's Apprentice
William Wild	Farmer (Fox House Farm),
Charles Kay	Farmer (Hall Farm)
George Kay	Maltster
Elizabeth Burton	Schoolmistress
Thomas Ridgway	Stonemason
Charles Ridgeway	Apprentice Stonemason
John Thompson	Farmer (Well House Farm)
Richard Brooks	Gardener
John Revill	Carpenter (Joiner)
Hannah Howell	Framework Knitter
Martha Clarkson	Framework Knitter
Robert Hall	Shoemaker
George Thompson	Blacksmith
William Clarkson	Framework Knitter
John Snipe	Wheelwright
Thomas Revill	Wheelwright (Raddle Lane)

Occupations – Braithwell 1891 Census

Francis Broom	Farmer (Field Houses)
Robert Dunstan	Farmer (Foredoles)
William Tindle	Farmer (Holly House)
Richard Dunstan	Farmer (Foredoles)
Sydney Weyman	Butcher's Assistant
J. T. Waterhouse	Farmer (Manor)
Edward Robson	Farm Foreman
John Markham (40)	Blacksmith
John Markham (66)	Horsebreaker
Thomas Thompson	Blacksmith
Albert Fidler	Blacksmith's Assistant
John Lawrence	Joiner/Wheelwright
William Payne	Police Constable
Edward Baker	Butcher
Robert Houghton	Farmer/Carrier
Annie Duckmaster	Nurse
John Marshall	Farmer (between Ashton Farm & Orchard Farm),
Hannah Sayles	Farmer

Edward Spencer	Farmer
Mark Clarkson	Painter/Paperhanger
George Spencer	Farmer
William Garbutt	Agricultural Labourer/Engineer
Frederick Burton	Wheelwright/Coach Builder
Eliz. Watson	Dressmaker
Francis Crawshaw	Farm Bailiff
William Turner	Farmer (Well House)
Joshua Norman	Pawnbroker (Rose Cottage)
George Crookes	Publican (Red Lion)
Helen Beck	Dressmaker
George Turner	Butcher
Henry Hall	Cordwainer
Robert Hall	Engine Fitter
Henry Colbeck	Publican (Butcher's Arms)
Charles Briscoe	Schoolmaster
Charles Colbeck	Tailor
Annie Little	Dressmaker's Apprentice
Charlotte Turner	Dressmaker
Emma Stevenson	Dressmaker
George Speight	Cordwainer
Joseph Moers	Joiner/Wheelwright
George Clarkson	Hosier/Grocer
William Wild	Farmer
Charles Ridgeway	Mason
Thomas Ridgeway	Bricklayer's Apprentice
Alfred Dove	Travelling Photographer (wood tent in farmyard, Braithwell)

Where they Lived
(Farm acreages in early 1900s)

FOREDOLES 300 acres
    James Shepphard (1752), Mary Amery, William Law,
    Fisher, R. Dunstan, Walker, Revitt, Lunn

MANOR FARM 186 acres
    Thomas Dyson, Waterhouse, Scrimshaw, J. Stones, Golland
    Chatterton, E. Braithwaite, C. Cooper Snr., C. Cooper Jnr.

HALL FARM (Milk Herd) 190 acres
    Charles Kaye, G. Spencer, Robert Dunstan, Edwin Dunstan,
    Derrick Dunstan and Dennis Dunstan

ELMFIELD (Milk Herd & Milk Round) 150 acres
    William Hawke, Yudon, R. Robinson, Spencer & Palmer

(farm men, lived in the house), E. Harrison, John Lidget, B. Robinson

WELL HOUSE FARM 30 acres
John Thompson, William Turner, Mottram, Arthur Spencer, Ron Robinson, Jim Gurney, Harper, R. Dye, David Musson, McAteer

CEDAR FARM (Milk Herd) & (Milk Round) 100 acres
George Kay, Ron Robinson, T. Belk, Frank Crawshaw, William Pickin, G. Lee, J.Thompson

FOX HOUSE FARM 60 acres
Thomas Wild, William Wild, Jim Parkes, Harry Parkes, Jack Parkes

ORCHARD HOUSE FARM (Milk Herd) 65 acres
Robert Thompson, Hardcastle, Albert Dunstan, Joe Dunstan

ASHTON FARM (Milk Herd) 58 acres
Richard Thompson, George Wells, Crookes, Smith, Cooke, Bailey, Vincent Hill, Peter Dunstan

MALTKILN FARM (Milk Herd) 52 acres
Nicholson, Herbert Allison, Leslie Allison, Randall Allison, John Stevens

LOW FARM (Church Grove) (Milk Herd, Milk round)
owned by Lord Scarbrough, (now demolished) Thomas Gandy, Leonard Waterhouse, Edward Dobbs

FIELD HOUSES originally 2 cottages. 30 acres
Frances Broom, E. Pawson (sen.), A. Pawson

AUSTWOOD HOUSE FARM
Isaac Root, E. Knowles, R. Lee

PEAR TREE FARM (3 milk cows) 12 acres
Sarah Thompson, William Fidler, Septimus Fidler, Albert Fidler, Robert Holmes

RUDDLE MILL FARM (now demolished)
E. W. Pearson, Geo. Wells, Palmer, Gooch, Drury

CARDWELL HOUSE Wood, Foers, Weyman, Inman

HAREHOUND HOUSE (Once an alehouse)
John Swift, Martha Marshall (came from the Plough at Micklebring), William Marshall, Aimee Marshall, Gordon Leigh

ROTHERWOOD
John Thompson, Bailey, Brunt, Denham, A. & W. Crooks

NAILOR'S COTTAGE
Holgate, Picton, Woffinden, Taylor, Arnold

FORGE COTTAGE
Thomas Westry, Thompson (father followed by son), Mark Jones

LION COTTAGES
William Snipe, John Snipe, Brookes, Beavers, Eddie Nicholls

ASHTON HOUSE
William Marshall, Lawrence (Wheelwright & undertaker, father followed by son), T. Causer

RED LION
George Hicks, George Turner, Harold Crowcroft, Eggleston, Eric Hughes, Willis Marsden, Jeff Rumbelow

BUTCHER'S ARMS INN
William Mason, Colbeck, Herbert Allison, George Morrel, Garrison Vasey, Jack Hallam, Edward Odlin, Graham Stubbs, Willis Marsden

WORKING MEN'S CLUB
Waring, Brewster, Johnson (when in Club Cottage garden), Neal, Butler (new Club)

SPRINGDALE COTTAGE
Wadsworth, Crow, Kitchen

MOAT HALL COTTAGE
Joe Crawshaw, T. Cutts, Myers, Plowright

HILLCROFT HOUSE
Wilson, Haigh, Wingfield, John Dunstan

VILLLAGE STORE
Thomas Thickitt, G. Clarkson, Travis, Peter Parkes, Bickmore, Annis Gill, Margaret Williams

NORTHFIELD
Bradbury (Sen.), Bradbury (Jnr.), L. Jones

MOAT HALL (now demolished)
John Vyncent, Thomas Toone, William Toone, W. Crawshaw

DAM HOUSE (Wild Duck Cottage) (now demolished)
Saxton, Ward, Dimbleby

ROOK HOUSE FARM (now demolished)
Nance Holmes, Fred Holmes

ELMHIRST
Joseph Clarkson, Edward Houghton, William Gooch, Robert Holmes, John Barker

CHAPTER 36

Entries Taken From Old Accounts Book of Charles Kay
who farmed Hall Farm, Braithwell

Remember – 1s. then is worth 146s (£7-30) today

1829 June 7th   Pay for casual labour

1½	days	leading manure	3s – 0d
1½	days	mowing clover	3s – 0d
2	days	howing[1] turnips	4s – 0d
3½	days	thrashing wheat	7s – 0d
1	day	getting stuck in	2s – 0d

May 30th. *Hired to Thomas Ridgeway**

2 horses to fetch stone from Roach Abbey	5s – 0d
2 horses to fetch lime from Roach Abbey	5s – 0d
Sharpening 4 chisels	3d

* He was an old stonemason in Braithwell and built
many of the houses
His name appears on a cottage in the Village

1830 June 28th. House let to Markham at 1s – 8d per week

May 30th. 2lb cheese at 8d per lb	1s – 4d
May 6th. George Godber's mare came to clover	6d per week
May 11th. Mr. Hall's horse and foal came to clover	10d per week
Feb 2nd. Ploughing ½ acre	4s – 0d
Leading 2 load manure	2s – 0d

1830 July

2 stone troughs	4s – 0d
2 pecks seedling tatoes[2]	1s – 4d
4 chisels sharpened	3d
3 score plants	4½d
2 horses to fetch grave stone from Roach[3] Abbey	5s – 0d

[1] hoeing; [2] potatoes; [3] Roche

1831 January 26th. William Wastney Toone promised marriage to Charlotte Kay in the presence of his brother Thomas and said he would never marry anybody else

1831 January 28th. Hired for 1 year
Mary Wilkinson of Rotherham – wages£6 – 0s – 0d per year
John Mitchell of Wombwell   £7 – 10s – 0d per year

1831 June 3rd.		s – d
½lb	butter	5
1 lb	currants	9
3¼lb	cheese	2 0½
6	Pigeons	2 0
	Fat calf	90lb at 5½d

1831 June 8th   *Funeral Expenses for my father (Charles Kay)*

	£ –	s –	d
¾ yd flannel		3	3
Shrowd[1]		7	0
Bisquites[2]		7	0
Pipes[3] and Tobacco		1	5
Cheese			9
Leg Mutton 15lb		9	4½
4lb Beef		2	4
Wine		12	0
Paid Bearers		12	0
My Trouble	1	1	0
Berrying[4] Fees		5	0
A "Mortium" to the Parson		10	0
Paid Sarah Grindle[5]		3	0
Coffin	1	10	0

[1]*Shroud* [2]*Biscuits* [3]*Clay* [4]*Burying* [5]*This family is still in the Village*

1831 December 19th. Wagon Coals to Tickhill   £1 – 18s – 0d
                    Wagon Coals to Braithwell £1 – 8s – 0d
                    Cart Coal to Conisboro   14s – 0d

1834		s – d	
April 11th.	2¼lb Beef at 6d per lb	1–1½	(One and three ha'pence)
12th.	10¾lb Beef at 6d per lb	5–4½	(Five & four-pence ha'penny)
June 3rd.	Sheep's pluck	1–0	(One shilling)
7th.	10½lb Mutton at 6½d per lb	5–8¼	(Five & eight-pence farthing)
July 25th.	10½lb Veal at 6½d per lb	5–8¼	(Five & eight-pence farthing)

217

1838	Grindstone	5s – 0d
	2 Carts	£5 – 0s – 0d
	1 Wagon	£8 – 0s – 0d
	3 Pig Troughs	7s – 6d
	10 Sacks	15s – 0d
	1 Straw Cutter	15s – 0d

1842

Nov 21 Hired James Foster for one year for £7 – 0s – 0d
had to be washed for

Nov 24 Hired Harriot Webster for one year for £2 – 15s – 0d
She left first week

Dec 5 Hired Elizabeth Bower for one year for £3 – 10s – 0d
Horse Shoeing 1s – 0d

Tincture of mur for a prick in a horses foot
For cuts and Bruises
4oz of Vinos Turpentine
3oz Rozin
1 pennyworth of Verdigrease
All boiled together

1844

January 30th.

Horse and cart to load tiles from old Vicarage 1s – 6d
June 12th 3 horse loads of stone from Brecks quarry 7s – 6d
June 17th Horse to ride to Doncaster (7 miles) 2s – 0d
June 23rd Horse to ride to Conisboro (4 miles) 1s – 6d
July 27th Horse to Maltby Stone and Sandbeck 1s – 6d
Aug 4th
3 horses & cart to Wickersley quarry for rig stones 10s – 0d

1844 December
2 loads wood leading from Maltby Wood 5s – 0d
2 horses and cart to Roach Abbey for Tombstone 5s – 0d
3 Rood Fallow Ploughing 5s – 0d
Bricks from Conisboro (500) 6s – 0d

**1833 Recipe written by Charles Kay, born in the Village
May 29th. 1806**
How to skin a horse and make him up for sale
The names of the stuff
Mitre and flour of sulphur and cream of tarter and horse spice

and penny grit sand.

You must get an equal quantity of each sort and it must be given either in balls or in a little wet mash.

Give each horse a table spoonfull every other night an hour after water and they must have no more water till next morning.

Give them alf a buckitt of water and put one handfull of salt in it then give each horse ½lb. of salt petre 2oz at a time disolve in a little warm water and mix it in a little mash and when you go out if it be cold you must give each horse a table-spoon full of carraway seed and it will keep their inside warm.

It is a medicine that any Christian may take or I would not give it to a horse

CHAPTER 37

The Governance of The Township – Before Parish Councils

Parish Councils were not constituted until the last years of the nineteenth century. Before then Parish matters were in the hands of the clergy, "responsible citizens" and some rate-paying householders. This "council", which met regularly, appointed parish officials to carry out the necessary duties of the Township. All except the vicar and the Parish Clerk were vol-untary appointments. This council was known as The Vestry and in the case of Braithwell the Vestry Account Book remains intact, showing balance sheets regarding Parish expenses, the earliest records dating from 1717. The chief elected officials appointed by the Vestry were the posts of Constable, Churchwardens and Overseers of the Poor.

The Parish Constable
Three lists of nominations survive for Braithwell and Constables appointed were:

1848	Edward Spencer	Micklebring	from a list of eight
1853	William Wild	Braithwell	

objections to being on the list had to be made in writing and taken to the Mansion House in Doncaster.

The Constable had to maintain law and order within the community and he was responsible to the Churchwardens and J.Ps. His was one of the most hated posts in the village and, although when elected one had to serve, often others were paid to take the job that another didn't want! The appointment was for one year – from Michaelmas to Michaelmas and balance sheets (from 1735 to 1830) written by the Braithwell Constables are in existence. All the reports deal with the usual business – fetching warrants, attending Brewster Sessions, attendance at Courts Leet and Baron at Conisborough and the drawing up of lists but other items of interest are mentioned.

It would seem that as well as his many regular duties, the Braithwell Constable was also a "pest control officer". The going rate seems to have been:

2d.	per dozen sparrows
4d.	for a fourmart (polecat)
1s. 0d.	for a fox

In one instance he was presented with: "48 dozen sparrows" – useful ale money for some Villager!

About 1751 there is a record of the Village Pond being "mended" at a cost of 8d..

In 1752 an entry states "myself for Common Day Work ale 3s. 6d..

In 1762 Richard Amory took pity on those doing common day work to the extent of:

John Bayes for ale	3s. 0d
Ann Lockwood for ale	3s. 0d.
John Jackson for ale	3s. 0d.
Samuel Parkin for ale	3s. 0d.

How much ale did one get for 3s. 0d. in those days?!

John Coulton's entry in 1773 leads one to wonder if the Constable had a uniform:

"Constable's staff painting	13s. 9d.
Brass ball for same	2s. 0d.
For turning same	1s. 8d."

The entry for 1781 needs little explanation: "For well gutter cleaning 5s. 6d. ..... for ale for men as was cleaning it 1s. 6d." but some entries do leave one to speculate... "given to sufferers by water 9d." Had there been storms and flooding?

In 1781 the Constable's report was brief and many of the

expenses relate to liquor – they must have had a merry Christmas that year:

"December 24th   1 gallon red port   9s. 4d.
                    4 bottles   1s. 0d.
                    bread and fetching   10d"

Even on official business, ale seems to have been a necessity. On October 18th. 1786 the Constable reports taking:

"3 persons at Conisborough Court 2s. 0d., Liquor at same time 2s. 6d."

It is about this time that Braithwell Fair is mentioned. 1788 seems to have been a year to note – on 4th. May there is an entry: "handbills for Braithwell Fair, and paper 3s – 6d." but of more interest is the entry for 9th. July which simply says: "paid at Braithwell Feast in quelling a riot 1s. 0d." ... an entry which leaves you wondering what really happened! It seems the custom was to ring the Church bells to publicise the Fair and there are numerous entries giving payments to the ringers – the usual price was 3s. 0d.. Again, "paid for ale at Braithwell Fair" appears also to have been a common occurrence. On 3rd. may 1791 John Armitage wrote: "Braithwell Fair cried twice 10d." and in July of the following year we learn that trouble again occurred in the area: "paid to the Chief Constable the Parishes proportion of damages on account of Sheffield riots £11 3s 11d.".

The Village pumps at both Braithwell and Micklebring were in constant need of repair: "Paid for wood casing for Braithwell pump 7s. 8d. (1819)" Micklebring Pump repaired twice. New bucket and 2 new spouts (1828).

The stocks seem to have been in constant use and often in need of repair. If it wasn't new stone supports, it was minor expenses for staples and locks. In 1747 the Constable paid for "work done at the new stocks, and ale, 7s. 6d." and "for leading stones and a new lock 1s. 2d." In 1827 another stone post was fetched for the stocks at a cost of 2s. 6d. We have a record in 1824 of "paid for handcuffs 10s. 0d.". Fun and games were had in 1752, the Constable being paid 4d. for carrying out a hue and cry.

The most time-consuming part of the Constable's duties appears to have been dealing with the regulations regarding the Militia. This temporary force was organised locally and Militia men lived and worked at home but had to go when the call came. They had to attend a camp each year for two weeks' training and they were intended specifically for home defence. This force came into being in the thirteenth century – the Dad's Army of its day!

Under the 1757 Act Parish Constables were ordered annually to record names of all men between the ages of 18 and 50 (excluding Peers, clergy, teachers and apprentices). From this list a ballot was held and a given number of men were enlisted (reluctantly) from each Parish. Later the upper age limit was reduced to 45. This military service was hated by all and in some cases led to rioting. Opposition steadily grew and in 1829 service in the Militia was again on a voluntary basis. Each Braithwell Constable mentions drawing up the lists, organising the ballots, taking the enlisted men to Sheffield for swearing in, along with his expenses for these duties. On February 9th. 1810 William Wordsworth, Constable, reports: "going to Sheffield to swear militia men 9s. 6d." Later the account reads "going to Rotherham to lot for lawcal milishaw". It would seem that this was an onerous job and to curry favour, the enlisted men were well treated by the Constable. A good example of this reads:

"To Rotherham to swaer them in	2s. 0d.
Expenses with them	12s. 0d.
Gave Sargent	1s. 6d.

Richard Smith gave the information that on 21st. July 1819

"my day to Rotherham to hire a militia man in harvest	3s. 6d.
Paid for militia man	£2 2s. 0d.

He was obviously finding a replacement for a Village resident, chosen by lot, who did not wish to serve. This was common practice – as long as you could afford it!

Overseers of the Poor

From the middle of the twelfth century onwards, the great monastic houses began to be established across the country. Over the next three centuries, thanks to gifts and endowments, they grew rich in both land and property. In an unorganised way they coped with the endless needs of the poor who beat a path to their door. They were fitted out with charity in the form of food, dole and clothing. With the dissolution of the Monasteries during the reign of Henry VIII, the monastic lands were sold. It was then left to the conscience of the Squire or Landed Gentry to decide whether to continue this practice. Some felt that the care of the village and its inhabitants was their responsibility but others were not so charitable. Towards the end of the reign of Elizabeth I, legislation was passed creating the Poor Law to be paid by compulsory rates levied on the individual parishes according to their needs, sometimes called the Assessment. The main aim was for the Overseers using funds provided by the Assessment to purchase materials to fund work for the able-bodied poor. They also sought apprenticeships for the children of poor families to ensure that they in turn did not become a burden "on the Parish.". The established system was not perfect but it kept the poor from starving. England was the only country in Europe to have such a system and many historians believe that the Poor Law was one of the reasons why public unrest and rebellion did not break out in England as it did on the continent at the end of the eighteenth century.

The post of Overseer of the Poor was a voluntary one requiring a great deal of time and dedication. In many cases the post-holders were also the Churchwardens of the Township. As can be seen from the existing Braithwell documents, the job changed hands almost every year. Accounts for the Township are in existence from 1735 and most have survived up to 1812.

The only record of poor relief within the Township before 1735 was to be found in a book called "Yorkshire from AD 1000". In it we learn that "poor people set up houses on the wastes and commons, especially in the Western parts but even on the Magnesian Limestone belt, where a survey of 1652 found "foure pore houses" built on the Lord's waste at Braithwell." As has been detailed in Archbishop Herring's Visitation Report of 1743, there were two alms houses in existence at that date in the Parish.

From the records kept by the Overseers of the Poor we can glean a great deal about life in the Township and the hardships encountered daily. Many of the recipients were widows, the amount they received varying according to the number of dependant children. In 1738 the entry reads: "Widd Simson 3s. monthly.". All needs were catered for including clothing, fuel, food, ale, doctor's bills, furniture, house repairs and burial expenses:

1738	Paid John Rowell for hiss coffin	6s.
	for woll to winde him in	6d.
	Paid Widd Stool for layin him out and attending	1s.

1741	Mare Guy buriell.		
	Coffin	6s.	
	Bread and drink	3s.	
	Clark and parson two and foverpens		
	lingeher ut on shilon	3s.	4d.
	for woll and my atendons	1s.	4d.
1745	for repairing ye alms house. 8 score of		
	thacke	8s.	
	paid ye thacker for 2 days	1s.	8d.
	for leading and watering and thacke		
	getting in all	2s.	6d.
	John Hodsham 2 pecks of wheat	2s.	2d.
	Paid for a pare of shoos for him	4s.	
	paid for a pare of blankits	7s.	6d.
	for Barle a ved. 6yds. at 7 pens a yars	3s.	6d.
	for making it and filling it	1s.	
	for my trobell		8d.
1750	2 sheepharts and eds for Hames Burla		6d.
1752	Bought James Barley a Chaff bed	4s.	
	a coverlet for James Barley	5s.	2d.
1756	Gave Eliz Palethorp when she was badley	1s.	
	Eliz Palethorp 2 pecks of wheat and 1s		
	when she baptised her child	3s.	
	paid for burying Sarah Fryer	14s.	
	Paid Mary Revill for laying Eliz Palethorp	2s.	
	paid Ann Lockwood for ale	1s.	
	Eliz Briggs. pd. for her burell	2s.	4d.
	for her cofin	5s.	
	for crape for her		6d.
	for wakening and bread and ale	3s.	
	for my trobll		8d.
	pd. for a cofin for Bet. Palethorps child	2s.	6d.
	bread and ale	2s.	
	buryal fees	2s.	
(...a bad year!)			
1764	Thomas kemp. paid his rent	15s.	
	going for his goods to bramley	3s.	
	for his wife bord 3 days	1s.	
	John Wadsworth for mendin bed and		
	setting it up		4d.
	Widow Sails a post leter to botry		9d.

John gye for going cunsber with a mad woman		6d.
1774 John Guys reposeing metearials and workmans wages and casage		£2. 11s. 4d.
John Guy for ringing bell at 5 and 12 o' clock		£1. 3s. 0d.
1779 Paid Elizabeth Laycock for mending Amory's shirts and washing a shirt for him that was John Guys		1s. 6d.
1798 - for ale for cross setting up		3s. 0d.
Widow Amerys funeral. Pd. to clerk		5s. 0d.
Mr. Thompsons fee		1s. 0d.
paid singers		2s. 0d.
paid for flnel and pines		2s. 4d.
Pd. John Wordsworth for coffin		13s. 6d
pd. to Braithwell clerk		2s. 6d.
1803 (This was at the height of the Napoleonic Wars and the "standing army" was engaged on the continent.)		
paid for John Show for the Armey of Resarve		5s. 6d.
paid for the men for the armey of resarve		£26.10s. 9d.
spent at a meeting for valintires		7s. 3d.
the valantires, ale, bread and cheese		3s. 4d.

To defray the costs as much as possible, jobs were given to the able-bodied poor as they were called. Many people mentioned above as being paid for work done were themselves on Poor Relief (e.g. John Guy and M. Holmes). Also widows on Poor relief were paid to look after other ill paupers.

The documents also show that work was created and sponsored by the Overseers to provide some income. Here are two extracts:

"1790 A wheel and reel for Mary Jackson		7s. 0d.
For spool and for her wheel mending		6s. 0d.
Yarn sold to Mark Clarkson		£1. 7s. 0d.
Yarn 11 lb. @ 1s. 2d. per pound spun by Ann Dyson		12s.10d."

The high rate demands needed to support the relief system as it was caused great unpopularity. This was one of the main reasons why in 1834 a new system of Poor Relief was instituted.

Under this law it was forbidden to give dole to the able-bodied poor as had previously been the case under the Speenhamland Judgement. Relief from then onwards was only to be given to those in the workhouse. New workhouses were built to meet the growing need and this system lasted until well into the present century.

Apprenticeships

In order to minimise the cost to the inhabitants of the Township, one of the duties of the Overseer of the Poor was to find apprenticeships for the children of those families receiving poor relief. The Archives at Doncaster have 12 original documents relating to such apprenticeships dating between 25.4.1727 and 17.11.1834.

If for some reason the master wished to terminate the agreement, a fine was imposed. The Township records show that Richard Sharpe of Micklebring, instead of taking Elizabeth Lowcock as a Parish Apprentice, agreed at a Parish Meeting to pay John Sheppard and William Amory (Overseers of the Poor) the sum of £10. (Elizabeth was said to be a "poor family child whose parents were not able to maintain her.").

Whilst on the subject of fines, the laws were also strict on the parents of children born out of wedlock, the impression being that a child brought up by a single parent could become a liability to the Parish. The records show that at a Parish Meeting on 10.7.1768, "William Haywood, son of John Haywood (farmer), the father of a bastard child, born on the body of Susanna Cooper of the Township of Micklebring", was ordered to pay the Overseers of the Poor and the Churchwardens the sum of 1s. 0d. per week "maintainance for the said child, William Haywood." Susanna Cooper, the mother, was also ordered to pay 6d. per week, in order to have the 1s. 6d. that it was deemed necessary to look after the child.

❧

CHAPTER 38

Extracts from The Minutes of The Parish Council

Braithwell Parish Council
At A. Parish Meeting held this 4th day of December 1894.

according to the Notice pasted on page one of this Book.

Proposed by Mr William Wood and seconded by Mr William L. Tindle. that Mr. John Thomas Waterhouse. of Braithwell Manor. take The Chair. Carried unanimously.

Mr. Waterhouse took The Chair at 10 minutes past Seven O' Clock.

The following Gentlemen were forthwith Nominated as Parish Councillors.

Viz.		
Mr. Robert Dawson.	*Gentleman.*
Mr. Robert Dunstan.	*Farmer.*
Mr. Henry Hall.	*Shoemaker.*
Mr. George W. Spencer.	*Farmer.*
Mr. Richard Spencer.	*Farmer.*
Mr. John Ward Turner.	*Farmer.*
Mr. John Thos. Waterhouse.	*Farmer.*
Mr. William Wild.	*Farmer.*
Mr. William Wood.	*Farmer.*

After opening and arranging The Nomination Papers and giving of due time for more Nomination Papers to be handed in according to Instructions as per. Local Government Board Order. (of Nov. 28th. 1894) the Several Nominations were duly put to the Meeting with the following Results___

Viz,			
Mr. Robert Dawson.	7.	
Mr. Robert Dunstan.	22.	Elected.
Mr. Henry Hall.	13.	
Mr. George W. Spencer.	21.	Elected.
Mr. Richard Spencer.	5.	
Mr. John Ward Turner.	14.	Elected.
Mr. John Thos. Waterhouse.		withdrawn.
Mr. William Wild.	29.	Elected.
Mr. William Wood.	21.	Elected.

After giving the full Time allowed by The Parish Councils Act. 1894. The Chairman finding no Poll was demanded. Therefore closed Tlhe Meeting.

Signed

(JNO WATERHOUSE Chairman)   Book 1 Fo. AB

At the first Parish Council Meeting held this 13th. day of December, 1894. according to Circulars sent by Mr. Waterhouse the Chairman of the Parish Meeting held on December 4th 1894.

After Each Member had Signed The Declaration accepting Office ___

Proposed by Mr. William Wood. & Seconded by Mr. Robert Dunstan. that Mr. William Wild be the provisional ___ & afterwards that he ___ Mr. Wild. be The Honourable. The first Chairman of the Braithwell Parish Council.
Carried Unanimously.

Proposed & Unanimously Resolved that Mr. Waterhouse be recorded with the best Thanks of This The first Council Meeting. for his Courtious & Impartial Services as Chairman. & conducting first Publick Meeting.

Proposed by Mr. Dunstan & seconded by Mr. Wood that Mr. Mark Clarkson be asked to take the duties of Clerk to The Parish Council until the March Meeting 1895. which was Carried Unanimously.
Mark Clarkson. accepting ___

Proposed by Mr. Spencer & seconded by Mr. Wood __ that Mr. Robert Dunstan be appointed Vice Chairman ___
 For Mr. Dunstan ___ Mr. Spencer.
                    Mr. Wood.
                    Mr. John Turner. was Nutural.

Signed   WILLIAM WILD   Chairman
                                      Book 1, Fo. CD

Parish Council Braithwell 1895

Copy of Circular calling Meeting to be held Feby 28th

I hereby give you Notice that a preliminary Meeting of the Council will be held in the Schoolroom, Braithwell, on Thursday next at 7 o'clock in the evening Feby 28th 1895

228

Business
1st. To decide as to the future custody of the Parish
Documents
2nd. "Also", Inviting the Recter & Churchwardens to attend
the said Meeting, to consider & discuss the Charities
of, & belonging to the Parish of Braithwell
The Council will be pleased to see copies of all Wills &
– belonging to the said Parish_____

Feby 23rd. 1895
Signed pro. William Wild.   Chairman
M. CLARKSON. Clerk.   Pro. Tem.
Book 1, Fo. E

1894 First Parish Council was held, in the Schoolroom, December 4th. Before that year it had been an Open Parish Meeting.

Meetings.
The Chairman to open Parish Meeting was chosen on the night. They seemed to be held only when necessary not every month as now. Sometimes once a year, sometimes four times, sometimes every month if something urgent arose. Members were elected to the Parish Council every year from December 4th. 1894 until 1901. Then it became 3 years.

1895 April First Treasurer appointed: Mr. William Wild
First Minuted mention Overseers: "G.W. Spencer & Mr. Henry Hall". "Assistant Overseer & Clerk "Mark Clarkson at a salary of £6pa and all fees connected with the office.".
October Request Birchwood Lane being put into reasonable repair as a highway and not as a bridle road and the bridle road from Fordoles to Lilly Hall be repaired.
£1 paid to Mr. Robert Dunstan by Mrs. Fisher for the Parish Treasurer (this must be for the Bull Piece at Foredoles)
December 5th. (Authority granted to) Repair Pinfold walls and impound stray cattle – whether this Authority lies with the Parish or District Council.
Reference made to "a School built by The Parishioners about the year 1871.".
Resolved that all Members attend Church on December 15th.

1896 Two oil lamps were in the Village: one attached to the Village Cross and one in the centre of the Village – presumably by the Butcher's Arms. Oil and lighting and repairs of same done by Mr. Fidler, Blacksmith.

1897 Another lamp was bought. (These were only lit in winter months November – March).

January First list of Charities – 32 Recipients . . . . "after paying of Claims by Will   TOTAL £15 – 9s. – 0d." Braithwell Council to plant trees above and below the Town Well in commemoration of H.M. The Queen's Diamond Jubilee Reign (what happened to these?)

March First Precept set at "1/2d in the £ giving £4 – 14 – 0."

Meetings were held in the old Church School (now a doctors' surgery) and members were usually elected by show of hands, sometimes by ballot but done on the premises the same evening. Some time was always given (15 mins., legal time) for a poll to be demanded. Mark Clarkson, Clerk to the Council from 1894 to 1902, had been the Poor Rate Collector for 28 years and Assistant Overseer of the Parish. He resigned due to ill health.

Cow Close Inquiry held 9th. May, 1895 (taken from the Charities Report)
"By Deed bearing date September 23rd. 1613 Rob Waterhouse and Maximillian his son of consideration of £20 paid by Philip Waterhouse, charged a messuage* and certain land held therewith, and a close called Cow Close, in Conisboro now the property of Mr William Nicholson with the payment of 20s. a year to be distributed by the vicar, churchwardens and overseers of the poor of Braithwell.".
  * *messuage – dwelling house with outbuildings and land*
My cousin Allen Smith found this field – to reach it you go down Kearsley Lane Conisbrough, cross Kearsley Brook and follow the public footpath to beyond the land behind the Conisbrough cemetery. It's on your right in the corner. Of course the hedges have been removed.

Bull Piece (From the Charity Report, dated 15th. May 1895)
"Mention was made at the Inquiry of a payment of £1 a year made by the owner of a certain farm in Braithwell, and believed to be charge upon a particular field, now or formerly called the Bull Close. The payment is probably made in discharge of an

obligation upon the owner or occupier of this field to maintain a bull for the use of the parish, but no certain evidence was forthcoming upon this point.

The money is paid to the churchwardens in the church porch and applied by them to the general expenses of the church. This application of the money appears to have the sanction of long usage, but the existence of the payment was apparently brought to the knowledge of most of the persons present at the Inquiry for the first time on that day, and it is possible that an inquiry into the matter will be instituted by the Parish Council." This has also been lost since Mr. Revitt left. Nobody seems to know its exact location. I did ask Mr. Ashley (Clerk to the Council) when I was Chairman. He didn't know but still kept collecting the £1 – bless him.

The Minutes always refer to "the lanes being let as usual." I can only think that this was the grazing of the lanes by animals and this must have been by some means of tender or spoken word, as a special Meeting was always called within the next few days. Obviously this was let to the farmer or smallholder who paid the most and of course there would be plenty of grass in the lanes, which would be good feed for cows or sheep etc.. They would have to be tented (watched) so they didn't stray.

1902 15th. April Mark Clarkson resigns as Clerk, thanks, Mr G.W. Turner takes over

1906 March Papers in the Parish Chest
Braithwell Common and Enclosure Award and Map
dated 1763
Valuation of Braithwell Parish for Rating purposes
dated 1816
ditto   1838
Book for Collecting Land Tax   1861
Braithwell Open Field Inclosure and Award with Map
dated 1858
Schedule of Claims for same
Agreement for catching moles   1838

1908 July Closing of old churchyard opposed for a few more years. (No further information in Minutes of when, or if, it was ever officially closed.)

1910 January A mole catcher was advertised for by the Parish Council. (This must have been the Council's responsibility) Braithwell Council asked for the Maltby Railway to be opened for passenger traffic.

They also asked that the Pinder (Mr. J. Brooks), keeper of the Pinfold, be asked to clean it out and the Cross, too.

1911 August It was proposed that The Clerk write Mrs. Marshall re. the Parish Choke Rope and that it was to be taken to the Butcher's Arms, the place where it was formerly kept.

This must have been the rope used for cows when they were choking. A rope with a small wooden end, narrower at one end than the other and put down a cow's throat if it was choking, usually from eating whole raw potatoes.

1913 A dispute arose about rights of way bordering the Mill Dam. Twenty-two people signed the Petition saying that they had used this path, some for 22 to 60 years.

1914 April Proposed a cart be sent round every month to collect rubbish and Doncaster asked to look at the tip up Ashton Lane.

1915 March. Lanes Letting Reasby Spencer and William Marshall

1916 November A resolution be sent to the County Council that application be made for a new school – AT ONCE

1918 February A Food Committee was formed – obviously due to the shortage during the war.

Land was offered by Mr. Crowcroft (landlord of the Red Lion) at £3 per acre which was accepted and the 3 acres of land was measured out for allotments. (Playing Field £1250 per acre, 1978).

1919 February Another 2 acres was rented from Mr. Crowcroft for more allotments, let at 8/- per year. Mr. Crowcroft to pay the rates of 12/-.

1st. March Poor Land Fields let – first time this was mentioned These are still let by the Parish Council to this day.

November Proposed that a War Memorial be put up in the Village. The Monument to have the following inscription:

"Tell Britain ye who mark this Monument
Faithful to her we fell and rest content"

but this was never done. I wonder why?

27th. December When the soldiers and sailors all returned from the war, a dinner at the Butcher's Arms was given for all of them and their wives and sweethearts.

1921 16th. April. Saturday at 3pm. Monument unveiled and Service in church followed by the Procession:

Rev. Seed the Vicar and Rev. Canon Bean to take part in short service in church.

Procession to Memorial:

> Clergy and Lord Scarbrough
> Choir
> Relatives of fallen men
> Ex soldiers
> Churchwardens and Chairman and Members of the Parish Council
> Children
> Rest of Congregation

In all the Minutes, it mentions two Councillors being voted in as Overseers of the Parish (officers concerned with the levying of the Poor Rate and the Poor Law). In most Parishes this had long since been done away with but not in Braithwell. Mentioned from 1890s to early 1920s. Also two Councillors responsible for "Letting the Lanes."

1920 Sewage to be emptied more frequently.

1923 26th. April First time it was recorded that "Minutes be passed as correct"

1924 December List of papers found in Parish Chest:
(Chest held in Church and still there but now empty)

"Map on Place of Braithwell Common	dated 1765
Award Dated on Parchment	1766
Map old	1858
Braithwell Open Field Enclosure Award	1857
Claim under the Award	1838"

1928 Enquiries made re. street lighting and domestic lighting from Yorkshire Electric Power Station. Villagers canvassed on lighting of public places (1929 cost too high, so not done until 1933).

1928 Braithwell Parish Council were offered 3½ acres of land for allotments in the field next to the Rectory for £184. This was not accepted.

1929 A fire hose was bought by the Council with nozzle costing £40 and housed in the Pinfold.

1930 A new sewage scheme was suggested but turned down by the Council as the land was too costly for the Parish.

1931 Ask for repair of the Cross.

1932 Council ask for public telephone. Carbon book bought for Clerk to use.

1934 Again the Sewage Scheme was mooted but turned down as it was to cost each parishioner 8d on his rates for the benefit of a few.

(Today's cost would be £82 for sewage based on ratable value of £119 (Band D).

"That George Ashley be Clerk", succeeding his late father-in-law, George Turner

November Several wells gone dry in the Village due to weather. Request for Parish Pump to be put in order.

1935 Man named Smith from Harthill wrote to say he had the "Parish Award of Braithwell" and for £10 they could have it. Chairman Mr. R. Robinson and Mr. E. Littlewood went to see him but refused to pay. They left it in the hands of the West Riding County Council.

(No mention since, what a pity. To have been lost for ever for £10.).

February Old Rate Books kept from Braithwell Overseer's time and stored in Mr. Baker's boot shop were destroyed in Mr. Albert Fidler's (the blacksmith) furnace.

May A flagpole was erected at the Cross with money left over from Jubilee Celebrations. The work done by Mr. J.W. Copley at a cost of £1. 10s. 0d.

The Jubilee was of his Majesty King George V. Cross railings and War Memorial railings painted for £1. 2s. 10d. by Mr. Copley. A Cup was purchased for each child up to 14 yrs. old. Fancy dress parade and a free tea. £10 Precept for Celebration and a special church service.

November When any business was left over for another Meeting, it was marked: "This business be left on table" One heading in November 26th. 1935 reads:

"Sewage be left on the table."

1935–36 Street lighting discussed and letters of complaint re. traffic – 30mph signs requested for the Village due to the narrowness of the Village street.

Village Pump to be restored.

1937 Meetings now in the Church School Room.

March Mr. Ronald Robinson retires after 18 years.

Last Meeting when nominations to vacancies allowed

April Typewriter bought for Clerk to use.

May Coronation Celebrations. 20doz Mugs bought, Church sports, fancy dress etc..

1938 May 12th. Mr Littlewood was very desirous of buying the

Pinfold & had seen R. Bowers Esq. Clerk to R.D.C. who informed him to ask the Parish Council if they would sell same, this being the case, they were advised to write the Ministry

Members of Council: Mr. W. Pickin (Chairman), Mr. Copley (vice Chairman), Mr. E. Littlewood (Treasurer), Mr. Jacques, Mr. Richardson

(The Pinfold was next to Mr. Littlewood's house (The Poplars, High Street).

1938 September Mr. Copley was asked to make the Village Pump safe

Printed letterheads used for the first time.

1939 January 17th Village Pump dangerous.

November 14th If Pump not made safe by R.D.C. the Parish Council felt it was incumbent upon them to proceed with the matter.

1940 Collision with Micklebring Village Pump "Lead exposed and has a very good market value.".

1944 October 23rd (R.D.C.) Bus company agreed to bus stops at Birkwood Terrace provided bus stop was at the south end and the north end of the houses. Police to be informed.

1946 February Mr Lidgett's (of Elmfield Farm) horse ran away with the cart and damaged the railings and curb (sic) at Braithwell Cross.

May Parish Well – Public Meeting in Church School

Parish Well to be either filled in or capped with concrete to make it safe.

Birkwood Terrace was still on closets – request for these to be emptied more frequently.

1947 March No 'busses came through Braithwell for six weeks due to snow

April Meetings in The Council School.

Keep left sign on Cross as the causway on Red Lion corner had been widened.

June "R.D.C. to purchase a plot of land adjoining the Council School for road widening purposes, the present owner had notified some members of the Parish Council that he would be agreeable to sell"

The above applies to the Lump (Lumping) in front of the iron gates to the Braithwell First and Middle School. Mr Albert Fidler of Pear Tree Farm owned it.

Many people have asked me how we lost the Pinfold. Here is

the answer now, collected together and out of Minuted sequence. Were we to blame? Yes!

1947 June 3rd. Mr Littlewood made an offer of Twenty Pounds for the purchase of the Pinfold in High St. Braithwell, the Parish Council were agreeable to sell at this price, Mr. Littlewood informed the Council that he had be in communication with Mr. Meldrum at the R.D.C & in his opinion the Parish Council were quite in order to sell.

Signed Chairman

Signed E J LITTLEWOOD

(Mr. Littlewood first made this offer on May 12th. 1938)

(Council Members:

Chairman Mr. Littlewood, Mr. Shaw, Mr. Lidgett, Mr. A Dunstan, Mr. Goodman)

July 8th. The Council were advised by the D R D C to write the Clerk of the West Riding C C. re the offer of twenty pounds for the Pinfold made by Mr. Littlewood, prop Mr Shaw & Sec Mr Goodman all in favour that the Clerk be instructed to write the West Riding C. C for their permission to sell the pinfold.

Signed. Chairman E J Littlewood

August 19th A letter was read to the meeting from the Clerk to the West Riding C C. in which he stated that the Pinfold was the property of the Parish & did not need the consent of the County Council to the sale. It was also pointed out that the consent of the Parish Meeting was required, & the consent of the Minister of Health, the money received from the sale of the Pinfold must be applied in such a manner as the Minister of Health may approve towards the discharge of any debt of the Parish Council or otherwise for any purpose for which capital money may be applied

Signed. *Vice Chairman* Frank Shaw

October 21st. In accordance with instructions received from the Clerk to the County Council re the sale of the Pinfold *this meeting was a Parish Meeting but none of the Parishioners with the exception of the Council attended* it was therefore proposed & passed to proceed with the sale of the Pinfold to Mr Littlewood subject to the approval of the Minister of Health

Signed. Chairman E J Littlewood

Where were we, the parishioners? We should have been at that Meeting and stopped that sale.

1948 April 9th. Minutes Parish Meeting held in the Church School Room. 9th April 1948.

There was a very poor attendance at this meeting & Mr H. Allison took the Chair at 7- 10PM.

The Chief business of this meeting was to discuss the sale of the Pinfold to Mr E J. Littlewood.

Sometime ago Mr. Littlewood made an offer of Twenty Pounds for the Pinfold & after several letters to various bodies namely the Doncaster RDC. The West Riding County Council, & the Ministry of Health, the Parish Council were ultimately informed by the Ministry of Health that a Parish Meeting should be held.

Mr Shaw. proposed that the Pinfold be sold to Mr Littlewood & was seconded by Mr Goodman all in favour.

This ended the Parish Meeting & the Council then went into committee to follow on with Council matters.

(Mr E J Littlewood now took the Chair)

July 22nd. A letter was read to the meeting from the Ministry of Health sanctioning the sale of the Pinfold to Mr Littlewood for £20 Twenty Pounds. It was pointed out in the letter to what uses the proceeds of the sale could be used for Viz., National Saving Certificates, Post Office Savings account on behalf of the Parish, or for the General expenses of the Council.

A resolution was passed by the Council that the money be used to meet the general expenses of the Council.

Signed. E J Littlewood Chairman

September 23rd. After all the preliminary details which had taken some months to complete re the sale of the Pinfold to Mr. Littlewood for the sum of (Twenty Pounds), Mr Littlewood produced the agreement at this meeeting for signing by two councillors & the Clerk, this was accordingly done & the Sum of Twenty Pounds was paid to the Clerk, this sum of money as previously arranged with the Ministry of Health was to paid into the Parish Account to help to defray the rates

Signed E J Littlewood Chairman.

1949 December 29th.

"The Pinfold has been sold so it is now necessary to find a new site for the noticeboard. It was ultimately decided that the most suitable place would be on the piece of waste ground in front of the Old Hall Farm."

TO RESUME THE CHRONOLOGICAL SEQUENCE FROM
THE MINUTES:

1947 August 19th

Water supplies Ashton Lane & Fourdols *(sic)* Farm Prop Mr
Shaw & Sec Mr Goodman all in favour that we write to the
Doncaster R.D.C. & ask them to press further for the supply
of water for Ashton Lane & Fourdoles *(sic)* Farm, & also
invite Mr Hunpel the Doncaster & Tickhill Joint Water
Board Manager to attend our next Council Meeting to discuss the water question.

War Memorial

The Meeting was informed that the work on the War
Memorial was now completed & Mr. Guest & Son had presented thier *(sic)* a/c of Seven Pounds Seven Shillings. The
money collected so far amounted to Eight Pounds Eleven
Shillings & Threepence. handed in by Mr Littlewood £3. 3.
6. Mr. Goodman £3 – 0 – 6. Mr Lidgett £2. 7. 3.

October 21st. The first business of the meeting was a discussion
on the proposed water supply for Ashton Lane & Fourdoles
(sic) Farm. Mr Shaw said that whilst the water question was
on the table he would like to say that it was not too satisfac-
tory in some parts of Micklebring. A resolution was therefore passed the Doncaster RDC be asked to reconsider this
Ashton Lane Scheme to incorporate the whole of
Micklebring.

June 10th. Request for sign to keep traffic left of Cross

September 23rd. A letter was read to the meeting from
T. Williams M.P. Secretary to the Ministry of Agriculture in
which he explained that the increased production which
might be derived from a water supply did not merit the
excessive cost that the scheme would entail.

Mr. Shaw & Mr Littlewood brought to the notice of the
meeting that the work of scavenging at Birchwood (sic)
Terrace, Braithwell, & Micklebring was being badly neglect-
ed. After some discussion on the matter it was decided that
Mr Shaw should put a complaint in to Mr Reynolds at the
next meeting of the Doncaster R.D.C.

1949 March 30th. "Representation of the Peoples Act 1948":
.....term of office of Parish Councillors would expire on the
20th May 1949, and that the election of Parish Councillors
could no longer be carried out at a Parish Meeting or at a

poll consequent thereon, but the Election would in all cases be conducted by means of nominations and, if necessary, a poll......"

November First Poppy Wreath bought for War Memorial by Councillors themselves.

1951 August Since fixing two Keep Left signs on Market Cross it appeared to be confusing at this point. A Halt sign was requested on Holywell Lane as the major road was deemed to be Maltby Lane.

1952 July To celebrate Coronation of Queen Elizabeth II, it was proposed by Mr. Vincent Hill a Village Hall be bought and erected. A Committee was then elected.

August Brass plate with inscription to be fixed to Village Cross.

September Mrs. Humphries' book on Braithwell History to Mr. Meldrum (RDC).

October Go Slow sign already on Maltby Lane.

November A request received to move the Village Cross further down Holywell Lane since sending traffic round the south side had made it difficult for lorries. A Public Meeting was called.

A lively Meeting. Mr. W. Marshall said: "Move the bugger? Not likely!" 37 **against, 10 for**

The newspaper report regarding the request to move the Braithwell Village Cross said "Mr. William Marshall, aged 72, resident of Braithwell, fired verbal arrows at the Council.". What a lovely description!

1953 March Trees were planted on the Village Green in Commemoration of Queen Elizabeth's Coronation.

May Meetings in the Church School.

1955 March Blacksmith's Shop still in working order.

March An urgent Meeting was requested with the Highways to widen Ashton Lane due to accidents. Grass verge, The Hawthornes – Highways Dept. cleaned up this corner.

July Highways to purchase The Lump (sometimes called "The Lumping") at the top of High Street for road alterations.

(In November it was referred to "The Mound" – top of High Street).

1956 Request closets be converted to WCs – £2000.

239

1957 June In future Clerk to send letter of condolence to nearest relative of any ratepayer who dies in the Parish on behalf of the Parish Council (rescinded May 1966).

1958 Whole Village to be connected to sewerage mains.

1961 March First record of an "Annual Parish Meeting" Chairman Rev. E.P. Eccles

1962 January Meetings in County Primary School

1963 "Inattention to cesspools be reported.".

1964 July Old School doors hanging off, windows broken – "an invitation to certain characters for obscure practices.".

1965 August Parker Rhodes & Burgess drew up an agreement to the effect that the Play Area would not be used for building purposes.

See 27.10.65 – Council to hold a copy.

1968 October A plan was produced to widen High Street, knock down old property and put grass verges in front of new houses in Braithwell High Street. This was dismissed as ridiculous by the many parishioners who attended – it was a very heated meeting. It was at this time also when the new building in the Village and behind Cardwell House and Willow Crescent were passed.

1977 1st. July Mrs. D. M. Swift takes over as Clerk (G.H. Ashley served 43yrs.)

October Meetings in the Darby & Joan Room

1987 1st. January Mr. J.H. Wortley took over as Clerk

1993 29th. October Mr. M. D. Arnold took over as Clerk

❖

CHAPTER 39

Councillors from 1894

There is a remarkable familiy tradition within the Parish Council:
George Turner   Clerk for 32 years 1902 – 1934
George Ashley (son-in-law of G. Turner) 43 years 1934 – 1977
not forgetting: Robert Dunstan, Albert Dunstan, Joyce Milnes (nee Dunstan), John Dunstan.

Listed as they appear in each hand-written Volume. An asterisk indicates the Councillor served as Chairman during the period.

240

FROM VOLUME 1 4th December 1894 to 15th. March 1937

*Mr. William	Wild	Farmer	Fox House Farm
Mr. Robert	Dunstan	Farmer	Foredoles
George W.	Spencer	Farmer	Micklebring
Mr. John	Turner	(later Clerk to the Council)	Landlord, Red Lion
Mr. William	Wood	Farmer	Well House Farm
Mr. Mark	Clarkson	(Clerk to the Council)	Village Shop
Mr. Henry	Hall	Shoemaker	Pear Tree Cottage
Mr. David	Bentley	Farmer	Manor Farm Micklebring
*Mr. John T.	Waterhouse	Farmer	The Manor
Mr. John	Green		Micklebring
Mr. William Arthur	Spencer	Farmer	Lambcote Grange
Mr. John. W.	Foers		Cardwell House
Mr. E. W.	Pearson	Farmer & Mill owner	Mill Dam (Ruddle Mill)
Herbert	Allison	Farmer	Maltkiln Farm
Mr. G. K.	Dodds	Farmer	Low Farm
Mr. J. W..	Hardcastle	Farmer	Orchard Farm
*Rev. William	Seed	Vicar	The Rectory
Mr. A.	Youden	Farmer	
Mr. James	Parkes	Butcher & Farmer	Fox House Farm
Mr. L.	Kelly		Micklebring

Mr. Ross, Mr. Weyman and a Mr. J.H. Bracegirdle did some proposing and seconding Feb 1918

*Mr. Ronald	Robinson	Farmer	The Cottage
Joseph	Crawshaw	Foreman, Cedar Farm	Moat Cottage

POOR TRUSTEES (2) Mr. Allison and Mr. Crawshaw
L. Waterhouse

Thomas C.	Shaw	Landlord	The Plough, Micklebring
Mr. Albert	Fidler	Blacksmith & Farmer	Pear Tree Farm
William	Pickin	Farmer	Cedar Farm
Richard U.	Robinson	Flour Mill owmer	Croft End

241

Joseph William	Copley	Builder	Doncaster Road
Edward John	Littlewood	Winder (Colliery)	The Poplars
Mr. Robert	Dawson	Gentleman	
Mr. Richard	Spencer	Farmer	Micklebring
Thomas Russell	Bracegirdle	Maltby Colliery	The Hawthornes

FROM VOLUME 2 22nd April 1937 to 11th. January 1956

*William	Pickin	Farmer	Cedar Farm
*Edward John	Littlewood	Winder (Colliery)	The Poplars
*Joseph William	Copley	Builder	Doncaster Road
Charles	Ja(c)ques	Maltby Colliery	Ravenfield Common
Albert Edward	Richardson	Blacksmith	Micklebring
Stanley	Thompson		Micklebring
J. Thomas	Goodman	Grocer	Village Shop
*Mr. A.	Dunstan		
*Mr. E. E.	Pawson		
Mrs. E.	Smith		
Mr. J. W.	Barratt		
Mr. V. J.	Hill		

FROM VOLUME 3 8th. February 1956 to 15th. September 1966

*Mr. E. E.	Pawson
Mr. V.	Hill
*Mr. J. W.	Barratt
Mrs. E.	Smith
Mr. Albert	Dunstan
A. A.	Fidler
*Charles	Denham
Mr. E.	Byron
Mr. T. W.	Scales

FROM VOLUME 4 3rd. November 1966 to 11th. April 1975

*E.	Pawson
*T. W.	Scales
Mr. E.	Byron
Mr. C.	Denham
Mr. A.	Dunstan

*Mr. J	Barratt	
Mrs. Joyce	Milnes	(co-opted to replace Mr E. E. Pawson, September 1970)
Mr. Arnold D.	Pawson	

FROM VOLUME 5 21st. May 1975 to 17th. December 1986

*Mrs. J.	Milnes
*Mr. A. D.	Pawson
Mr. Charles	Denham
Mr. John	Barratt
Mr. Tom	Scales
*Mr. William	Varah
Mr. John	Parkes

FROM VOLUME 6 21st. January 1987 to 24th. April 1996

*Mr. John	Parkes	
*Mr. W.	Varah	
*Mr. A.D.	Pawson	
Mrs. Joan K.	Overett J.P.	Micklebring
Mr. John B.	Dunstan	
Mrs. Helen T.	Parkinson	
Mr. Roger	Greenwood	Micklebring

❖

EPILOGUE

There is still much missing from this account. Many tales from old residents are handed down and cannot possibly be true. For example, that the underground passages from Hall Farm lead to Moat Hall and then on to Roche Abbey. My father went down these as a youth and was brought out gasping for air. They certainly did go under the drive – there is an air grate on the side of the house from these passages but, surely, the air would be far too foul to venture much further. Small cells, which were about 6' square with a grid in front and with iron hooks on the wall (I saw these), were seen under the floor when the sitting room wooden floor collapsed. I was about eight years old. These were quickly filled in with rubble stone (dad fetched cart loads from the fields) at that time. No great interest was shown in such things then and money was short and the room wanted to be got back into a family room as quickly as possible. Tales are told of pewter tankards being found down there in the late 1800s. Also stocks – but where are they now? An old friend of the family, Brenda Harden, told me that her mother used to tell of them when she lived in the House. It is nice to hear these old tales and one would like to believe just a little of it.

And so for my lovely, happy life, I thank God, my Family and friends, this Village and its people. How I wish that all children could have my wonderful childhood.

And I finish with the wisest of sayings.

**GOD GRANT ME THE COURAGE TO CHANGE
THE THINGS I CAN CHANGE
THE SERENITY TO ACCEPT THOSE I CANNOT
CHANGE
AND THE WISDOM TO KNOW THE DIFFERENCE**